D0556319

Hands

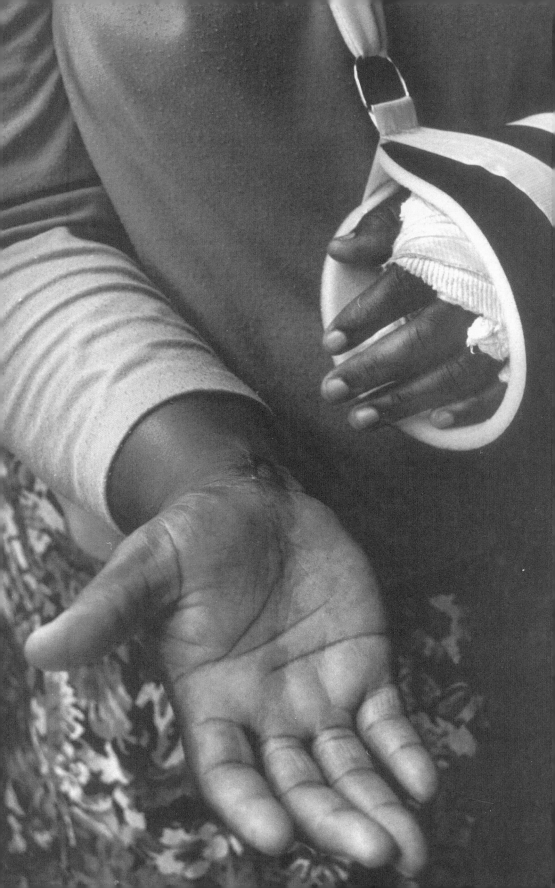

Hands

Physical Labor, Class, and Cultural Work

Janet Zandy

Rutgers University Press
New Brunswick, New Jersey, and London

Library of Congress Cataloging-in-Publication Data

Zandy, Janet, 1945–
    Hands : physical labor, class, and cultural work / Janet Zandy.
    p. cm.
    Includes bibliographical references (p.   ) and index.
    ISBN 0–8135–3434–8 (hardcover : alk. paper) — ISBN 0–8135–3435–6 (pbk. : alk. paper)
    1. Working class writings, American—History and criticism. 2. American literature—20th century—
History and criticism. 3. Working class—United States—Intellectual life. 4. Social classes in literature.
5. Working class in literature. 6. Working class in art. 7. Work in literature. I. Title.
    PS228.L33Z365 2004
    810.9'920624—dc22

                                                                        2003019801

    British Cataloging-in-Publication information for this book is available from the British Library.

Manufactured in the United States of America

for
Bill, Anna, and Victor Zandy
my world's center

William Zandy, *Planting Tomatoes*.
Courtesy of the photographer.

Contents

Acknowledgments

No book is a solo act. While the writing may be solitary, shaping meaning out of the tangled relationship between class and culture in America is a communal act. This book originates in a deeply rooted belief in the dignity and strength of working-class people. I could not sustain this work without that crucial connection, particularly the working-class legacy of respect and love of learning from my deceased parents, Millie and Charles Ballotta. I am equally indebted to those in the academy who have offered the necessary support and time to complete *Hands*. I especially wish to thank Paul and Francena Miller for their Miller Fellowship, which permitted release time from a yearly nine-course academic schedule. To the community of Hedgebrook Farms, a small paradise for writers on Whidbey Island, my thanks for three precious weeks. At Rochester Institute of Technology I thank colleagues Sandra Saari, Diane Hope, Loret Steinberg, and, especially, Mary Sullivan. I thank my students for their intellectual challenge and their belief in a better future, particularly those who allowed me to quote from their writing. My appreciation as well to the writers, artists, and photographers whose work is quoted or reproduced here. Colleagues in working-class studies mutually construct a space within the academy for this work. I especially thank Laura Hapke, Carole Anne Taylor, Nicholas Coles (my co-editor of a forthcoming anthology of U.S. working-class literature), and I appreciate the work of Edvige Giunta, Larry Smith, Sue Doro, John Russo, Sherry Linkon, and Michael Frisch. John Crawford and Florence Howe were critical and insightful readers of early chapters: many thanks. I thank Tillie Olsen for her love and inspiration. The late Larry Chisolm, brilliant American Studies practitioner, recognized this work at a very early stage and made a difference. My Rochester friends have listened to my ideas and tolerated my work-driven schedule for decades. I thank especially Chojy Schroeder, Dolores Kleinberg, Sylvia Gasoi, and Marilyn Anderson. I thank my sister, Carol Ann Bamdad, for taking me back to the site of Trubeck Labs and for supporting my work. This is my third book with Rutgers University Press. My appreciation to the staff at the Press, particularly Marilyn Campbell and Anne Hegeman. I thank Susannah Driver-Barstow for her expert copy editing. My gratitude to Leslie Mitchner, trusted editor and friend, for her support of this book at every stage, and for her sustaining recognition of the importance of class to the shaping of knowledge and the formation of culture. Most especially I thank my immediate family—my husband, Bill Zandy, and adult children Victor and Anna Zandy. They are inseparable from *Hands*.

Prologue
The Epistemology of the Hand

Historically and linguistically, the human hand emanates protean meanings. The *Oxford English Dictionary* lists sixty-three nuanced definitions. Foremost is the hand as instrument of agency, Aristotle's "instrument of instruments." Hands are tools of measurement as in the height of horses, indicators of capacity, skill, artistic performance, or handiwork, as well as calculators and spellers. Hands embody the tactile: they shake, embrace, stroke, touch, applaud, point, handle, reach out, possess. They encapsulate human emotions—wildness (out of hand) and signify power relationships of control (in hand).

Hands are maps to history and culture as demonstrated in the elegant exhibit "Writing on Hands: Memory and Knowledge in Early Modern Europe" staged at the Folger Library from December 2000 to March 2001. Hands, as the earliest modernists understood, are also maps of memory, aids to retrieving or associating ideas. Hands are microcosms of the whole human. Lined palms

Janet Zandy, *Folger Exhibit.*

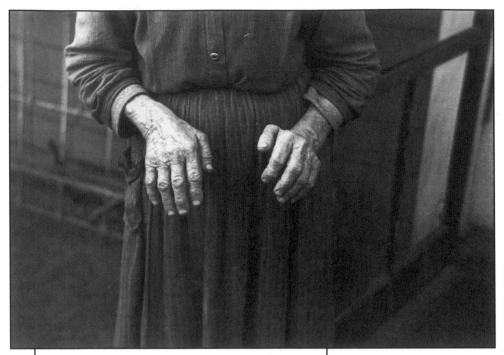

Russell Lee, *Homesteader's Hands,* 1936.
Reproduced from the Collection of the Library of Congress,
319270, LC-USF3301-011121-M1.

reveal life paths, dispositions, essences, and the future—long and short. Hands raised from the grave, as appliances for medical diagnosis, as dangling signifiers, as defenders of faith, and as embodiment of knowledge and skill, indeed, seem to say it all.

These myriad meanings from earliest history denote connection, indeed, inseparability of mind and hand. But probe more deeply, and see how homages to the human hand also mirror hierarchies of power, control, and ownership. Dismantle the philosopher's hand and underneath one uncovers not the instrument of instruments, but the transformation of human beings into nothing but instruments, just so many hands. The first OED reference to hands as metonym for labor is from 1655: "a person employed by another in any manual work; a workman or workwoman." In 1721 manufacturers employed "hands," and in 1771 Benjamin Franklin recorded in his autobiography that his son "lost his principal hand by death." Olmsted in *Slave States* (1856) reports a chronology of hand labor "where children begin as 'quarter hand,' *advancing* [my emphasis] to 'half hands' and then to 'three-quarter hands' and finally to 'full hands.'" Also there is the gendered division of hands having hands, that is, wives and children.

Prologue

In 1936 Russell Lee shot the photograph reproduced here of a homesteader's hands. What narrative of instrumentality does it tell? The hands are huge. Isolated, they appear genderless; we know they are attached to a woman only because they appear before the stage curtain of her apron or skirt. They tell a story of unremitting labor—washing, scrubbing, digging, cooking, canning, building, repairing, sewing—prematurely aged hands, hands that did not know rest. Russell Lee may have been genuinely sympathetic to the woman attached to these hands, but by using her hands as emblems and severing them from her head he reinforces the body/mind split. Some people get to use their heads; the rest *become* their hands.

I begin with these two images: the hand of the institutionalized account of history and culture as staged at the Folger and the hand of the homesteader, albeit framed and presented, but also revealing a physicality of labor that is elusively represented in academic culture. I trust that most readers carry in their bones and skin, consciousness and memory, the capacity to embrace both hands. That embrace necessitates alternative forms and configurations for academic writing. The organization, relational parts, and rhythm of this book offer a new, hybrid methodology for working-class studies, a bridging of interior and exterior, of variegated kinds of knowledge. This evokes a call and response between labor and culture that is more than juxtaposition, indeed, that illuminates their inseparability. Illumination is critical to my intent, but that cannot happen without the recognition of shaded and dark spaces. Penetrating the actualities of class difference within or without the academy is still unsafe ground for writers and readers. But these discomfort zones open possibilities for expansion and connection.

College professor and working-class person, both identities claim me. But I am not neutral or distanced. Ultimately, this book is a hand's turn, a stroke of work, that seeks to uncover meaning embedded in those large working hands. It claims a grounding, an epistemology, crucial to the construction of knowledge and culture. We are all sustained because of the labor of hands; what is undervalued, overlooked, and often discarded is how much they have to teach.

Hands

before they die the brave have set their hand on rich particular beauty
for their heirs. —Muriel Rukeyser, "Citation for Horace Gregory"

the dead which exists in our imagination has as much fact
as have we ourselves —William Carlos Williams, *In the American Grain*

"I made a drawing of a guy once, lugs coal into alleyways.
Unbelievable pair of hands. I've caught a couple of sets of hands,
that's all in twenty-five years. Still trying it!"

—Ralph Fasanella, in Patrick Watson's *Fasanella's City*

. . . mill hands, farm hands, factory hands . . . hands . . . hands . . . hands . . .

—Eugene V. Debs

No man with a starched face
asked of Effie
how many shirts it took
to make a washer woman *—Wilma Elizabeth McDaniel, "Shirts"*

Introduction

H ands speak. In sign language they do the work of tongue and voice box. In greeting, they iterate multiple meanings. They augment orality. They reveal identity—the long fingers of the pianist, the rough, stubby hands of the bricklayer. The most advanced technology cannot completely eliminate the daily tasks performed by hands. Hands are reductive identifiers and lucid maps to the geography of human complexity.

Hands are evocative. Ask someone to describe a parent's or a grandparent's hands and out will pour stories. The hands of an Italian laborer are remembered as "solid calluses . . . hands like a 2 x 4." The hands of a mother embroidering remain vivid to her daughter sixty years later. Hands are class and cultural markers. Missing fingers attest to the dangers of farm labor or factory work. Working-class hands are rarely still. They often embroider spoken language with subtlety and emphasis, anger and love.

Once noticed, hands are everywhere in working-class literature. Richard Wright's paean, "I Have Seen Black Hands" combines the historic sweep of generations with the specifics of action, of the reach of "tiny black fingers," of laboring hands "jerked up and down at the throbbing machines" and hands "raised in fists of revolt."[1] Agnes Smedley's Marie Rogers describes the hands of her washerwoman mother in *Daughter of Earth* as "big-veined and almost black from heavy work."[2] In *China Men* Maxine Hong Kingston's father was born with long hands and fingers, "made for holding pens."[3] Tillie Olsen's Jim Holbrook who cannot speak "the things in his mind so vast and formless, so terrible and bitter, seeks articulation through hands—"till the day that hands will find a way to speak this: hands."[4]

Factory hands. Field hands. Illegal hands. Redundant hands. The death of the hired hand. 'My hand will do it,' says the employer who hires or owns the function of hands. Human beings reduced to working parts, just so many hands. This book develops out of the synecdoche of the hand as obscured and undifferentiated stand in for human labor and moves toward cultural retrieval and reclamation. Within this figurative frame, *Hands* begins thematically with loss and dis/memberment, that is, with the actual physicality of labor. Out of loss emerge cultural responses, recoveries, remembrances, and articulations. Tensions between presence and absence, visibility and invisibility, voice and silence provide the necessary underpinnings and design. In linking forms of cultural expression with physical labor, *Hands* centers what is usually de-centered—the variegated, unstable, and complex culture of workers.

The concept of building is crucial to this book, from the assembly of its various parts as a text to the materiality of physical construction, to the deconstruction of industrial work sites, to the tectonics of cultural relationships in time and space, and to all the complex ways hands mold and shape. Through a sequence of essays and intersecting collages, I construct a form that seeks a dialogue between the tactile world of work and the textured world of the academy. I combine literary analysis, pedagogy, memoir, and cultural critique to probe the myriad ways class circumstances affect the making and reception of culture. Each part can stand alone, but read sequentially, these meditations reveal larger patterns of historical witnessing and recovery. They also present modes of discernment, ways of acknowledging class difference, particularly through encounters with the physicality of labor.

Some of my themes, concerns and intentions include an examination of literary and visual representations of the physicality of labor, the insertion of the actuality of unsafe work into cultural and literary studies, a recognition of the inseparability of body and mind, and commentary on how working-class cultures emerge, forms of representation, cultural antecedents, and working-class aesthetics. This collection of writings seeks reconnection: of the metaphorically dismembered working hand to the whole body, of the representational to the real, of labor practices and working-class lived experiences to academic and cultural institutions. I address both the problematic of representation and its necessity. I emphasize how the working-class body itself is an historical witness and subject by including memoir, factual documents, and labor statistics on occupational injuries and deaths with literary and visual representations. The intended tone is cautionary, not celebratory. I am testing new forms, using collage and juxtaposition, story and analysis, as tools to penetrate the wall of bourgeois cultural assumptions and sensibilities. I am attentive to possibilities for worker self-representation and always concerned with the risk of colonizing my subject. I offer a process of recovery and retrieval, a struggle for reciprocal visibility, for sustained relationality, for humble witnessing.

I began writing these essays as early as 1991 and completed them as recently as 2002. I violate boundaries of genre and form, beginning with personal story not because of an obsession with my own biography, but because I believe it is a necessary revelation of my own grounding. I straddle borders between working-class lived experience and institutionalized knowledge. Loss cannot be compensated, but it can be answered and understood through finding meaning within cultural and historical contexts. My thirty years as a teacher have a presence in these essays as well, directly through the integration of students' commentary, and indirectly in the didactic impulse implicit in my examination of literature, photography and painting. My long and deep-rooted feminism is not so much a separate theoretical category as an expression of solidarity with working-class and poor women, with my own family legacy.

Consider these writings as necessary hybrids, organic filaments of connection and structured conceptual frames. I approach theory as lever or guide. I am no Jude the Obscure carrying on imagined conversations with scholarly "worthies." Rather, I turn frequently to Raymond Williams, Mikhail Bakhtin, and Antonio Gramsci because they illuminate the relationality of class and culture. Williams's synthesis of intellectuality, historicity, and human empathy (too easily dismissed as nostalgia) and his recognition of structures of feeling and experience have informed all my writing. Bakhtin's concept of architectonics and answerability, relationships of parts to wholes, texts to lived experience, fit the tectonics of this book and the interpreted meanings of working-class culture. Gramsci offers a model of an alternative *Bildung*, a journey out of disprivileged material conditions into the wider world that affirms but does not romanticize working-class potential and knowledge. If Gramsci leads the way out, then Lewis Hine is a ferryman taking me back through his photographs into worlds of no one's choosing. Here are alternative models to individual exceptionalism.

I am also writing consciously to a growing community of working-class scholars, teachers, and students. This new field of working-class studies is not dependent solely on an aggregate of academics from the working class, nor does it necessarily speak with one theoretical and political voice. Rather, working-class studies emerges at a critical moment, a time of ruthless economic disparities, of disappeared jobs and struggling cities and towns, of political and corporate oligarchies, and fear of America's vulnerability and its imperialistic power. As an academic field of study the centering of a variegated working-class history and culture complicates and deepens class analysis and provides a space for reciprocal visibility across divisions of race, ethnicity, citizenship, and geography. At its best, working-class studies bridges communities and nonacademic workers to institutions of knowledge.

To say that working-class bodies speak is more than a rhetorical flourish or theoretical gesture. I argue that laboring bodies harbor an epistemology, a way of knowing and understanding the world that comes out of the physicality of work. This is a tricky and complicated position and risks reduction and essentialism. But consider how anyone's training as scientist, violinist, computer engineer, physician, not to mention academic, can shape one's perceptions and ways of knowing. This is not to say that work identity equals human sensibility, but rather to draw attention to something that has been dismissed and ignored in what constitutes knowledge. If you use your body in a physical way year after year, the body speaks back not only in terms of sore muscles or swollen legs, but also out of know-how. The laboring body speaks the language of fatigue and frivolity, of sacrifice and shared experience. It is a vocabulary of gestures, an idiom of collective experience. On noisy work sites, communication through the body is the grammar of safety. Bodies also contain an assemblage of familiar and inherited postures. Actors surely study the physical stances that define a character. The architectonics of human bodies, the ways they lean, sit, walk, embrace, gesture, the masking and unmasking of emotion through the face, the imprint of work on the body inform the essays of this book. Bodies also carry memory. Consider the shock of recognition of seeing a long-dead relative reappear in the gait of his son or the hand motions of her daughter. This is a language of the body that while not unique to working-class people is particularly important to their articulation of who they are, and it is represented and affirmed in working-class literature, painting, and photography. Writing out of body memory of women scrubbing laundry, Wilma Elizabeth McDaniel says her poem "Shirts" "helps me handle my grief and anger when I see their wet faces and swollen red hands in my memory."[5]

The divisions of this book reflect particular movements, actualities, formations, and rhythms of working-class culture. These are offered as alternatives to periodization or specific author or genre approaches. I begin with the physicality of jobs and how memory and culture respond to loss. Next, articulations demonstrate forms of working-class cultural presence and the complexities of representing working-class experience. How artists and writers recover useable working-class and cultural history as subject and catalyst for their work follows. The last section situates technology as complex systems operating on laboring bodies through various zones of history, culture and experience. These essays experiment with juxtapositions, quotations, and intertextual references, and question assumptions about aesthetics and cultural formations.

What are two hands worth? I begin with a brief account about a woman who was a machine operator in a plastic-molding factory. Through no fault of her own, her hands were crushed and destroyed by a faulty machine in a preventable industrial accident. This case highlights the importance of recognizing the actual risks workers face on the job, and also serves as reminder of the difficulty of approaching such stories of private injury. Questioning the worth of hands, not as a monetary matter for personal injury lawyers, becomes a means of probing the capacious symbolic meaning of hands. The very inaccessibility of this story serves to enlarge our awareness of what can be known and what constitutes knowledge in the space between presence and absence.

Many critics comment on the difficulty if not impossibility of representing laboring bodies in literary texts. Some acknowledge how the critical act itself distances further the body from the text. Few, though, recognize the deep and unacknowledged resistance to working-class experience in the academy, the persistent elitism that delimits knowledge and the study of culture. Working-class people cannot be trusted—physically, culturally, politically, linguistically—to behave within a constructed ideological and theoretical frame. For all the rhetoric of praxis and transformation, of interdisciplinarity and border crossing, academic practices tend to elide the laboring body. But by examining the great symbolic weight of the human hand, by recognizing labor's stamp on the body, we can begin to claim the complex epistemology embedded in the body.

No book can reattach the human hand severed on the job, but it can trace the process of dis/memberment and remembering, and see the hand's potential for graceful movement, its delicate rough beauty, and its hidden wisdom.

How Much Are
Two Hands Worth?

The hand is not simply a flat paddle adorned with a row of fingers. It is a complex matrix of bone, sinew, and muscle, operating within an elastic covering of skin. Understanding the relationship of those parts and their range of movement is integral to conveying the effects they have on the external contours of the hand.

—Simon Jennings, ed., *Ways of Drawing Hands*

Mrs. C. worked for nineteen years as a machine operator at Newburgh Molded Plastics.[1] She was paid $6.45 an hour to pull plastic containers out of a twenty-year-old molding machine.[2] On August 3, 1993, alone at her machine, she did not know that the three internal safety systems in the machine were not working, or that her employer may have deactivated these devices in modifying the machine. That night the safety system on her machine failed, and Mrs. C. did not pull her hands away in time. Two hundred tons of pressure smashed her arms and crushed her hands.[3] The police received the emergency call at 8:20 p.m. Emergency workers tried to stem the bleeding by tightly wrapping bandages around what was left of Mrs. C's arms.[4] News reports identified Mrs. C. as a fifty-nine-year-old widow, mother of four, and grandmother. Reconstructive surgeons described her injury as a "world-class case" because of the extraordinary difficulty of reconnecting blood vessels, nerves, and bones of crushed limbs.[5] At the work site, OSHA (Occupational Health and Safety Administration) investigators uncovered thirteen examples of hazardous working conditions, including failure to conduct safety inspection of the injection-molding machines, unmarked fire exits, and some machines without safety guards. The owners, Sally and Peter Polhamus, were fined $5,460.[6] After Mrs. C.'s hands were destroyed, the owners did not notify the manufacturer of the machine about the accident. The machine was sold and eventually was found in Central America.[7]

Surprisingly, even some skillful figure artists claim to have difficulty drawing hands. Perhaps to those artists, hands are almost an afterthought, mere details that do not command the attention given to drawing a portrait. In fact, hands provide a great deal of subliminal information.

How much are two hands worth? A question for attorneys. Two years later, fitted with artificial arms, Mrs. C. won a $4 million settlement from the molding company and the machine's manufacturer (minus court costs and lawyer's fees). Her lawyer said that "none of the three safety systems worked, and she didn't know they weren't working."[8] Three years later Sally Polhamus appeared before a Senate labor committee to complain about the high cost of workers' compensation. She never revealed that the machine that crushed Mrs. C.'s hands did not have an inexpensive safety interlock. Instead she described Mrs. C. as "a relatively unintelligent sixty-two-year-old woman who is on her own with $4 million" and who could be "living in a trailer park."[9] There was no reported commentary from Mrs. C.

> Close scrutiny of the fingernails can reveal something about a person's occupation. Clean, manicured nails suggest a life of comparative leisure, while broken, discolored nails are more likely to belong to a laborer. Don't forget the cuticle.

I knew none of these facts when I noticed the photo of a very gaunt, white-haired woman on the cover of an AFL-CIO pamphlet urging workers to contact their New York state legislators to resist the disregarding of legal precedents which offer workers some defense against unsafe work places. Mrs. C. looks straightforwardly into the camera. Wedding rings are looped through a chain circling her neck. Her arms extend forward as if she is offering them for the world to see. At the end of the shortened forearms are no hands. By bravely showing herself Mrs. C. speaks through her body in a language that workers can understand.

Perhaps less compelling, but for the purposes of this book no less important, is the narrative of the incomplete retrieval of Mrs. C.'s story. I contacted the state office of the AFL-CIO (American Federation of Labor-Congress of Industrial Organizations) and requested information about Mrs. C. and the lawsuit. Seven years after the actual incident, no one had any details except for the name of her lawyer. I called her lawyer and was able to arrange an interview with Mrs. C. in his office some two hundred miles from my home. The day before the meeting, I received a phone call postponing the meeting because Mrs. C. was "busy" and "had other commitments." I rescheduled the meeting and made new travel arrangements. Shortly before the rescheduled visit, I received another call informing me that Mrs. C. did not want to talk to me.

I reacted without resistance. Mrs. C. had every right to say no. I was disappointed that I could not communicate my intentions better or speak to her directly. I had written to her lawyer: "I would like to understand the circumstances of her injury as fully as possible. Please realize that my interest is in Mrs. ___'s working conditions at Newburgh Molded Plastics, not her private life before or after the settlement."[10] I thought then and still believe that if Mrs. C.'s story could reach an audience outside of personal injury lawyers or labor unions, in a context concerned with working-class experience, it would show

how job safety is a marker of class difference and crucial to any analysis of working-class culture.

At the same time, I realize that Mrs. C.'s story, any story of the physicality of labor and the risks and losses workers and their families face, has to be partial and elusive. Such experiences are not so many fruits to be plucked for academic purposes. Nor are they necessarily part of society's shared narrative. What is familiar is the language of winning and losing, four million for two hands (minus legal fees). What is foreign to those who control the language of the marketplace is the crushing force on Mrs. C.'s hands and the ghosts of those missing hands. Like the difficult task of drawing hands, that "complex matrix of bone, sinew, and muscle," much depends on the relationship of parts to the whole.[11] As I navigate the space between reality and representation, presence and absence, I wish to preserve the legitimacy of not knowing, a respectful not knowing that acknowledges the limitations of textual analysis, no matter how practiced, and yet wills an imaginary leap into deeper understanding. To be sure this is not about guilt, easy sentimentality, or even sympathy. Rather it is the deliberate construction of a methodology to expose linkages, those crucial intersections between experience and expression.

Workers to commemorate those who've died on the job

Three killed in collapse of scaffold over river

2 killed, 49 hurt in power plant blast

One killed in plant explosion

"We went flying"

Georgia
Worker dies after plant explosion

U.S. admits radiation illnesses, raises possibility of con

Teens unaware of job dangers

Bereaved Hunting Bodies of Friends
(Continued from Page 1)

MILLER PARK TRAGEDY

Workers had argued about safety of

Worker in hospital after legs crushed

Jot

Cider mill fined for boy's injury

Victims' kin say mine ignored warnings

ll. The day of the acci-
tas James' first near the
ery, she said.

ing off the books, acc
an agency statement.
The Occupations
and Health Admis

Explosion at Mass. foundry injures 1

someone blown up   at least five
Howard County and ripped the roof

Nation's Deepest Coal Mine Now Ranks Among Deadliest

ill does not
n work because
ples from other
ld said.

downe said. He is
gle his fingers, but th
mains numb.

"We're not sure
going to be 100 pe

ENTOMBED!

Many crushed to death in hard hat hell

4 dead, 9 missing in coal mine blasts

Miner Killed at Leisenring

Michael Hordos, a Greek employe
in the mines of the H. C. Frick Co
Company at Leisenring No. 1, was ru
over by a pit car yesterday mornin
shortly before 5 o'clock and was i
stantly killed. His neck was broke
his right arm and left leg were also
most severed from his body. His che
was also badly mashed. The bo
was removed from the mines to h
late home at Leisenring and was p
pared for burial by Funeral Direc
J. L. Stader.
Hordos was born in this country an

After fire, survivors struggling

Workers Sensed Danger Before Garage Collapse

Atlantic City Garage:

Philadelphia

Garage collapse hurts 8 workers

N.C
pie
The Ad

5 more bodies found
BRIDGEPORT, Conn. —

the
ining
and un-
ill burn.

officials of the mine company,
Jim Walter Resources, Inc.
The Blue Creek mines are
considered "ultra-gassy" by the
federal government because of

Fellow Workers
Join in rendering a last and solemn of sympap
and affection for the victims of the Triangl
Fire. THE FUNERAL PROCESSION wil
place Wednesday, April 5th, at 1 P. M
Watch the newspapers for the line of march

city mourns sanitman

Angry Citizens Demand End to Ceaseless Sacrifice of Workers

Death at wo

Operai Italiani

Unitevi compatti a rendere l'ultimo pi
fana alla vittime dell'enome sciagura dell
Triangle Waist Co. Il CORTEO FUNEBR
avrà luogo quotando, 5 Aprile, alle ore 1 P I

Violations foun

Loss

Circumstances and Choices

Ours is a culture that celebrates choice and barely acknowledges circumstance. Yet choice and circumstance are intricately bound, like swirling sea hitting hard rock. Such boundaries and borders fade out in the class geography of American culture, where acknowledgment of obstructions or advantages cuts against the ideological cloth of success and progress.[1] The ideology of individualism is impatient and intolerant of a deeper understanding of circumstance. Instead we have a reification of choice—whether having it our way on hamburger toppings or entitled entry to the best universities and circles of power. The privileged know or can easily find out what they need to know to move out into the wider world; the disprivileged, through no fault of their own, are clueless.

Circumstances cannot be separated from the social, the communal, and the obligatory. Individualism, on the other hand, cuts linkages. Each new generation is urged to make it, or go for it, or be all they can be. The instrumentality of the cliché shields us against the burden of history and the needs of the present. Material circumstances provide the architecture of individual lives. Class circumstances shape—literally and figuratively—the working-class body.

This beginning section looks at the costs to the body because of the physicality, risks, and dangers of work. It also forges linkages, reconnecting that injured or lost body to cultural expression. Tracing known and unknown risks, pursuing medical records, testimonies, imagining the linkages between "god job" and human lives require a writer to be also ethnographer and witness. The fragmentary personal story "Trubeck Labs" claims a particular yet common labor legacy. Linking cultural analysis and expression with the harsh and gritty consequences of unsafe work is not the sequestered work of one generation either. Under the heading "Books of the Dead," I examine the fate of the "Dialpainters," young women poisoned by radium-laced paint and the labor risks Audre Lorde faced operating a commercial x-ray machine as described in her biomythography *Zami.* The third sequence analyzes Muriel Rukeyser's stunning collection of poems, *The Book of the Dead,* that documents the building of a hydroelectric power plant in West Virginia and the dry drilling that caused the silicosis deaths of over seven hundred workers, mostly African American migrant men. Next, "God Job," the most pedagogical essay, merges commentary on Lewis Hine's photographs, bits of memoir, and students' responses with the physicality of work in two immigrant novels. I conclude this section with "Workers Memorial Day," an explanation and meditation on this annual national commemoration of workers killed on the job.

This literature is a necessary encounter with violence—not the packaged kind of tabloids and crime shows—but the violence of work that the human body endures. Like the ceremonial intent of Workers Memorial Day, it is remembrance, but also creative catalyst for other writers. It attests to the legitimacy of unsafe work as a subject for literary and cultural expression. And so, this necessary, discomforting beginning.

"I have always wished that my children could see me at my work. . . . That they might see how articulate we are in the accomplishment of what we do.

—Alistair MacLeod, "The Closing Down of Summer"

Trubeck Labs

No place to stop. This is East Rutherford, New Jersey, the southern tip of Route 17 where it is broken by Route 3 and reemerges in Lyndhurst as Ridge Road. Neither suburb nor city, working-class north Jersey breathes in tight spaces. The speeding cars and potholes are unforgiving on this stretch of Route 17. I look for familiar landmarks, noticing new small businesses and clusters of urban commerce on either side. I am on a small quest to find my father's company. I remember family visit days at Trubeck's in the environmentally unconscious 1950s and tours through the safer parts of the plant. Making our way around gray pipes and open drums, we stepped over snaky cables on damp ground. Vats of chemicals bore the stern warning "No Matches!" This was a masculine world of work, of 24-hour-a-day, 7-day-a-week chemical production. Nearly fifty years later, visual memory unreliable, I recall the chemical smells. This unconscious olfactory link joined my father's workplace and our home. That smell evokes absence, not only of my father's presence, but of the knowledge of the kind of work he did for nineteen years.

This ride is no tour. Impatient New Jersey drivers impose a speed too fast for my slow eyes. Suddenly I see the baseball diamond on the left, the meager bleachers and sparsely green field. I can't see the car dealership and diner, maybe I've missed them or maybe they're gone. My eyes are now fixed on the right side because I know it's just ahead. Square building follows square building and then suddenly a flat zone. There it is. There's the spot. A large gray foundation protrudes behind a perimeter of weedy vegetation. I strain to see inside, to glimpse the remains of broken and cut-off pipes. In this crowded stretch of Route 17 with no unused commercial space, it stands empty. Why?

I guessed before I knew for certain. Nothing could be built there. The ground is too toxic. I wonder how many of my father's work buddies, the long line of working men, white and black, who offered us their condolences at his wake in 1965, are still alive.[1] What was once Trubeck Laboratories is now this empty lot, a ghost plant. In my childhood it was the family's bread and butter. And more. My sister and I won the company scholarship, which freed us from unsafe work. Later I learned that we were the first "children of workers" allowed to apply for the scholarship, which had been reserved for "professionals" and managers.

New Jersey traffic urges me forward past the remnants of Trubeck Labs. I stop this time in memory only.

SAFETY RULES

On the following pages are listed rules regarding Safety as well as Cleanliness and Losses. In order to convince anyone who might feel we prefer to take a few chances rather than lose production in a given instance, we present the following, which will serve as an outline for the proper operation of the plant.

1. SAFETY

We wish to state, as emphatically as possible, that we consider the safety and health of our employees to be the No. 1 consideration, without question. We make every attempt to install the latest devices for full and adequate protection, and will, as outlined herein, be glad to act upon any suggestions which we might receive. Of course, all these devices are useless if they are ignored. We also want to emphasize that any employee SHOULD NOT UNDERTAKE WORK OR OPERATE ANY PIECE OF EQUIPMENT WHICH HE FEELS IS UNSAFE. IN CASE OF DOUBT, CONSULT A SUPERVISOR.

—*The Trubeck Laboratories Employees' Handbook*[2]

It must have been a good postwar job. I imagine the relief my father felt to find something steady with a nine-month-old baby (me) and another one soon on the way. Trubeck's was a big leap from the temporary jobs he took after returning from Germany and the war he never talked about. On the inside of the company handbook, someone wrote his name, Charles F. Ballotta, date of

Charles Ballotta (center) with co-workers, late 1940s or early 1950s. Collection of Janet Zandy.

employment, July 22, 1946, and social security number, 140–01–1781. On one of the back notebook pages, my father reinscribed the day in his own hand: "Started work on July 22, 1946."

He died on March 7, 1965. He was unlucky or God was cruel. For a long time I could not decide which, and I thought it did not matter. That the cause of his death matters, not just to my family, but in a larger public sense, was a late recognition. His generation, born at the cusp of the First World War, coming of age during the Great Depression and the second great world war, knew they were historical participants, but had neither the articulated education nor the necessary space and time to step back and comment on the power of external forces to shape everyday lives. His ethos was family and work. Combined, those values sustained not only our family, but also an extended one of surviving parents, brothers, sisters, nieces, and nephews. Working three shifts, alternating every two weeks, my father never secured what he called the "sheepskin," a high school diploma, so important and elusive. Contrary to the assumption that the GI Bill was the great gateway out of the working class, my father, as was true for many working-class vets, had very few options given his extended family responsibilities, his ninth-grade education, and the family's urgent need for a steady paycheck.[3]

2. CLEANLINESS AND ORDER
Since we are convinced that these two items are very closely tied up with safety, we feel that they rate next in importance. A messy plant is bound to be an unsafe plant, and therefore, we also feel that the task of keeping the plant orderly is of *extreme importance*.

The private concerns of my parents were felt in the climatic changes of the household, but never said aloud. And I was too dreamy, too much living in my head and heart, to notice. I was the scholarship girl, living at home, attending a state teachers college. I relished conversations with my father about this new world of learning. So much to learn, who even thought about a sophisticated literacy of critique? I live now with the memory of unasked questions. One day my father entered the hospital for surgery and never returned home. He was forty-nine, nearly fifty, seemingly healthy. He died from a pulmonary embolism the day after prostate cancer surgery.

It took nearly twenty years after his death for me to assemble the causal circuitry.

I became convinced that had he not worked in a pre-OSHA chemical plant (that produced the ingredients for expensive perfumes) he might not have gotten the cancer, he might not have needed the surgery, he might have survived to see his grandchildren born. All the workers at Trubeck's had the right to know about the dangers of the hazardous materials they handled and were exposed to. One now-retired former manager informs me that Trubeck "was not a 'schlock' chemical operation," and safety was a primary operational concern.

Plant Explosion.
Collection of Janet Zandy.

Perhaps so, but I suspect that he never poured chemical materials into open vats or breathed their fumes on a daily basis. Production workers may or may not survive the invisible, toxic, chemical assaults on their bodies. Safety concerns have an immediacy and visibility; industrial hazards and occupational diseases are hidden and long term. It may be too late for an epidemiological study, but it is not too late to recognize the class lines that divide safe and unsafe work. The safety concerns in the handbook and the safe work signs in the plant are just so much, perhaps well-intended, verbiage. Such signage places the burden on workers to work safely under circumstances where they are not aware or informed of the real and consequential dangers they face immediately and long term.[4]

3. PRODUCTION
Naturally, we are interested in securing the maximum production from our
equipment, but again we wish to emphasize that we want no production at the expense of the first two items listed—that is why we have listed PRODUC-TION as No. 3.

My chronology is sketchy and unnuanced. Near undeveloped tidal marsh-
lands Trubeck Laboratories began as Aroma Chemical Labs in 1932. In 1955 it
started operating a solvent chemical facility, storing recovered chemical wastes
as well as constructing a wastewater treatment plant which utilized two wastewater treatment lagoons. In 1960 Universal Oil Products acquired Trubeck's. In
1971 the wastewater treatment plant and the two lagoons ceased operations.
Universal Oil closed the company site in 1979 and demolished all structures on
the seventy-five acres in 1980. In 1983 it became a Superfund cleanup site. In
1999 I followed the trail from the ghost plant on Route 17 to the EPA (Environmental Protection Agency), where my suspicions were confirmed. According
to the EPA's Record of Decision Abstracts (RODs), various hazardous substances
seeped into the soil and shallow ground water "due to the operation of wastewater lagoons and the routine handling of raw materials and wastes" and "a
number of State investigations revealed PCB-[polychlorinated biphenyls],
PAH-[polycyclic aromatic hydrocarbons],VOC-[volatile organic compounds],
and lead-contaminated soil and VOC-contaminated leachate." The estimated

EPA cost for the remedial action to contain the toxic pollution of Trubeck/Universal Oil Products is $9,600,000, with an annual O&M cost of $1,025,200. The remedial answer to the problem was containment of contaminated soils and long-term management.[5]

If the Right-to-Know law does nothing else, it forces a company to document what it does with its waste, an act viewed as a safeguard against the creation of future toxic-waste dumps. New Jersey already has 110 major toxic dumps—Superfund sites—and hundreds of other dumps of lesser but still pressing concern.[6]

CLEANUP IS A STEP IN THE RIGHT DIRECTION

May 27, 1990

Dear Editor:

"One small step for man" is the beginning of a statement used for a dramatic accomplishment, when a man first stepped on the moon. It is, however, appropriate to use in describing activity currently under way on vacant property in East Rutherford.

Workers have begun to clean up the toxic waste left on the property of the former Universal Oil Products Co., a designated Superfund site on Route 17.

Under the supervision of the state Department of Environmental Protection, two large lagoons filled with a mixture of toxic wastes such a benzene,

Janet Zandy, *Revisiting Trubeck,* 2003.

Janet Zandy, *Revisiting Trubeck*, 2003.

chromium, and PCBs are being pumped out, dehydrated, the water treated, and organics shipped to disposal sites out of state.

It is hoped that this cleanup is the first step in a series of steps taken by government and business to remove the chemical wastes and pollutants that have been left to poison our environment by a series of corporate polluters.

The tragic record of irresponsibility has left us in the south Bergen area with a legacy of at least three Superfund sites and a record of current polluters that are among the worst in the state.

The cleanup of this UOP site has taken almost a decade to begin; for the sake of all the residents, employees and employers of this area, I hope it doesn't take another decade to continue the removal and reduction of pollutants and the restoration of our community.

Donald M. Pitches, Carlstadt[7]

This book is dialectically grounded between the values and sustaining labor of my parents and other working-class people and their places of labor, toxic waste sites (metaphoric and actual) with all the occupational hazards and dangers those workers knowingly or unknowingly faced. How that dialectic exposes and expresses itself as culture informs the writing that follows.

My answer to the unpuzzle of my father's death is not containment, but exposure. Sandra Steingraber, in *Living Downstream*, describes our "body burden," an accumulation of environmental contaminants that our bodies carry.

Janet Zandy, *Revisiting Trubeck,* 2003.

Experienced dendrochronologists, she writes, can identify comparable subtle patterns in slices of tree trunks, indicating "an ecological chronicle of the entire community."[8] Bodies prematurely ended because of unsafe work are not recoverable, but the inscribed burden of those bodies on our living consciousness and continuing histories can be excised, reclaimed, and culturally transformed.

Addendum

In March 2003 my sister, Annie, drove me back to the site of what was once Trubeck Labs. We circled twice before she found a nearby spot to park the car and wait while I walked through the highway debris toward the remaining foundation of the plant. The rusted fence, overgrown weeds, private property sign allowed for a mere glimpse at first. But then, I could see that the sign itself was near collapse, and nothing blocked the rutted road gouged no doubt by trucks and people sent to monitor the chemical waste containment. Nothing was particularly contained in this wasteland, though. Marsh grasses nonchalantly emerged from foundation cracks, birds complained about my intrusion. Piles of rusted pipes, remnants of somebody's work. A necessary return, my snapshot memory enlarged now into a wider panorama. I sought connections. And listened, not to ghostly voices, although they may have been there, but to the best of laboring lives.

These touching radium and the luminous poison,
carried their death on their lips and with their warning
glow in their graves.

—Muriel Rukeyser

Books of the Dead

Dialpainters

Hazel Vincent Kuser, Irene Rudolph, Katherine Schaub, Marguerite Carlough, and Amelia Maggia were among about two thousand women who worked as dialpainters, a war-related occupation.[1] Luminous watches with dials that glowed in the dark aided soldiers fighting in the trenches in 1917 and later during World War II. They also were a gimmicky fad at home. Measured against the physical strain of most factory jobs, dialpainting had to be appealing. It was relatively clean; the young women workers—"factory girls"—could sit rather than stand; they socialized; the work site was called a "studio" rather than a factory; the piece work pay was fairly good for the time; and these young women could use their fine manual dexterity creatively by painting luminous numbers on watch faces and other dials. Plus they were doing their bit to help the soldiers at the front.

In 1917, fifteen-year-old cousins Irene Rudolph and Katherine Schaub worked together at a dialpainting studio of the Radium Luminous Materials Corporation in Orange, New Jersey. They carried home the glowing residue of their daily work. In the dark they were not just working girls, but luminous, starry. To apply the paint to the dials, the girls "lip-pointed" their brushes. "The method of pointing the brush with the lips was taught us, to give the brush an exceedingly fine point," Katherine Schaub recalled in 1932.[2] Hand to mouth, lips as tools, watch after watch, the cousins worked for three years as dialpainters. In 1922, when they were both twenty years old, they became ill. The trouble centered in the mouth—first a swelling, a tooth removed, an inflammation, an unhealing sore, and then the whole jaw infected accompanied by a debilitating anemia. Irene Randolph died in July 1923 after what Katherine described as "a most terrible and mysterious illness."[3]

Amelia Maggia worked with Irene and Katherine. Described as a particularly productive piece worker, she began to have similar problems with her teeth and mouth in 1921. Her dentist removed her entire mandible before she died in 1922. Her death certificate listed "ulcerative stomatitis—inflammation and tissue destruction of the mouth—with syphilis given as a contributory cause."[4] As Claudia Clark, in *Radium Girls*, quietly comments, later autopsies on her exhumed remains found no evidence of syphilis, but did find traces of radium deposits in her bones. Imagine the life of Amelia Maggia, one of seven daughters, who worked with her four sisters at Radium Luminous Materials. Imagine her strong work ethic, the extra pay she earned, the craft she employed, the money she handed to her parents. A good Italian daughter? "Syphilis as a contributing factor" is the cruel, deceitful, racist footnote to her stolen life. Her death marked the first of many deaths of young women caused by radium poisoning.

Clark carefully documents the cross-class, gendered campaign of the Consumers' League, particularly the efforts of Katherine Wiley, executive secretary of the Consumers League of New Jersey, a voluntary women's organization. Wiley and others in the Consumers League were interested in industrial diseases and improving working conditions for women and children in 1920s, and were inspired by the pioneering work of Progressive Era reformer-physician Alice Hamilton, who published a survey of occupational diseases in 1910.[5] They sought to prove the existence of radium disease, gain some compensation for its victims, and prevent future cases. They fought against not only business interests, including scientists with close ties to businesses, but also government agencies, especially the New Jersey Department of Labor, as well as conservative unions who dismissed the health concerns of women workers. Clark does not overstate her case for the Consumers League, demonstrating how much class and gender prejudice impeded recognition and compensation efforts.

The newspapers at the time of the dialpainters' lawsuit in 1927 highlighted the victimization of the young women, their disfigurement, and the impediment of the disease to their societal roles as wives and mothers. Enduring, blaming fate, trusting in God, not complaining, not releasing anger were the societal and familial lessons taught to working girls in the 1920s.[6] But Katherine Schaub's direct commentary belies the stereotype of the passive victim. In her 1932 autobiographical essay, "Radium," Schaub carefully delineates the steps she took toward public recognition of her radium poisoning, her frustration at the delaying tactics of the defense, how she spent her monetary reward (in part, on reducing the mortgage on her parents' house), and her determination to help herself through a regime of fresh air, physical activity when possible, and continuing, painful medical treatments. Schaub's writing fragment vacillates between the clarity of her recognition of the depths of her disease—"there was no way by which the radium could be separated from the [dead] bone tissue. Imagine, then, the difficulty of trying to eliminate radium from the human body in life!" (139)—and her determination to live what life she had in the face of a death sentence. She took home-study courses from Columbia University and decided to write her story. As is true for many writers of the working class, she writes a double story—retelling her own experiences and speaking for and to other workers and a larger familial and communal audience: "It has been my purpose and my job to be of service to others, if only in the small measure permitted me" (157). Despite their sufferings, Schaub and other dialpainters insisted on a recognition of their own bodies as witnesses to the causality of their occupational diseases.[7]

The lawsuit was settled in June of 1928 after many defense delays. Under the settlement, the women received some financial compensation, but U.S. Radium did not have to admit guilt.[8] As Clark points out, one flaw of the settlement was the stipulation that a board of physicians would control settlement disbursements (136–137). Putting the decisive authority in the hands of (not necessarily unbiased) doctors and scientists delimited the authority of the women workers' own experience, not only displacing their own knowledge but causing them to prove once again through their damaged bodies their eligibility for recompense. Clark stresses the importance of workers finding their own medical experts and acquiring their own resources for investigative research.

In her preface to *Radium Girls*, Clark asks the acute question, "what is a senseless death and what is a meaningful one?" (vii–ix). Scientists and physicians also perished from radium poisoning. Marie Curie died from leukemia likely caused by her long exposure to the radium she discovered. In her poem "Power" Adrienne Rich singles out Marie Curie, "a famous woman" who, the poet avers, denied her "wounds" from radiation sickness, "denying / her wounds   came   from the same source as her power."[9] Rich's poetic linkage of wounds and power evoke for the reader other singular, extraordinary women— Anne Sexton, Sylvia Plath, Virginia Woolf—suicides caught, perhaps, in the paradoxical connection between creation and destruction. Rich suggests a quiet heroism in Curie, who "must have known she suffered from radiation sickness" (3). Rich's homage to Curie read in the context of what we know about the dialpainters also reveals the complexity of class assumptions. A single extraordinary woman is separated and remembered; her disease imagined poetically as "wounds," a saintly, heroic sacrifice. Whether this description truly fits the scientist Marie Curie, I do not know. But what is clear is that it does not speak to the lives of the women dialpainters, whose circumstances and choices were ordinary, not extraordinary. They were not "wounded"; rather, they were unknowingly exposed to a deadly occupational disease. What power they had as working-class women was stolen from them. This is a larger collective story rarely told in a individualistic society even by our best poets.

Clark argues, convincingly in my mind, that the deaths of the dialpainters were more than senseless deaths. It is no easy task for working-class women to stand up to authority. They don't have formal education and the linguistic tools of officialdom. Yet some of the dialpainters did precisely that. They fought not only for survival, but also for the legitimacy of their own stories, forming alliances and facing obstacles along the way. Their struggle to represent themselves as injured and dying workers is connected to a much larger story about worker self-representation.

Dialpainters

Mandible bones rest on dusty museum shelves
untombed from the earth, the length of a woman's forearm,
white testaments to deep history.
Mandibles, young and small,
jawbones
surgically removed
from radium poisoned mouths.
Where are they buried?

In 1917 in Orange, New Jersey
O New Jersey, industrial garden state,
your working people cheap crops,
Cousins Katherine and Irene worked
At Radium Luminous Materials
As dialpainters.

They were fifteen.
It was a clean job
so delicate
dipping thin paint brushes
into radium, luminous paint
so soldiers could read
their watches in the darkness of the trench.

Lips and mouth as tools
Lippointing
inserting the brush into the
mouth, carefully using the lips
to point the brush for the paint
dexterity and speed
no time to rinse the brush
lips, point, paint   lips, point, paint.

Katherine and Irene were luminous
carrying home their glowing residue
like young stars.

Hand to mouth,
lips extend hands
watch after watch.

In five years they were twenty
and terribly sick.
The trouble centered
in the mouth
that trusted tunnel.

First a swelling, a tooth extracted,
an inflammation,
more teeth, then all teeth,
unhealing sores,
then the infected jaw
and crushing anemia.

Mysterious.
One of the girls
Dial painter Amelia Maggia
died first in 1922.
One of seven daughters
worked with four of her sisters
at Radium Luminous Materials
such a strong work ethic
the extra pay earned, the money handed to parents
her death certificate
listed syphilis as a contributing cause
a doctor's racist lie
her bones exhumed
evidenced no syphilis, but radium, luminous radium.

Hazel Vincent Kuser, Irene Rudolph, Katherine Schaub,
    Marguerite Carlough, Amelia Maggia.
Dialpainters. Small canvases.
Our luminaries.[10]

Audre Lorde, X-rays, Acceptable Risks

Like superficial spirituality, looking on the bright side of things is a euphemism used for obscuring certain realities of life. . . .

—Audre Lorde, *The Cancer Journals*

In her biomythography, *Zami: A New Spelling of My Name* (1982), Audre Lorde narrates her work experiences in Stamford, Connecticut.[11] Arriving at a community center named for Crispus Attucks, Lorde inquires about openings as a medical receptionist and immediately gets the message that employment options are limited for colored girls in Stamford. She is sent to one of the factories on the other side of town where she is hired by Keystone Electronics to run a commercial X-ray machine. Keystone processed quartz crystals used in radio and radar machinery. Lorde describes the dirty, noisy work:

The two floors of the plant rang with the whine of huge cutting and refining machines. Mud used by cutting crews was all over everything, cemented by the heavy oil that the diamond-grit blades were mounted in. Thirty-two mud saws were always running. The air was heavy and acrid with the sickly fumes of carbon tetrachloride used to clean the crystals. . . .

All the help in the plant, with the exception of the foreman and forewoman, were Black or Puerto Rican. . . .

Nobody mentioned that carbon tet destroys the liver and causes cancer of the kidneys. Nobody mentioned that the X-ray machines, when used unshielded, delivered doses of constant low radiation far in excess of what was considered safe even in those days. (125–126)

Work is not a central story in *Zami*. It is embedded within larger, spiraling, internal and external narratives about family, independence, lesbian identity, erotic expression, racism, language, and power. Reading *Zami* as working-class literature, consider how Lorde illuminates her strategies of economic survival in the face of race, gender, and class—probably in that order—oppression. She is directed toward a job situated within an inflexibly structured system of race-segregated labor. Unlike white classism, where workers are shut out because of limited education and training opportunities, racism domineeringly displaces Lorde's literacy and skills. But Lorde does not displace the reader; she takes us directly onto the factory floor and meticulously reconstructs the processes of production:

The cutting "boys" made the first cut through the thick grease and mud of the machines, and then brought rough two-inch slabs to Ginger or me to be read for an electrical charge before they set the axis of their machines. The reading was obtained by a small X-ray beam passed through the crystal. There was a hood to be flipped to cover your fingers and prevent the X-ray from touching you, but the second that it took to flip it down was often the difference between being yelled at for being too slow and a smooth-working relationship with the cutters. (126–127)

Lorde and the other women workers engage a strategy of risk. To a small degree, it is an informed risk; flipping the hood would have provided some shelter from the X-ray radiation. They could obviously figure that out, although the residual effects of the radiation on their bodies was unknown and untold. Yet the exigencies of economic survival and cooperative relationships with the male cutters on one level and the very processes of production and constructed system of labor on another, more dominant level pressure Lorde and the other women not to flip the hood.

Representations of labor from outside its lived experience may offer a still life of worker as cutter or worker as X-ray technician, but rarely reconstruct the subjectivities of human beings getting through a work day. Lorde not only describes the exterior physicality of work, but opens up the interior strategies of enduring another day. Inserted into the Taylorized clock of production, Lorde sets up her own timed survival system. She "sets herself" to make it in two-hour intervals—from 8:00 a.m. to 10:00 a.m., the first break, then setting herself for another two hours to make it to lunch, and then two more hours to the 2:30

p.m. break, the hardest stretch of the day, and then finally the last two hours and she would tell herself, "you'll be free" (127). How many workers (not to mention bored school kids) set the same internal clocks every workday? Lorde writes, "After the first week, I wondered if I could stick it out. I thought that if I had to work under those conditions for the rest of my life I would slit my throat" (127).

Lorde leaves her job and Stamford temporarily when her father dies in New York. She returns to Stamford after the funeral fiercely determined to make enough money to finance a move to Mexico. And so she accepts more risk.

> I was moved on to an X-ray machine in the reading room, where the finished electronic crystals were fine-read according to strength of charge, then racked for packing.
>
> Although this job paid the same $1.10 an hour, all the jobs in the RR [reading room] were preferable and sought after. The room was in the middle of the floor, enclosed by glass panels, and the fierce sensory assaults of the rest of the plant were somewhat muted. . . .
>
> But working in the RR meant there was a chance to make piecework bonus. (144)

Piecework is another kind of worker tyranny. A tiny monetary carrot dangles in a system of unliving wages. Output above and beyond the already high pace of production earns much-needed bonuses. Desperate to leave Stamford and claim another kind of life, Lorde tests her own body and strains her relationships with other workers. She also deepens the reader's understanding of the structure of her labor by enunciating each task and action of the X-ray reader:

> Each reader obtained her crystals from the washing cage in boxes of two hundred. Taking them back to our machines, we inserted the tiny, ¾-inch squares of wafer-thin rock one by one into the throat of the X-ray machine, twirled the dial until the needle jumped to its highest point, powered by the tiny X-ray beams flashed across the crystal, snatched it off the mount, racked it in the proper slot, and then shot another crystal into the machine. With concentration and dexterity, the average amount one could read in a day was one thousand crystals.
>
> By not taking the time to flip down the protective shield that kept the X-ray from hitting our fingers, we could increase that number to about eleven hundred. Any crystals over twelve hundred read in one day were paid for as piecework, at the rate of $2.50 a hundred. Some of the women who had been at Keystone for years had perfected the motions and moved so swiftly that they were able to make from five to ten dollars some weeks in bonus. For most of them, the tips of their fingers were permanently darkened from exposure to X-ray. Before I finally left Keystone Electronics, there were dark marks on my fingers also, that only gradually faded. (144–145)

Lorde's actions and those of the other workers were not careless acts of worker indifference to bodily risk. Rather, they were necessary calculations for economic survival within a mechanized and measured system they did not control or own. If it is a game of chance, the house odds are stacked against them. And Lorde decides to go for broke. Her bonuses increase, drawing the notice of the forewoman and the other women workers. She defies the measurement experts and risks the wrath of her co-workers by upsetting the pace of their readings. Her girlfriend Ginger warns, "Don't you know those rates are set high like that so nobody can beat them? If you break your ass to read so many, you're going to show up the other girls, and before you know it they're going to raise the day rate again, figuring if you can do it so can everybody" (145).[12] Lorde risks herself and Ginger's friendship. Her daily rates get higher and higher, and she earns "an additional thirty dollars in bonus money in two weeks" (146). As one worker comments, "Just wait and see. She's going to burn her fingers off before she's through" (146). Like a Chinese railroad worker dangling in a wicker basket with a stick of dynamite, Lorde increases her bonuses by slipping crystals into her socks; she chews them up "with my strong teeth" during her bathroom breaks, flushing "the little shards of rock down the commode" (146). Suspected by the forewoman and the efficiency expert, Lorde is fired. She leaves Stamford with two weeks' severance pay thanks to her union membership.

Lorde resists certain systems of labor oppression. Her discrete actions are embedded within a larger techne of labor constraints and circumstances. She claims ownership of her body and accepts partially realized risks. If she had been better paid, if racism had not closed other jobs, she might not have been compelled to take chances. Risk and endurance are integral to the physicality of working-class labor. This is why the language of slavery and sweatshops used by writers to describe Dilbert's corporate America, is, in my mind, too casual and historically hollow.[13] While recognizing a continuum of bad jobs, it is still important to realize that boredom and stress are not the same as physical danger. The white-collar middle class may endure long hours and job insecurity, but they do not lose fingers, destroy their mouth cavities, and poison their bodies because of their paid labor. And the rich, of course, never have to make such trade-offs.

Muriel Rukeyser, Hawk's Nest, Silicosis

What three things can never be done?
Forget. Keep Silent. Stand alone.

—Muriel Rukeyser, "The Book of the Dead"

X-rays and tunnels, interior costs and exterior results, apertures and closings, natural domination and human destruction comprise the architecture of Muriel Rukeyser's sequence of poems "The Book of the Dead."[14] The setting is a West Virginia valley; the story begins in 1929. In a record two years' time, workers ("muckers") dug a 3¼-mile tunnel under a mountain from Gauley's Junction to Hawk's Nest in Fayette County so that a river could be diverted as part of a hydroelectric power project.[15] The project was and still is an engineering marvel. New Kanawha Power Company, a subsidiary of Union Carbide, diverted water through the tunnel for a hydroelectric plant which then sold the power generated to another Carbide subsidiary, the Electro-Metallurgical Company. Of the nearly five thousand men who worked on the tunnel, 65 percent were Black, largely migrant workers who dug the tunnel, the most dangerous and dirty work. The rock of the mountain contained a high silica content, "a mother lode of 90 to 99 percent pure silica."[16] Silica was an unexpected, valuable bonus, a precious by-product for Electro-Metallurgical's steel processing operation in Alloy, West Virginia. For the tunnel diggers it was death. To cut costs and increase speed, the contracting company forced the men to drill dry. Normally, minimal safety requirements involved hydraulic water drills, safety masks, and frequent relief times. But with the depressed state of West Virginia's economy, the closing or abandonment of many local coal mines, and the migration of laborers in search of work, conditions were ripe for exploitative labor practices and disregard of basic safety practices. Reports also suggest that Black workers were physically coerced to speed back into the detonated tunnel before the toxic dust had settled. Under these combined economic and racist circumstances, workers were literally disposable. It was no secret at the time that silica dust is lethal to human lungs.

Martin Cherniack, physician and researcher at the National Institute for Occupational Safety and Health, and author of the comprehensive *The Hawk's Nest Incident: America's Worst Industrial Disaster,* demonstrates how Union Carbide and Carbon Corporation controlled the project, which was designed for its own use, and comments, "It remains remarkable, nonetheless, that a private corporation could buy parts of a major river system and effectively de-water more than five miles of riverbed without encountering significant objection from either state or federal government"(14).

Counting the dead in cases of industrial death (murder?) is complicated, and, in this case, compounded by the fact that national social security records were not yet established and by the dispersal of the work force, the suppression of information, and racism.[17] Estimates of dead workers ranged from 476 to 2,000 tunnel diggers, experts settling on 700 as a reliable number. Cherniack carefully reconstructs the process of estimation, concluding that a "toll of more than seven hundred men, arrived at through a series of necessarily speculative but consistently conservative calculations, may well be too small." However, he notes that "[t]here is no need to infer a tragedy of greater proportions. . . . The death toll of the disaster at Gauley Bridge was immense compared with any other outbreak of industrial disease in modern history. That toll was taken not by accident and a merciful sudden death, but by prolonged illness and physical deterioration" (104–105). Death is slow suffocation: "Silicosis is a disease that infects the lungs and gradually causes the cells to digest themselves."[18] There is no cure. It is not known how many of the migrant laborers moved out to die elsewhere. All the company housing was shoddy, but the segregated housing for Black workers was more expensive and more crowded. What is known is that assigned the dirty job of "mucking out" the tunnel after a blast, Black workers died in proportionately higher numbers. Their deaths were obscured even more because of local racism and the company's assertion, supported by company doctors, that they died because of pneumonia, not silicosis, caused by their own self-destructive life behaviors.[19] The Hawk's Nest incident demonstrates how human workers, especially people of color, are whited-out—at first, visible as labor costs along with equipment and supplies—but then erased, invisible as dead workers killed by the job. In wartime, the bodies of dead soldiers are counted; in class warfare, workers must count their own dead.

Compounding the tragedy of individual death and the financial ruin of families, workers faced the calculus of power differentials. Company doctors, local undertakers, and calculating attorneys colluded in minimizing the corporate damage. Bodies were buried quickly and secretly, many in a nearby cornfield in makeshift graves. However, the progressive press at the time broke the news of industrial deaths at Hawk's Nest. *New Masses* and *People's Press* published accounts that were later picked up by mass-circulation magazines. The first litigation on behalf of some of the seriously ill and dead miners began in 1932. Although courts ruled in favor of compensating the plaintiffs, the amounts were meager after lawyers' fees were deducted and they were also reduced according to race and marital status. In January 1936 congressional hearings on the dangers of silicosis began. Responding to articles in the progressive and radical press, Vito Marcantonio, a young congressman from New York and member of the Subcommittee on Labor, initiated the hearings.[20] In a 1936 article in *The New Republic*, Marcantonio passionately describes the physicality of this disease as it destroys human lungs: "Silica eats through tempered steel. What it does to the human lungs is almost beyond belief. One of the most dramatic committee exhibits is the lung of a worker who died of acute silicosis. Parts of it the size of your fist are petrified clear through—veritable chunks of silica rock."[21]

these men did not need to die   —Muriel Rukeyser, "The Doctors"

how small is the sum of good writing against the
mass of poisonous stuff that finds its way into the history
books; for the dead can be stifled like the living.
                    —William Carlos Williams, "The Virtue of History," *In the American Grain*

The twenty sequenced poems of "The Book of the Dead" (1938) emerge out of an aesthetics of documentation, witnessing, and history reimagined as poetry.[22] Muriel Rukeyser traveled to Gauley Bridge with her friend Nancy Naumberg, a photographer. A New Yorker born into a wealthy Jewish family, Rukeyser takes the reader on a journey, a plunge, really, into a specific place, time, and industrial catastrophe for workers. It is not a tour, a casual stop and then back on the bus. The poems make demands on the reader, calling for an active piecing together of voice, image, and event.

Beginning with "The Road" and ending with "The Book of the Dead," the movement is from one place, Gauley Bridge, a one-street town, to another, a cliff, a gorge, a precipice, Hawk's Nest, taking the reader down, down, down, tunneling into a steeper subjective and experiential geography. The first line, "*These* are roads to take when you think of your country" (my emphasis) stresses a more incisive map and obscured epistemology (10).

These poems, imagined as roads into history and human tragedy, are not easy or well-traveled routes. The polished literary ear of the listening poet hears the nuanced idiom of witnesses and survivors and recognizes the predictable and programmatic voices of officialdom—doctors, congressmen, corporate spokesmen. This long, sequenced poem, emulating the power of healthy lungs, breathes in and breathes out. The poet must speak, observe, witness, and yet hold back some of the rush of her own language so as not to colonize and dominate the event. The Hawk's Nest project harnessed technological power; Rukeyser's "Book of the Dead" unearths another kind of power. The lyrical—"O the gay wind, . . .O the gay snow . . .O proud O white O water rolling down" ("The Face of the Dam: Vivian Jones," 14–15) ironically abuts the actuality of the "locomotive rusted on the siding" (14). Rukeyser's poetic prowess creates multivocal and dialogic aural spaces. Voices speak.

Images. The camera's eye, the eyes of witnesses, the eyes clouded with dust inside the tunnel, the eyes of doctors reading X-rays, the eyes of the dead, the eyes that deny, refuse, obfuscate—all dialectically both re-present and obscure the brutal story: "here is a room of eyes / a single force looks out, reading our life" and "[t]heir hands touch mastery; now they / demand an answer" ("Praise of the Committee," 17). The near-ghost-town Gauley Bridge mirrors the fluidity of presence and absence. Glass, a supercooled liquid, not quite a solid, based on silicon, boric, and aluminum oxides dominates the poem "Gauley Bridge" (13-14). The town is seen through the camera's eye ("ground glass"), a boy "blurs the camera-glass fixed on the street." The hotel owner keeps his accounts "behind the public glass"; the waitress is "April-glass-tinted"; the bus schedule is pasted to the "plate-glass window" of the bus station; the "harsh night eyes over the beerglass." These accumulated images suddenly shift and the still life is broken up and the poet speaks directly to the reader, "What do you want—a cliff over a city?" From Walker Evans/James Agee sublime to the direct voice of the New Yorker, declaring, "These people live here." This is not a tourist stop, not a picturesque postcard, not bourgeois aesthetic pleasure, not a clear mirror reflecting accessible surfaces; this place holds brutal history.

How do we know? Facts, stories, memories, experiences, observations are deposited, deposed, written down. Sediments of experience and knowledge lived. In "Absalom" (18–20), a mother speaks for her three dead sons: "Cecil, aged 23, Owen, aged 21, Shirley, aged 17" lured by a "power Co. foreman" to "give up their jobs [in the mines] and take this other work." The youngest, Shirley, urges her to pursue his death's meaning—"'Mother, when I die, / I want you to have them open me up and / see if that dust killed me'"—and the first lawsuit. More sweeping and penetrating than a camera's eye, the mother names some of the dead:[23]

> There was Shirley and Cecil, Jeffrey and Oren,
> Raymond Johnson, Clev and Oscar Anders,
> Frank Lynch, Henry Palf, Mr. Pitch, a foreman;
> a slim fellow who carried steel with my boys,
> his name was Darnell, I believe. There were many others,
> the towns of Glen Ferris, Alloy, where the white rock lies,
> six miles away; Vanetta, Gauley Bridge,.
> Gamoca, Lockwood, the gullies,
> The whole valley is witness.

The mother, through the poet, speaks for her son: "He shall not be diminished, never; / I shall give a mouth to my son."

Rukeyser uses repetition to underscore the authorial power of the body as witness. In "The Disease" (20-21) a series of lung X-rays documents the disease's progression. This is not picturesque water cascading down naked rock, but rather the demolition of occupational disease: "This is" breastbone; "this is" heart; "this is" a lung mottled by disease "like a snowstorm struck the fellow's lungs." First stage. The poet commanding, reading the body: "Come to the window. . . . Here is the heart. . . . And now, . . . solid scars . . . thick on both sides. / Blood vessels shut. Model conglomeration." Second stage. And then: "There and there and there, there, there." Third Stage. And then the voice of the dying worker:

> It is growing worse every day. . . .
> . . . .
> That is what happens, isn't it?
> A choking-off in the air cells?
> Yes.
> There is difficulty in breathing.
> Yes.
> And a painful cough?
> Yes.
> Does silicosis cause death?
> Yes, sir.

Final Stage. What do we readers, then and now, do with this evidence? In "The Cornfield" Rukeyser admonishes us to participate and not just read the poem as object, but to read our own country: "Uncover," "Contemplate," "Voyage," "Think" (27).

Loss: Circumstances and Choices

George Robinson holds all their strength together:
To fight the companies to make somehow a future.

—"Praise of the Committee" (16)

No color. Gray. White. George Robinson, Black tunnel digger, maps the intersection of race and capital, in the poet's "George Robinson: Blues" (21–22): "thirty-five tunnel workers the doctors didn't attend, / died in the tunnel camps." If the men complained of their sickness they were fired, "the Cap and company come and run him off the job surely." The Black men forced back into the tunnel—"hurry, hurry, into the falling rocks and muck." Their drinking water coated with dust. Dust stayed. Unwashable. Death's minstrel show turning Black workers White:

As dark as I am, when I came out at morning after the tunnel
At night,
With a white man, nobody could have told which man was
white.
The dust had covered us both, and the dust was white.

Rukeyser concludes with a sequence of poems about power. In "Power" she turns to the technological sublime, the power plant. Dialectically, she moves from technical achievement—"Four generators," sun, a "day of heat"—to the human costs of the diversion of water power—the "river Death" (29–31). Documentation is displaced by the rehearsed voice of the poet. She returns, perhaps less effectively than in the earlier poems, to documentation in "The Dam." The power of water, "kinetic and controlled" (31) mirrors the ambitions of the poem. The silver screen of motion picture technique segues into "a screen of falling water / in film-silver . . ." (32). Rukeyser connects the historical equations: water harnessed equals industrial power. She does not forget that technological achievement rests on human backs, "The dam is the father of the tunnel" (33). But she attempts to answer corporate power, "A corporation is a body without a soul," with elemental and transcendant power, a "perfect fluid": Be born again. / Nothing is lost, even among the wars, / imperfect flow, confusion of force. / It will rise" (33). Will it? Who pays for power and with what? The congressional committee holds hearings, makes worthy recommendations, a bill proposed, blocked, further investigations, recompense, blocked. Rukeyser acknowledges the inadequacy of "Capitoline thunder" ("The Bill," 37). She calls for the freeing of "authentic power," rising out of the earth (37).

The final poem, "The Book of the Dead," is an evocation, an informed vision, and an expanding possibility. Rukeyser asks the young, the surveyors and planners, the collectors of facts, to "measure our times again" (39). She calls on her readers to carry the catalytic power of the poems forward in time to continue a long struggle begun for her in the 1930s. It is a struggle for justice and safe working conditions for workers everywhere. What Rukeyser offers anew is the strength that can grow out of anger grounded in historical knowledge. Look.

"[W]iden the lens and see." Listen. "Voices to speak to us directly." The poems are offerings to the dead tunnel diggers, "seeds of unending love" (40). Let them serve as epilogue to occupational death.

> You look at that tunnel there and you think it's a mighty fine thing. Just from looking at it, a man would never know how many lives were sacrificed.
>
> —Harless Gibson, deputy sheriff of Fayette County, 1928–1930[24]

"Work! Sure! For America beautiful will eat you and spit your bones into the earth's hole! Work!"   *—The Lean, in Pietro di Donato's* Christ in Concrete

So he threw it up, not yet knowing a job was God, and praying wasn't enough, you had to live for It, produce for It, prostrate yourself, take anything from It, for was it not God . . .   *—Tillie Olsen,* Yonnondio

I shall never forget where I came from, and I shall never deny that I was privileged to learn.   *—Rosa Crane, unpublished memoir*

Two really significant aspects of my work have been recognized: The acceptance of the common man in contrast to the white collar stuff and the value of the realistic photography which has for some time been displaced by the fuzzy impressionism of the day.   *—Lewis Hine*

God Job

The documentary photographer Lewis Hine never won a major grant, fellowship, or prize. In 1938, unable to find work, his son, Corydon, hospitalized, his wife, Sara, suffering from chronic asthma, facing foreclosure on his house in Hastings-on-Hudson, he applied for a Guggenheim Foundation grant. His proposal, "Our Strength Is Our People," said simply, "This project should give us light on the kinds of strength we have to build upon as a nation. Much emphasis is being put upon the dangers inherent in our alien groups, our unassimilated or even partly Americanized citizens—criticism based upon insufficient knowledge. A corrective for this would be better facilities for seeing and so understanding what the facts are."[1] The Guggenheim Committee considered, considered, promised, promised, and then finally turned him down. Hine then applied to the Carnegie Foundation with a proposal for a project on American craftspeople. Carnegie, too, rejected him. The bank foreclosed on his house and Hine was forced to go on relief. On Christmas morning in 1938 Sara died, and two years later, Lewis Hine, broke, and perhaps, broken, died. Such is the cruel, ironic conclusion to the life of America's greatest documentary photographer.

Lewis Hine died five years before I was born. His images are crucial to my self-education, the affirmation of working-class experience missing from institutionalized learning. I stand at appreciative attention before a Stieglitz image, but with Hine I slip and fall into that space where humanity trumps art. Hine's photographs are inexplicably familiar. I am drawn to the craft and beauty of Hine's images because they emanate a communitas, tendrils of connection between photographer and subjects. Hine's life in relation to his work, dying broke, commercially unviable, is more than a familiar story of the unappreciated-in-his-own-time artist. Hine's fate exposes deeper national fault lines, problems of selective and undemocratic vision. The genuinely heroic Hine becomes historically tamed, the social imperatives of his images hidden beneath a patina of patriotism or placed at a convenient and comfortable distance. Hine's photos of Ellis Island immigrants, "sky-boys" building the Empire State Building, street children, tenement mothers, and factory workers are easily and frequently appropriated for some national self-congratulatory celebration without credit to Hine or recognition of his deep commitment to social justice. Hine is an essential guide exactly because his photographs are about illumination, not celebration. His "photo stories" are both public and private: historical documentation and family album. Sometimes the portraits convey the blank look of exhaustion, sometimes the newcomer's shyness, sometimes an unexpected posture, even bravado, but almost always in these photographs there is the mark of labor on the human body.

Hine's dark photographs of "breaker boys" in Pennsylvania coal mines document the theft of childhood. Boys seven, eight, nine years old, wedged in tight rows, covered with soot, hunched over, are pushed to work and work, faster and faster, sorting and breaking, hour after hour.[2] The 1913 *Child Labor Bulletin* reported: "These boys picked out the pieces of slate and stone that cannot burn. It's like sitting in a coal bin all day long, except the coal is always moving and clattering and cuts their fingers. Sometimes the boys wear lamps in their caps

Lewis Hine, *Breaker Boys,* Pennsylvania, 1910.
Courtesy of George Eastman House.

Lewis Hine, *Breaker Boys,* 1911.
Courtesy of George Eastman House.

to help them see through the thick dust. They bend over the chutes until their backs ache, and they get tired and sick because they have to breathe coal dust instead of pure air." And Hine adds, writing in *The Survey*, May 1913: "There is a prevailing impression that in the matter of child labor the emphasis on the labor must be very slight, but let me tell you right here that these processes involve work, hard work, deadening in its monotony, exhausting physically, irregular, the workers' only joy the closing house. We might even say of these children that they are condemned to work."[3]

What happens to bodies that never unbend, that never feel the heat of the sun? These young lads, grown into men, were said to carry their "boy on their back." Their spines were often permanently crooked and their shoulders literally carried the hump of work. This is not a birth deformity. This is a work deformity.

I do not carry the hump of childhood work on my back. Like many children of working-class families, I was allowed, even encouraged, to study. My body does not bear the mark of labor as my parents' bodies did, as their parents' and grandparents' did before them. In snapshots of significant occasions in my parents' lives, the work clothes are gone, the injuries are hidden, and they smile into the camera. They choose to smile. I choose to look behind the smile, not because the smile is false; it is as genuine and real as what lies behind the smile. I choose to look behind, beneath, and around the smile exactly because I am safe. I will not be injured on the job; no chemical burns will tattoo my skin; no knife will slip and cut off my finger. I am physically safe and have time and space to think and write. In every sense, I can afford to do this and they could not—at least not in this textual way. This is about an ethos of working-class responsibility, not about guilt. Carrying the hump of memory about physical labor into polite and clean circles of knowledge and power is one way to practice working-class agency.

I remember standing in the doorway to my parents' bedroom in our small apartment in Union City, New Jersey. Each room has a doorway but no door. Only the bathroom with a tub and no sink has a door. My parents' bedroom is in the center of the apartment. On the right is the front or living room with its elaborate 1950s wallpaper of ferns and ivy. On the left is the tiny closet of a room I share with my sister. The center of our home is, of course, not the living room, but the kitchen. Every corner of this crowded apartment is clean and tidy.

I am standing in the doorway to my parents' bedroom because I am afraid to enter that space. Accustomed to my father's shift work at the chemical plant, I knew there were times when he had to sleep in the daytime because he worked all night. So, I was used to playing quietly, unseen, hushed so Papa could rest. On this particular day, when I was perhaps seven or eight, something felt different. Papa was in bed in the middle of the day but he wasn't trying to sleep. He was trying to get better. From what? And then, standing in the doorway, I saw it: the ugly red burns gouged into his chest. I remember he looked at me—maybe he smiled, that would be like him—but did I smile back or did I run away too scared by what I saw to speak?

This was a family where the children were not encouraged to speak up or back or question. From a very young age I knew the boundaries of what could be named and what was permissible for family kitchen talk. Papa getting burned at work was not for the children to hear about or know. . . . But I saw!

How to carry this memory without betraying it? It would be a violation of family trust if I told my story for rhetorical effect. I tell it because I know there are some readers who will recognize in it their own family legacies of missing fingers, uneven shoulders, varicose veins, deafness, blinded eyes, enlarged hearts, swollen hands—an encyclopedia of ailing or phantom body parts, work-related injuries, that collectively attest to untold stories of labor. These missing body parts and inscriptions on the body are crucial to our understanding of cultural formation and academically sanctioned knowledge. I also wish to expose the connection between culture and the "g" word—grief. How is grief culturally represented and negotiated? The *New York Times*'s "portraits of grief," paragraph-sized obituaries and photos of the victims of 9/11/01 is one way.[4] The oppressive emphasis on "closure" in the popular media sense of forty-five seconds of bad-news reporting and now on to today's "bright spot" is another way. By negotiating I do not mean silencing, forgetting, or hiding grief for the comfort level of other people. Nor do I mean sympathetic tears of condolence. I mean instead the difficult task of putting grief, private and collective, to democratic and cultural use. How do we move pedagogically and culturally between death and life, past and present, to create spaces of reciprocal visibility, to provide, in Lewis Hine's words, "better facilities for seeing"? To do my work in the academy I claim an epistemological grounding outside the elitism of privileged-class universities. This is a matter of knowledge base, not, as Roxanne Rimstead warns, a display of working-class "identity credentials" in order to speak for the missing voices in academic circles.[5]

Many academics from the working class experience psychological, social, and linguistic dislocation, an outsider subjectivity rarely visible to their middle- and upper- class colleagues. Fortunately, these differences are no longer completely closeted. We now have stories aplenty written by women and men who were born into the working class and were able, often because of their capacity to learn, their tenacity, and, perhaps, their good fortune, to acquire academic jobs that offer physical safety and security not even imagined by their own families. Our challenge is to craft curriculum and change classroom practices so that working people are included at the center of study rather than at the margins of a syllabus or not on the page at all. In order to practice a working-class democratic pedagogy one has to engage one's own story (either voiced or silently remembered), draw strength and knowledge from it, connect it historically to other narratives, and then use these multiple voices to transform the present and imagine a future of transnational economic justice. To be sure this is a pedagogy of hope and agency, but it is more than idealism. It offers an alternative to the usual American Dream menu of amnesia first and nostalgia next for working-class intellectuals.

All of us (even the owning class) carry within us traces of our family's work histories: paid or unpaid labor, underemployment or unemployment, seasonal work or steady work, legal work or illegal work. Consciously or not, this work inheritance shapes our own attitudes about work, sometimes in imitation, sometimes in rejection. From my parents I have inherited a strong work ethic, just as I have inherited brown eyes. I see my mother breaking the eggs, rolling the dough, shaping the raviolis. I also see her at the window, waiting anxiously for my father's safe return from work. I realize that their sense of pride in their work could also be used against them on the paid job, facing working conditions that were unfair and possibly damaging and dangerous. Would my father have died at the age of forty-nine if he were a professor instead of a pre-OSHA chemical plant worker? Possibly, but not probably. Work also kills.

In his classic *Working*, Studs Terkel begins with a declaration: "This book, being about work, is, by its very nature, about violence—to the spirit as well as to the body." But Terkel, with his usual dialectical acumen, adds, "Perhaps it is time the 'work ethic' was redefined and its idea reclaimed from the banal men who invoke it. In a world of cybernetics, of an almost runaway technology, things are increasingly making things. It is for our species, it would seem, to go on to other matters. Human matters."[6] How can these human matters, the safety and health of workers, surface in a literature course? How can exposure to representations of physical labor enlarge class consciousness?

On the Job in Academe

My private, technical institute takes justifiable pride in preparing students for state-of-the-art training in their fields. Red brick dominates the modernist campus, a contemporary architectural style called "brutalism." And the name fits. Students keep their heads down as they face the cutting wind between the sharp edges of the campus buildings. Although recent beautification installments of wide paths, inviting benches, and flowering gardens soften and humanize those thrusting bricks, there is still a no-nonsense clarity on the campus about goals and purposes. Students take their courses, pass their exams, work their co-ops, get their degrees, and land well-paying jobs. That's the script, particularly for students in technical, science, and business degree programs. Most students, whatever their field—graphic design, information systems, imaging science, electrical engineering, printing, packaging science, photography—have a strong work ethic; they have to, or they wouldn't make it over the finish line to graduation.

My students, like most Americans, are practical people; they want to learn what they need to know in order to obtain the best possible job. It is not that they're disinterested in history; they're just accustomed to its sanitized historical packaging. Mike Wallace, in *Mickey Mouse History and Other Essays on American Memory*, demonstrates how, on one hand, there is tremendous enthusiasm for the present, the new and the now. On the other hand, as Wallace points out, "we have been on a heritage binge and remain thoroughly obsessed with the past."[7] But this is a staged past—history as static diorama, pleasant visits to Colonial Williamsburg or Old Sturbridge—not history as struggle.[8] This comfortable historical distance dissolves when students read certain working-class novels that present disturbing descriptions of the physicality of labor.

For most of the 1990s, the national rhetoric of entrepreneurial opportunity combined with technical expertise persuasively convinced students that a technical/business education would literally pay off. Maybe it will; maybe it won't. Many students, however, resist being defined as the sum of their technical training. Student artists speak knowingly about splitting their future work lives between art for the market and art for themselves. Engineering students shoot photographs, play instruments, climb mountains. Some students, though, especially the younger ones who have logged innumerable hours before televisions, terminals, videos, and who have never eaten a meal without a humming machine in the foreground or background, are not accustomed to dialoguing with, not to mention imagining, people who are not copies of themselves. Even those students, who are the most indifferent to politics and history, who are most centered on their immediate needs, who are most captured by the latest techno toy, have a work legacy I can tap.

And then there are those students, a little older, who are split between jobs, family, and school. Often the women have business ambitions and want the degree to get to the next wage grade; the men may be technicians in local plants or recent vets returning to school not to acquire skills they already possess but to have those skills warranted, certified, credentialed, and degreed. These students have little patience with what they may perceive as liberal arts blather. Their lives are one long time clock. Invariably, these are the students most responsive to working-class texts and I rely on them to convey this understanding to other, perhaps more economically privileged, students.

Joe is a good example. Recently married and discharged from the Navy, he enrolls in my upper-division writing course. His first essay is a beautifully written narrative recalling his father's suicide from the perspective of his twelve-year-old self. When he submits his first draft for my comments, he remarks that he expects me "to tear it up." He is worrying about punctuation; I am staggered by his capacity to write so powerfully and personally. I return it to him, telling him there's nothing to tear. I do not think he believes me at first. At the end of the quarter he seeks me out as I am ending another class. He blurts out: "I didn't expect to like your class. You seemed liberal and the other students seemed liberal, and I'm conservative. But I love this class." Why? I cannot in good faith put words in Joe's mouth, but I can safely surmise that the course appealed to him because it seemed *real*; he did not experience a bifurcation between his tactile, experiential world and the classroom. Although in our readings we tested how perceived reality is shaped and coded by language, we did not wind up floating in some nonreferential postmodern space. And perhaps his assumptions about the liberal female professor were undercut by assignments that asked him to read, photograph, and write about the lives of working-class people. In contrast to most of the other students, Joe particularly appreciated reading Michael Wilson's screenplay, *Salt of the Earth*.[9] Joe had no difficulty seeing the parallel work lives of the husband and wife protagonists, the unsafe, exhausting paid work in the mines, and the unsanitary, exhausting unpaid work of the Mexican wives and mothers at home. He understood that when the men could no longer picket because of a Taft-Hartley court injunction, the women had to take over and hold the line. Roles were reversed at home and the men, forced to take up women's work of chopping wood, scrubbing laundry, and caring for children, finally recognized the justification for the Mexican women's demands for the same indoor plumbing the Anglo miners had. That it is unlikely Joe or anyone else in the class had ever examined seriously the impact of Taft-Hartley or studied the orchestrated resistance to union formation and collective bargaining that is part of their country's history is another matter.[10] Other students had to negotiate their own class positions vis-à-vis a text that challenged their unstated, market-shaped assumptions about business and presented characters they're most inclined to identify with—managers, owners, and the local sheriff—as oppressors. Rather than investigate their own ideological assumptions, these students would rather write off the film as hokey or dated. It's ideologically safer. Relating the film to contemporary economic realities, such as huge differentials between CEOs' and workers' salaries, I can see that I am trespassing on sacred ground. After all, some are aspiring to be those CEOs. Whether the corporate scandals of 2001–2002, the enormous greed at workers' expense, will stimulate a larger historical consciousness and alternative careers remains to be seen.

In assigning working-class stories, with their frequent descriptions of the physicality and dangers of work, I am retrieving not only a lost American labor history, but also many students' own transgenerational family work histories. Accustomed to sweaty bodies on the running track, the weight room or aerobic class, many students, like many professors, managers, and technocrats, barely see the working bodies in their daily lives—the men and women who clean their toilets, repair their machines, or pick up their litter. Just as consumers resist acknowledging the machine-tending human hand behind the products they buy, students resist the disquieting confrontation with physical work. Students who have cut their teeth on violence in every medium (TV, film, video games, music, dance) are squeamish in the face of industrial and work-related violence. Narratives of workplace violence, however, produce an emotional as well as intellectual awareness, the seeds for the cultivation of transportable historical memory. Such texts not only reacquaint students with their own family's labor lineage, but also cast a disquieting light on their own assumptions about safe work. In the midst of a de rigueur postmodern cynicism, I hoist the blue-collar flag, welcoming students back to what blacklisted writer Michael Wilson once called (as an alternative to the 1950s Hollywood 3-D fad) the "fourth dimension . . . called reality—the reality of working people's lives" (109).

"God Job"

One of the ways working-class literature is distinct from bourgeois literature is in its emphasis on the physicality of work. The white-gloved serving hand that might be glimpsed on the periphery in a middle-class novel is fully attached to the working body in working-class literature. Workers—so many hands—and physical labor are foregrounded in working-class autobiographies, novels, poems, and songs. Injuries and deaths accumulate in working-class literature. Narrative shifts hinge on work that kills and maims. Whatever their differences of gender, ethnicity, race, and regional perspective, Agnes Smedley's *Daughter of*

Earth, Tillie Olsen's *Yonnondio*, William Attaway's *Blood on the Forge*, Audre Lorde's *Zami*, Thomas Bell's *Out of This Furnace*, Pietro di Donato's *Christ in Concrete*, Maxine Hong Kingston's *China Men*, Edith Summers Kelley's *Weeds*, Helena María Viramontes' *Under the Feet of Jesus*, Jim Daniels's *Punching Out*, and Sue Doro's *Blue Collar Goodbyes* are all grounded in the physicality of work.

Debates about classification—whether to call this literature realistic, naturalistic, ghetto pastoral, brutal proletarian—matter to professors and students of literature, but I doubt if working people care about such categories. They care about jobs. And jobs are both the epistemological center of working-class writing and a force that threatens to quell or silence literary, perhaps all, expression. Tillie Olsen, Thomas Bell, and Pietro di Donato take up the burden of forging a language of the working body that simultaneously depicts the brutal dominance of jobs *and* presents the aesthetics of human relationships. In Olsen's *Yonnondio* the word *jobs* melds into a singular, unmodified, capitalized God JOB. This is a demanding, authoritarian, inescapable, exacting God, and the workers who must prostrate before it have little hope that their service, their loyalty, their sacrifice will ever be rewarded in the present, never mind, like their distant Biblical cousin Job, in the sweet by-and-by. Job is monster, and workers' bodies are served up to the devouring Minotaur of labor. In her poem "The Minotaur" Muriel Rukeyser writes sympathetically of the mythological monster as a creature betrayed—"Trapped, blinded, led; and in the end betrayed."[11] So, too, these workers, whether they package meat, shovel molten steel, or lay brick, must grovel and accept their own betrayal as human beings, having not only their surplus labor value sucked from them, but their very lives. But these narratives would not have sustaining power if they were merely litanies of victimization. Resistance to Job is through the culture and ethos of working-class people themselves, through unionization and collective bargaining, as evidenced in the union-building third generation in *Out of This Furnace,* and through small and large acts of solidarity with family and friends. Each novel offers moments of human kinship, tenderness, commitment, a not-so-quiet spirituality of humble people up against the mighty, unsafe, exploitative Job. *Christ in Concrete, Yonnondio,* and *Out of This Furnace* challenge classical definitions of tragedy and present the loss of human lives because of the job as a tragedy of singular and collective proportions. These worker tragic figures cannot claim a noble birth or fall or even offer a reader a cathartic response. Instead they call for a response to the conditions that killed them, a move beyond sympathetic identification of them as victims. Such a view of tragedy, as theorist Carole Anne Taylor suggests, is not a "liberal tragedy reliant on solidarity without commitment," a "temporary identification that bypasses relations of power because after all, 'We are all victims.'"[12]

Literary critics speak of the difficulty of representing embodied labor. I agree to a point, but want to suggest that it is no more difficult or easy than representing embodied anger or love or any human condition. The difference is that in the formulation of canons and a belles lettres tradition, human labor has been fenced off as something inappropriate, perhaps too vulgar or even grotesque for literary consideration. We do have vivid, harsh, and believable descriptions of labor in two novels of immigrant experience, Thomas Bell's *Out of This Furnace* (1941) and Pietro di Donato's *Christ in Concrete* (1939).[13] In these powerful autobiographical novels, of Slovakians at the bottom rung of big steel and Italians laying brick at the top of New York's early skyscrapers, labor is neither aestheticized nor distanced. Further, these working-class novels illuminate the interdependence of domestic work and paid work (Bell more so than di Donato) and convey the horrendous economic and emotional cost to a family of an industrial death.

Out of This Furnace, spanning three generations of Slovakian steelworkers living in Braddock, Pennyslvania, from the 1880s to the 1930s, is Bell's homage to the struggle of his parents and other relatives, too often betrayed and used up by the steel mills.[14] While the characters may feel alienated and removed from politics and power, Bell subtly and skillfully weaves a historical context for their lived experiences. *Out of This Furnace* documents the class warfare inherent to the history of U.S. steel and exposes the lie that technical progress translates into human progress. Labor history is lived, but workers deprived of their own history of earlier struggles, such as Andrew Carnegie breaking the Amalgamated Association of Iron and Steel workers in Homestead in 1892, lack historical knowledge as a tool for change. Instead they are forced to exist in what seems like the ahistorical time of speed-up production, especially for those at the lowest levels of racially tiered jobs, who are subject to numerous and ghastly industrial deaths and injuries. But images retain historical memory. Lewis Hine's photographs of Homestead, taken as part of the 1907 Pittsburgh Survey, document the dignity of workers as well as their oppressive working and living conditions.[15]

At the literal center of the book, the emotional binding of the novel, are the intertwined work lives of Mary and Mike Dobrejcak at the turn of the twentieth century. In this scene of July heat "baking the streets and courtyards of the First Ward," Mary collapses in her kitchen and the doctor is summoned. She is pregnant again. The doctor advises bed rest and no exertion and "Mary stared up at him. With six boarders, three children and a husband to look after, meals to cook, clothes to wash, her hours were from four-thirty in the morning to nine at night, seven days a week" (173). How could she rest? There is no rest for her husband either—now old at thirty—as he faces another twenty-four hour work shift: "The first twelve hours were much like any day turn except that sometimes, through a break in the mill's rumble, he could hear church bells. . . . The second twelve hours were like nothing else in life. Exhaustion slowly numbed his body, mercifully fogged his mind; he ceased to be a human being, become a mere appendage to the furnace, a lost damned creature. 'At three o'clock in the morning of a long turn a man could die without knowing it'" (167).

Working-class novels like *Out of This Furnace* are more than an accumulation of labor horrors; they also document the human capacity for resistance and for insisting humans are not "its," merely "check number[s]," "Hunky laborer[s]," or human appendages to the machine. Mike announces to his friend Stefan:

It's a terrible and beautiful thing to make iron. It's honest work, too, work the world needs. They should honor us, Stefan. Sometimes when the bosses bring their friends through the mill they watch us make a cast and when the iron pours out of the furnace, you know how wonderful it is, especially at night, I feel big and strong with pride. . . . I don't mind work. But a man should be allowed to love his work and take pride in it. There's good in all of us that would make our lives happier and the world a better place for everybody. But it's never asked for. We're only Hunkies. (196)

The next day Mike kisses Mary good-bye, heads for the steel mill on a spring-like, mild evening, enters the mill gate and goes to work. Before he can finish his shift, a furnace blows and Mike Dobrejcak is dead. Mike's death is reported to Mary; the reader "overhears" the details of the explosion, and experiences the aftermath—the burial, the paltry compensation, and then Mary's and the children's struggle to survive.

In response, one student writes, "I honestly felt a sharp jab in my chest and a loss of breath when I read that Mike was dead. I also became enraged at Thomas Bell. He killed my Mike, Mary's Mihal. I had not realized until that point how engrossed I had become in the story until I felt the tears in my eyes. Bell brought the emotions of this book out vividly and by doing so really gave the reader a clear image as well as feeling for what these men and women experienced. I never really thought of life as a daily struggle until I visited the Krachas. The spirit and will that these people possessed must have been extremely powerful" (Erin).Working-class novels like *Out of This Furnace* and *Christ in Concrete* jar some students into a recognition of their own class privileges and circumstances: "Butcher, baker, or candlestick maker—the choice has always been mine. *Anything* I wanted to reach for, towards any desired office of life that knowledge and passion could buy, I was encouraged to strive. I have no memory of a time without choice. Happiness, fulfillment and wisdom were my given goals, and elemental survival was my granted right" (Alexandra).

But for other students, exposure to such novels permits them to tell their own suppressed labor stories: "Di Donato's description of starting work so young struck a familiar cord with me. I remember a delivery from the bakery where I fell down concrete steps and hurt my back, bringing me to tears. I quickly regained my composure and went back to the car and said nothing to my boss . . . [about] what happened because he would have thought I was making excuses" (Jesse). Carlette writes: "I remember vividly cleaning 16 rooms a day at a Colorado resort. That job was the toughest, most physical job I have ever worked. In an 8-hour day, I scrubbed, wiped, vacuumed, dusted, and pushed a heavy cart for the guests. I know how it feels to be tired and worn out, muscles hurting for a few days. But the job never killed me." Job as warfare, and workers as unwilling soldiers, become in the words of engineer-activist Jesse Lenney, an "ancient, inherited enemy (I know I didn't choose this fight), and the casualties of this war are not metaphorical, but real and human."

Sometimes, as Terry Eagleton notes, "you do not need to leap our of your skin to know what another is feeling; indeed there are times when you need rather to burrow more deeply into it."[16]

Another student describes *Christ in Concrete* as "the saddest book I've ever read. . . . While I was reading [it], I could actually feel Paul's trowel in my hand, feel the texture of the mortar and the taste of cement dust. I thought this was kind of strange because I don't have a single Italian bone in my body" (Terry). To be sure, in this working-class Bildungsroman of Southern Italian immigrant bricklayers, who see themselves as builders of families, of new American lives, and as artisans in shaping the urban, tall-building landscape, there is no reader comfort zone.

The novel begins amidst a building boom in New York City on a brisk March day of Easter week in 1923. A work crew of immigrant Southern Italians lays bricks six floors up on a building with a shoddy foundation. As in Italian opera, we know them at first through their ribald language, jokes, and physical descriptions—Burly Julio, known as "Snoutnose," or Mike the "Barrel-mouth," and "Old Nick, the 'Lean' who did not love the 'great God Job'" (8). We meet Geremio, their respected foreman, proud husband to Annunziata, father of six children, and one more soon to come. Geremio is torn between the intensity of his pride in and duty to his family and the realization that this construction job is unsafe. He tries to stop the work: "Padrone—padrone, the underpinning gotta be make safe and . . ." And gets the expected response: "Lissenyawopbastard! if you don't like it, you know what you can do!" (9). And what can Geremio do? "The new home, the coming baby, and his whole background, kept the fire from Geremio's mouth and bowed his head" and he became "[n]o longer Geremio, but a machinelike entity." And "the men were transformed into single, silent beasts" (9).

On Good Friday Geremio "stared dumbly at the structure and mechanically listed in his mind's eye the various violations of construction safety" (11), and the concrete was poured. The inadequate building supports burst and the "floor vomited upward" (14). Geremio is catapulted in "directionless flight," landing upright with arms outstretched, crucified, and facing the huge concrete hopper and the gray gushing concrete. In five long pages, di Donato describes the agony of Geremio's death:

> His genitals convulsed. The cold steel rod upon which they were impaled froze his spine. He shouted louder and louder. "Save me! I am hurt badly! I can be saved I can—save me before it's too late!" But the cries went no farther than his own ears. The icy wet concrete reached his chin. His heart appalled. "In a few

seconds I will be entombed. If I can only breathe, they will reach me. Surely they will!" . . . He had bitten halfway through when his teeth snapped off to the gums in the uneven conflict. The pressure of the concrete was such, and its effectiveness so thorough, that the wooden splinters, stumps of teeth, and blood never left the choking mouth. . . . He tried to breathe, but it was impossible. The heavy concrete was settling immutably and its rich cement-laden grout ran into his pierced face. His lungs would not expand and were crushing in tighter and tighter under the settling concrete. . . . He screamed, "Show yourself now, Jesu!" . . . . and the fighting brain disintegrated and the memories of a baffled lifetime sought outlet. (16–18)

Pietro di Donato sums up the day after Geremio's funeral in this understated, powerful way: "The day that followed was lived" (30).

I know of no other working-class novel that so powerfully confronts the reader with the horror of death on the job. Colored cement gray and blood red, Job betrays artisanal pride and skill. In this masculine coming-of-age narrative, the first born son, Pietro (Paul) must take up his father's trowel to support Annunziata and the younger children, and, consequently, leave his education, childhood, and belief in Roman Catholicism behind. "Lay brick! Lay brick!" (84). Up and up, higher and higher, Job is Paul's sexual awakening and first holy communion of work. The novel concludes with Paul's epiphany that he, his father, mother, godfather, siblings, have all been cheated by Job, the American creed of work hard and you will be rewarded: "Unfair! Unfair!—Our lives—unfair!" (226).

And for some it is still unfair, as Jimmy Breslin demonstrates in *The Short Sweet Dream of Eduardo Gutierrez,* an account of the life and death of an illegal Mexican earning low, nonunion wages at a shoddy construction site in Williamsburg, Brooklyn, in November 1999. Cement was poured onto the third floor where Eduardo "pushed with his big spreader" and the building shook, and in an instant, "a shrug of concrete and metal, and the floor under Eduardo went." And,

Down Eduardo went, so quickly that he made no sound.
Down went Alejandro and Lucino and Gustavo and two Angels and Juan.
Down they went so quickly that nobody screamed.
The third floor fell into the second floor and the second floor into the first and
 everything fell into the basement. . . .
What were supposed to be metal beams holding up the floors were as strong
as aluminum foil.
Eduardo fell face first into three feet of concrete on the basement floor and
 drowned.[17]

It is difficult, perhaps impossible, to measure the impact of the literature of God Job on students. Sometimes students express a sense of helplessness at an unexpected and unwanted emotional burden. The point, I remind them, is not about evoking individual guilt, but, as Hine might put it, naming the guilty.

Perhaps for a few this literature will spark a catalytic leap into an expanded class-consciousness, even political agency. For most students, though, these working-class stories complicate and usefully confuse received ideological narratives of success through hard work. Students are asked to open themselves subjectively to the lived reality of these stories, to intellectualize the sorrow, and make the historical connections both private and public. And many do. About *Christ in Concrete*, one student writes,

> I really liked the novel. I was drawn into the book from the first word. My grandfather was a bricklayer and also the first generation of his family born in America, although he was Irish not Italian. He told many stories about his job, and this may sound really funny but I appreciate the architecture of RIT because my grandfather laid the bricks for many of the buildings. I, however, have a different take on the Job. Besides the danger of falling off scaffolds, there is also a hidden danger which ended up taking my grandfather's life. Years of working with cement and dust and asbestos, caused my grandfather to develop emphysema, which took his life at age 63. My grandfather's story is much like Geremio's. He was taken advantage of by the Job, safety precautions were never taken and they both experienced discrimination by the American bosses. . . .The Job took both of their lives and left little in return. My family as well as Geremio['s] had to say good bye way too early and the compensation board offered little support, . . . [leaving] both families struggling to survive in this great country of America, the land of opportunities and dreams.

In a 1933 letter to Florence Kellogg about "human values in photography beyond mere illustration," Lewis Hine comments:

> Just now I think it is a very important offset to some misconceptions about industry. One is that many of our material assets, fabrics, photographs, motors, airplanes and whatnot "just happen," as the product of a bunch of impersonal machines under the direction, perhaps, of a few human robots. You and I may know that it isn't so, but many are just plain ignorant of the sweat and service that go into all these products of the machine. . . .
>
> One more "thought"—I have a conviction that the design, registered in the human face thro years of life and work, is more vital for purposes of permanent record, tho it is more subtle perhaps, than the geometric patterns of lights and shadows that passes in the taking, and serves (so often) as mere photographic jazz.[18]

Hines's photographs of Pittsburgh steelworkers and New York ironworkers and bricklayers combined with powerful narratives of working-class lives offer possibilities for an inclusive democratic visibility. When Hine wrote "our strength is our people" he was as he always was, the good teacher. If this is to be more than a digestible slogan, we have to ask ourselves whether we have the strength to take these worker stories as our own and in so doing take up the struggle against God Job.

Pray for the dead and fight like hell for the living.   *—Mother Jones*

Workers Memorial Day

April 28

Ceremony

Workers Memorial Day is the underside of Labor Day. Not a celebration of labor, not a free work day, not an occasion for department store sales, Workers Memorial Day commemorates the thousands, perhaps millions, of workers whose deaths, bodily injuries, and occupational illnesses are the direct result of their jobs. Outside the shrunken world of labor unions, activists, and a handful of educators and labor lawyers, Workers Memorial Day barely exists. But in its tone of mourning and continued struggle, it is the closest we Americans have to a worker-centered May Day. That it is known to some and nonexistent to others as a national day of remembrance attests to the peripheral status of workers and to the power of the state, media, and corporations to control the discourse about work. It is also undermined as a day of remembrance and recognition by the dearth of a labor education in schools and the academy and by an ideology of individualism and victim blaming.

Perhaps Workers Memorial Day more closely resembles Memorial Day, a commemoration of war dead. I suspect this unconscious connection explains why in 1997 a paper I proposed on Workers Memorial Day was assigned to a panel titled "War and National Identity" at the American Studies Association Conference "Defining Public Cultures." When I protested this placement, the executive director of ASA agreed to insert the word "class" into the session title. The insertion of "class" into hundreds of academic titles belies the fact that at best it is little more than simply that—an insertion—rather than a genuine engagement. Nevertheless, I came around to seeing how it could be an occasion to draw connections between war and workers in the formation of national identity. Factory fodder or cannon fodder, the working class takes the orders to fight in wartime and produce in peacetime. And there are multiple forms of war. The struggle for safe working conditions, for all workers—unionized or not, citizens or not—is part of the long class war that is the unexposed marrow of American history.

About six thousand workers went to work last year and never came home because they died on the job.[1] This fairly consistent statistic (considered a conservative estimate) and implicit call to action is a familiar refrain to national and regional labor councils, local COSHs (councils on occupational safety and health), and unionized workers. Intended as both a day of mourning for workers killed, injured, or made sick on the job and a renewal of the fight for strong safety and health protections, Workers Memorial Day merges statistics on job deaths and injuries, private memory, and public history with shared grief and outrage over preventable deaths and injuries to working people. Each April 28 in cities across the country, union members, politicians, and ordinary citizens gather for public rituals to remember and mourn workers killed and injured on the job.

The first Workers Memorial Day was observed on April 28, 1989. April 28, 1970, is recognized as the day Richard Nixon signed into law the Occupational Safety and Health Act which created OSHA (Occupational Safety and Health Administration, an executive agency under the Labor Department) and NIOSH (National Institute for Occupational Safety and Health, a supporting research agency).[2] While an extensive analysis of OSHA is not my subject, it is important to remember that OSHA's actions have never equaled its rhetoric. Appealing to the blue-collar vote, Nixon somewhat reluctantly signed the OSHA bill at a time before the conservative onslaught against federal government regulations begun in the Carter administration and boldly advanced by the Reagan and Bush administrations.[3] Since its passage, OSHA's effectiveness has been thwarted by insufficient inspections (fewer than one thousand investigators countrywide, able to inspect the average workplace once every eighty-seven years), insufficient funding (the savings and loan bailout cost $87 *billion*; the same year OSHA got $289 million), inadequate coverage for all workers, and meager punishments and penalties for business violators.[4] This is not to say that OSHA does not matter; on the contrary, its very existence does save lives. It has enabled unions to place more emphasis on prevention and safety training programs and has brought increased attention to what occupational illness pioneer Alice Hamilton once called the "the dangerous trades,"[5] as well as the more recent recognition of repetitive strain injuries.

The genesis of Workers Memorial Day can be traced to a 1987 AFL-CIO conference where a speaker was listing the number of worker deaths: 100,000 a year to occupational disease, another 10,000 killed in workplace accidents (labor union statistics tend to be higher than the Department of Labor's). At that meeting, George J. McDonald, then health and safety director for the New York City transit workers unions, overheard people mumbling, "We . . . hear the same thing [each year] and nothing happens." Frustrated by politicians' indifference to workplace injuries, the closing of OSHA offices, and the neglect of OSHA standards, "an incensed McDonald rose to offer a resolution at the conference that the AFL-CIO focus public attention on the issue with an annual Workers Memorial Day, similar to the one established in Canada in 1986."[6] Since this beginning, trade unionists around the globe have recognized April 28 as an international day of mourning, remembrance, and call to action. Each

WORKERS MEMORIAL DAY AFL-CIO

needs to **LISTEN!** SAFE WORKPLACE We're not machines!

STRESSED OUT!

OUR JOBS ARE KILLING US

UNION YES

IN HONOR OF ALL ROCHESTER-AREA WORKERS
--PAST, PRESENT AND FUTURE--
KILLED, INJURED OR DISABLED ON THE JOB

"Pray for the dead and fight like hell for the living."
Union organizer Mary "Mother" Jones

God bless our brothers and sisters

APRIL 28, 1989
ROCHESTER & VICINITY LABOR COUNCIL, AFL-CIO
Ronald G. Pettengill, President

Photo credits: *Left: top,* Marilyn Anderson;
middle and bottom, Janet Zandy.
Right: middle, Marilyn Anderson;
bottom, Janet Zandy.

year ceremonies of remembrance, rallies, conferences, memorial services, marches, demonstrations, and work stoppages occur in cities across the United States. In 1997 the rallying cry was "Stop the Pain" and the focus was the fight for prevention of repetitive strain injuries (RSIs) and back injuries caused by ergonomic hazards. This emphasis on RSIs is indicative of technologically shaped changes in work.

In Rochester, New York, Workers Memorial Day has been held at the site of one of Rochester's "dirty dozen," the companies with the most safety violations in the area and, in 1995, at the Rochester Federal Building after the Oklahoma City bombing. Usually, though, it is held in a public space—on a windy knoll in Highland Park.[7] Our gathering includes activists, union leaders, at least one academic, and working people. We hold red carnations and carry postcards with the names of workers who were killed on the job or died from occupational injuries and diseases. Later these cards are sent to elected government officials. We form a long line of mourners and one by one we step up to the podium, read a name, and then place a carnation on a small memorial inscribed with Mother Jones's exhortation, "Pray for the dead and fight like hell for the living." And year after year, this always-expanding litany of names links us as if they were our own kin:

> John J. Vadas, Firefighter, Line of Duty, 1969
> Nancy Wheeler, 48, Social Worker, Murdered by Client, 1992
> Dennis Bosley, 24, Buried in Sewer Project, 1988
> Vernon Molefe, 30, Taxi Driver, Shot in Robbery, 1992
> Gerald Dill, Died from Asbestos Disease, 1983
> Tom Johnson, 38, Killed in a Trench Collapse, 1993

This annual reading of names, a familiar ritual at many tragic events, offers a counterbalance to the media's undemocratic lack of recognition and coverage of workplace accidents and deaths. The same year a worker is buried alive, perhaps because of inadequate shoring, a Rochester businessman has a heart attack at his country club. The businessman gets front-page coverage, the worker's death is ignored in Rochester's one daily newspaper. As Mother Mary Jones once put it, "It's the same old story, as pitiful as old, as true as pitiful." What is ultimately at stake, though, is not so much media attention, but the right of any worker, citizen or not, skilled or not, unionized or not, to safe work.

Further, this ceremony of remembrance is an occasion for the sympathizing audience members to recognize each other. It is an enactment of what anthropologist Barbara Myerhoff calls a "definitional ceremony," a performance of collective identification. These definitional ceremonies are social drams that "allow people to reiterate their collective and personal identities, to arouse great emotion and energy, which . . . [is] then redirected toward some commonalties, some deep symbols, and stable shared norms."[8] Less spontaneous than the ceremonies described in Myerhoff's classic study of Jewish elders, *Number Our Days,* and certainly more secular, the ritual of Workers Memorial Day is a shared reading and interpretation of the world. We gather to advance an identity that links individual circumstances and loss to collective consciousness based on an ethos of just labor. The participants bear witness not only for the dead, but for themselves. Workers who are disabled have a rare chance to be seen and to tell others their stories. The ceremony encompasses simultaneous worker time: the past is remembered, the present struggle is acknowledged, and a safer future for workers is demanded. The emphasis is on becoming, on promise, on struggle, and embedded in this small ceremony is catalytic power for social change.

Testimony

We found that in one year 526 men were killed by accidents of employment in Allegheny County [Pennsylvania]: 195 steelworkers, 125 railroaders, 71 miners, and 135 miscellaneous workers.　　　　　　　　—Crystal Eastman, *The Survey,* 1910

Researchers at Mt. Sinai Medical School have estimated that 50,000 to 70,000 workers die each year as a result of major occupationally acquired diseases like cancer, lung disease, and coronary heart disease.　　—*Journal of the American Medical Association,* 1991

Workers Memorial Day is an antidote to victim blaming and class shame. If it is indeed true, as E. P. Thompson writes in his famous preface to *The Making of the English Working Class,* that the working class is present at its own making[9] (and unmaking?), perhaps it is also true that the working class is present at its own masking and unmasking. Workers Memorial Day unmasks workplace injuries and deaths in a culture that is on one hand saturated by smiley faces, and on the other controlled by powerful corporate, state, and media structures that deprive workers of their own history. Testimony is an important tool with which to recover this suppressed labor history. Consider the case and testimony of Camella Teoli. Camella Teoli was one of a group of teenage textile workers from Lawrence, Massachusetts, who testified at congressional hearings in March 1912, at a critical moment in the six-month Lawrence "Bread and Roses" strike:

THE CHAIRMAN. Now, did you ever get hurt in the mill?

MISS TEOLI. Yes.

THE CHAIRMAN. Can you tell the committee about that—how it happened and what it was?

MISS TEOLI. Yes.

THE CHAIRMAN. Tell us about it now, in your own way.

MISS TEOLI. Well, I used to go to school, and then a man came up to my house and asked my father why I didn't go to work, so my father says I don't know whether she is 13 or 14 years old. So, the man says you give me $4 and I will make the papers come from the old country saying you are 14. So, my father gave him the $4, and in one month came the papers that I was 14. I went to work and [in] about two weeks got hurt in my head.

THE CHAIRMAN. Now, how did you get hurt, and where were you hurt in the head; explain that to the committee?

MISS TEOLI. I got hurt in Washington.

THE CHAIRMAN. In the Washington Mill?

MISS TEOLI. Yes, sir.

THE CHAIRMAN. What part of your head?

MISS TEOLI. My head.

THE CHAIRMAN. Well, how were you hurt?

MISS TEOLI. The machine pulled the scalp off.

THE CHAIRMAN. The machine pulled your scalp off?

MISS TEOLI. Yes, sir.

THE CHAIRMAN. How long ago was that?

MISS TEOLI. A year ago, or about a year ago.

THE CHAIRMAN. Were you in the hospital after that?

MISS TEOLI. I was in the hospital seven months.

THE CHAIRMAN. Seven months?[10]

Camella Teoli went (as working-class people say) as far as the sixth grade before she dropped out (because of economic circumstances and not individual choice) to go to work and help support her Italian immigrant family of five children.[11] Her reticence, given her limited education, age, and fluency in English is understandable, but her responses are also revelatory for what they emphasize and omit. She responds in some length to the legality of her situation, and how her father was persuaded to pay for a paper claiming an earlier birth date so she could go to work in the mills. When she is queried about her scalping she misunderstands the question about where she was hurt and answers by naming the place—Washington Mills—rather than the physical location of her wound. This confusion, I suggest, is not evidence of an ignorant mill girl, but rather springs out of a working-class sensibility of not drawing attention to oneself, of minimizing one's own pain, and a tacit recognition that injury and death on the job are integral to working-class life. After all, what choice is there but to return to the mill, the mine, the pit, the line, to earn a living? Some may call this immigrant fatalism; others understand it as necessary to survival.

Consider as well this experience as told by a freshman writing student. When asked to describe a significant personal experience (a chestnut composition assignment), this student wrote "The Accident." He begins his story by saying, "I was young and very proud of my father." But the writer, whom I'll call Luis, had a premonition and grabbed his father's hand and begged him not to go to work on that particular afternoon. As it happened, the boy's premonition proved true. A press machine crushed Luis's father's hand at work that very day. As Luis visits his father in the hospital and approaches the bed, he describes his own interior state:

I felt like as if thousands of ocean waves pounded in my interior trying to break out. . . . I could feel the pride that I had for my father abandon me. . . . When I saw my father without his left hand I freaked out. I felt like a bad luck charm because, my subconscious was repeating, "you touched it last.". . . I also felt ashamed. Ashamed of having a handicapped father. I thought of all my friends making fun of him. I saw my friends not wanting to play with me because of his accident. I was mad at my father for losing his hand.

Luis's sense of shame can be read as a child's desire for the normative, as fear that the work injury will somehow spill on him and thwart his own life, and as an abrupt awareness that somehow he will have to carry the stigma of suffering and loss into an apathetic, victim-blaming society. It is not until he is a young adult that Luis can unmask this story, and end his paper with "as time went on, I felt my pride come back to me little by little. . . . Now I'm older and even prouder of my father." This conclusion of acceptance—indeed, the fact that he would expose this story in written assignment—suggests his own growth as a young man capable of dealing with familial adversity. But, read in juxtaposition with Camella Teoli's understated response to the committee, the public exposure of her scalping, it is also representative of a complicated structure of feeling, a pattern of masking and unmasking worker injury and death in relation to the power of the state, business, and the media.

In 1976, journalist Paul Cowan presented Camella Teoli's daughter with the transcript of her mother's 1912 congressional testimony. Every day this daughter had combed her mother's hair in such a way as to hide the bald spot and scar. But the daughter knew nothing about her mother's past, nor her testimony, what Cowan suggests "must have been the proudest moment of her [mother's] life."[12] Because of Cowan's intervention, Camella's daughter was able to see the intersection of private experience with public history and literally claim a past: "Now I have a past," she said. "Now my son has a history." Why wasn't Camella's heroic story known, at least to the family? The answer lies embedded in a long history of political and economic oppression, intimidation, and exploitation that particularly affects immigrants and nonunionized minorities—and not merely in the modesty of an Italian immigrant woman. As Paul Cowan uncovers, Camella raised her children in a Lawrence where reprisals against politically active workers, especially immigrants, were severe. Labor memory was masked, forgotten, even punished. Cowan writes, "Like her, most of the former strikers I met in 1976 were loath to discuss the event. And the few who did were afraid to let me quote them by name. Their comments suggested that Camella Teoli had remained silent in order to protect herself—and her young—from reprisals."

Camella Teoli's story is threaded with multiple parallel stories, largely lost and forgotten. As one other example, labor journalist Mary Heaton Vorse, writing for *Harper's Weekly* in 1912, reports this incident:

John Ramay, a young Syrian of nineteen, went out on the morning of the 29th of January at six o'clock. He joined a crowd of strikers which the militia moved along. He was at the back of the crowd. At fifteen minutes past six he was brought into his mother's house with a bayonet wound in the back and he died at seven that night. The name of the militiaman who killed Ramay is unknown, nor has any action been taken against him. He was not held for murder or complicity of murder as it was decided that he was within his rights.[13]

Workers are murdered in the struggle for unionization and on the job because of unsafe working conditions. Camella Teoli, John Ramay, Luis's father, names to be uttered on Workers Memorial Day, disappear into the vat of history not because they individually lack class consciousness, but because the system is rigged against them. To remember them is not an exercise in sentimental nostalgia. Rather, it is an embrace of a fragmentary, but critical, residual culture and set of experiences and feelings invalidated and suppressed by the dominant culture.

What Camella Teoli, John Ramay, and Luis's father hold in common is the lived experience of loss. What Luis and Camella Teoli's daughter inherit is a deeper epistemology than the visible wounds of their parents. However, this knowledge, lived and embodied, is impoverished as knowledge because it is, on one hand, written off and suppressed, and, on the other, deprived of the means for articulation beyond the personal. This kind of knowledge, identifiable as structures of feeling, or structures of experience, to draw on Raymond Williams's language and theory, can be reclaimed and reformed, and articulated personally and privately as resistance to shame and publicly and historically as culture and agency.[14] This recovered formation of class self-consciousness can be taken up by another generation, some of whom become, according to Williams, "new semantic figures" (134). These figures, let's call them writers or activists, then construct a circuitry of connection in time, enabling an articulation of both their own exposure and their parents' lived experience of loss. As Williams hypothesizes, they then speak, write, and act "at a reduced tension: the social explanation fully admitted, the intensity of experienced fear and shame now dispersed and generalized" (134).

Luis's feelings of shame might be understood, then, as literary theorist Pamela Fox suggests, as a process of demystification, a step in the formation of class consciousness.[15] Fox draws on Helen Merrell Lynd's 1958 monograph, *Shame and the Search for Identity,* to present a case for shame as a potentially emancipatory emotion that can break through the "dominant culture's transmutation of working-class shame into classless, individual guilt" (15). What are the mechanisms, tools, mediations where shame transforms into collective consciousness?

Workers Memorial Day acknowledges vulnerability and agency and offers an actual space and time where shared feelings and experiences (mind and body) might disperse private shame. It says to Luis that not only was it not your fault that your father lost his hand, it was probably not his fault either. It says to Camella's daughter that the covering of the wound marked metaphorically the continued oppression of the workers of Lawrence. The unmasking of wounds, the reading of names, the justified anger, all affirm private loss within a larger critical context of class struggle. In trusting the reporter with her mother's story and the teacher with the composition on the "Accident," Camella's daughter and Luis risk their private unmasking and exposure for a larger social, class-shaped narrative and historical purpose. As Fox elaborates, "[s]elf-aware-ness and confidence become possible because in the process of revealing the shame of being shamed, often one is exposing oppressive societal norms and values as well" (16). Workers Memorial Day cannot assuage private grief, but it can become a space for mutual recognition of loss and shared struggle and values, for the unmasking and remaking of the working class.[16]

Ultimately, the lesson of loss is how we listen to our dead. During the hot summer of 2002, the media embraced the heroic rescue of nine miners trapped for three days in a flooded (nonunion) Pennsylvania coal mine, where only ten months earlier and thirteen miles away hijacked Flight 93 had crashed into a Shanksville field. The miners survived because of the technical expertise of deep-mining engineers, the grit and determination of volunteers, and the soli-darity of the miners themselves. Sharing food, pressed against each other for warmth, and literally tethered together so that no one would die alone, they implicitly understood and enacted the necessity of solidarity—not as slogan—but as integral to survival.[17] At the same time that politicians were sharing the spotlight with the relieved miners and their families and the media was absorbed with the best feel-good story of the year, George W. Bush's adminis-tration was planning to cut the budgets of the Mine Safety and Health Admin-istration (MSHA), the federal Mine Safety and Health Review Commission and the Abandoned Mine Lands Program.[18] The media did not cover that story.

A year before this dramatic miners' rescue story, on September 23, 2001, thir-teen miners were killed in a deep mine methane explosion at Jim Walter Resources Blue Creek No. 5 Mine in Brookwood, Alabama. Here, too, the soli-darity of miners shapes the story. It seems that miner Gaston Adams Jr. was trapped by an initial methane explosion. Twelve fellow miners went down to rescue him and all were killed in a second powerful methane blast and fire. In reporting this story in *Mother Jones*, Aram Roston claims that if it hadn't been eclipsed by the tragic events of 9/11, this story would have been national news.[19] I wonder. On what page would they cover this story? Would they tell that according to MSHA inspection reports, the "Number 5 mine had a history of excessive safety hazards and 31 outstanding violations at the time of the acci-dent"? Would they investigate how the Bush administration has stacked MSHA with mining industry officials and former managers? I think not, nor do I underestimate the power of corporate-controlled media to suppress such ques-tions and stories. And yet, as Raymond Williams understood long revolutions, "however dominant a social system may be, the very meaning of its domination involves a limitation or selection of the activities it covers, so that by definition it cannot exhaust all social experience, which therefore always potentially contains space for alternative acts and alternative intentions, which are not yet articulated as a social institution or even project."[20]

Naming the dead is not enough. As a society we are adept at ceremony; we gather, we view, we gaze, and then we go home and turn on the television. Is it possible for a supine, materialistic society to take a leap into a wider consciousness? Perhaps not without a subjective understanding of loss and struggle. Workers Memorial Day emerged as a public event at a time when workers were (as they still are)downsized, deindustrialized, and discarded. As symbolic action and organized struggle for worker health and safety, Workers Memorial Day could evolve into an expanded field of vision encompassing workers globally as well as nationally, especially as its union organizers forge links with students, environmentalists, women's rights activists, community organizers, and others in democratic global movements. Hope, and perhaps the future, lie in these coalitions. But that would take a very great societal coming of age, energetic organizing, and recognition that there are alternatives to quiescence, militarism, and fear.

This essay is dedicated to the memory of Tony Mazzocchi (1926–2002), organizer for worker safety extraordinaire.[21]

Labor Books Program

WORKING CLASSICS

Expanding Workweek Makes Exhaustion an Issue

Pink-slipped worker just packed up and got out

BLUE COLLAR REVIEW

Slump at Boeing will cost 20,000 more jobs

DOWN AND OUT IN SILICON VALLEY

PEOPLE'S CULTURE

WORKING PEOPLE

Major layoffs on the increase

Hand in Hand Training

The Federation of Worker Writers & Community Publishers

Old, Young Worker Writers Share Dream

Kodak cuts 10,000 jobs

Articulations

Culture Is Not
Negation

In "The Hand of the World" (1912), Helen Keller lauds the human hand as foundational to all society: "All our earthly well-being hangs upon the living hand of the world."[1] Working-class presence and resilience answer historical patterns of loss, silence, and dislocation. Working-class culture is not about the absence or deprivation of bourgeois sensibilities. This observation is analogous to the recognition that Deaf culture is not about the absence of hearing, but rather is the embodiment of a presence, and is a distinctive culture based on the beautiful language of sign. While not about deafness and class (a subject worthy of deeper study), the meditations that follow seek to negate negation,[2] to resist shame, to reveal processes and distinctions in the formation of working-class cultural expression, and to query forms of representation and self-representation.

"Worker Writers: Where Do You Keep Your Writing?" begins with the assumption that workers write and highlights various modes of cultural production including small presses, worker publications, and the British Federation of Worker Writers and Community Publishers. It then focuses on specific writers, particularly the radical poetic humanism of Wilma Elizabeth McDaniel. "In the Skin of a Worker" offers an analysis of working-class aesthetics through comparative readings of novels by Tillie Olsen and Michael Ondaatje. It emphasizes strategic elements of working-class writing, those external forces that shape a text as well as those internal elements, residual and emergent, that represent working-class lived experience. Representation is the critical hinge of "Worker Ghosts," which uses the trope of the ghost to present a metacommentary on the complexities of documenting the disappearance of jobs. It explores the tensions between "ghosted work" and "embodied workers"—quiet victims or rowdy ghosts?—and examines perspectives from which stories of purportedly deskilled, displaced, and deindustrialized workers are told. "Worker Ghosts" speaks to the larger question of how texts provide aesthetic spaces for worker self-representation.

Shush—Mum's Writing

Sit down be quiet read a book
Don't you dare to speak or look
Shush Mum's writing

She's left the dishes in the sink
All she does is sit and think
Shush Mum's writing

Nothing for dinner nowt for tea
All she ever says to me is
Shush Mum's writing

But what's all this Mum's wrote a book
Why not buy one have a look
No need to shush now we can shout
And tell all our friends about
MUM'S WRITING

> —Pat Dallimore (1978), Women Writers Workshop Bristol Broadsides,
> Federation of Worker Writers and Community Publishers

Worker Writers

Where Do You Keep Your Writing?

Thieve time to write," Tillie Olsen urges.[1] Time begrudged and words unwritten is the elegiac theme of *Silences,* Olsen's moving rumination on unnatural silences, the "thwarting of what struggles to come into being, but cannot."[2] *Silences* adumbrates a powerful and widely referenced trope of absence and omission, particularly in women's writings. Cultural critics have been less attentive to working-class cultural formations, the multiple utterings, voicings—cacophonous and euphonic—that attest to the *presence* of working-class cultural expression. Whether through small presses and regional alliances, in trade union newspapers, labor magazines, or local and community publications, some working-class people have found the means to break silence and produce a veritable heteroglossia of writings about their own lives, communities, jobs, families, and struggles. The actual writing may take place alone, in time stolen at work or at home, but the context and often the content of the writing is communal.

"Where do you keep your writing?" This was the lead question I heard repeated during a 1997 visit to England and the annual gathering of the Feds, the Federation of Worker Writers and Community Publishers (FWWCP), where worker writers, readers, community publishers, and organizers assembled to talk about the work and pleasure of community writing and publishing. *Where do you keep your writing—under the bed? in a shoebox? out in the open? or hidden away?* Such questions assume human expression and recognize the generative quality of working-class culture. Perhaps because it reflects experience unrecognized by dominant, mass, or academic cultures, the chemistry of working-class writing is catalytic. That is, a working-class poem, as one example, might be answered—not with analysis—but by a story or another poem. It is less the particularized valorization of a single poem, author, or even book—although the appreciation is genuine—than the sparks of connection a good story or poem trigger. After my anthology on working-class women's writings (*Calling Home*) was published, I received calls and letters from strangers saying—"I enjoyed your book, AND I want to tell you about . . . my mother's secret shoebox filled writing . . . OR would you care to read more poems. . . ." In other words, the finished product or book matters, but equally important is the agency of possibility it evokes, to bring writing out of the closet—quite literally in some cases.[3] It also invites an appreciation, even collective ownership, of others' writing. At conferences and community readings I invited women to choose and read selections from *Calling Home*. These were small ceremonies where we (none of us seasoned performers) drew strength from each other, from the power of the language, and the affirmation of working-class expression. Moments of collective confidence.

Not every worker writes, obviously, but the example of worker writings attests to the variety, depth, and range of human expressivity located outside the academy and outside institutions of high- and middle-brow culture. Much critical attention has focused on culture as *purchase*, the construction of identity through consumption. Not far removed from analyses of material culture and market forces is a recognition and appreciation of indigenous cultural expression (consider the interest in outsider art, rap music, or the plethora of books on Black hair). Less notice, or indeed respectful attention, is given to the desire for beauty and the quiet shaping of words, wood, clay, cloth, music—the stuff of daily life—by ordinary people grounded in their own lived experiences using tools accessible to them.

In her poem "Out of the rubbish" Marge Piercy writes of discovering among her mother's things (presumably found after her death when she was sorting out her possessions) a "bottle-cap flower: the top / from a ginger ale / into which had been glued / crystalline beads from a necklace / surrounding a blue bauble."[4] Piercy's poem is a recognition not only of "working class making do" but of the desire to answer the drab brown and gray of the external world with the hand-shaped artifacts, affordable fabrics covering tables and chairs, and bold wall paints that add cheer and beauty to their lives. Piercy writes:

If we make curtains
of the rose-bedecked table
cloth, the stain won't show
and it will be cheerful,
cheerful. Paint the wall lime.
Paint it turquoise, primrose.

Not the thing itself but the process. Small gestures attest to the aesthetic desires all humans possess. But such hidden gestures and artifacts are trapped in a no-value zone, formed but hidden, awaiting the archeologist's tools in some future dig. Consider how Piercy's last stanza reimagines her mother's creative act:

One night alone she sat
at her kitchen table
gluing baubles in a cap.
When she had finished,
pleased, she hid it away
where no one could see.

It is important to remember not just the secreting away, but the "pleased," the pleasure taken in the act of creation. What needs reclamation is not so much the nostalgic memory of the object, but the circumstances of its creation and the linking of circumstances and context to creation. The dominant society congratulates the very rich for their "good taste," accumulated collections, or in Tillie Olsen's words, how they "languidly lie on couches and trill 'How exquisite.'"[5] But it fails to acknowledge the material circumstances of plenty permitting such expressions of refinement. What is permitted is the exotic—the beaded belt beneath the glass case in the museum gift shop, the raw "primitive" paintings of backwoods artists—and all the aesthetic trophies of travel. But the cultural work of working-class reclamation involves the stitching of beauty onto the ordinary, the joining of use and aesthetic value, and the enlargement of circumstances for creative expression.

Consider the Kizaemon Tea-bowl. In *The Unknown Craftsman* Soetsu Yanagi describes his much-anticipated glimpse at a sixteenth-century Korean Tea-bowl.[6] Buried securely in box after box, wrapped in wool and silk, the Tea-bowl embodied—not "the essence of tea" but rather the most fundamentally ordinary, the "commonest crockery." At first Yanagi is disappointed at the shabbiness and unrefinement of the bowl: "The work had been fast; the turning was rough, done with dirty hands; the throwing slipshod; the glaze had run over the foot" (7). Then he looks again, but with different eyes. "The plain and unagitated, the uncalculated, the harmless, the straightforward, the natural, the innocent, the humble, the modest: where does beauty lie if not in these qualities? . . . More than anything else, this pot is healthy" (7).[7]

Healthy is an unlikely word for cultural criticism, but I wish to claim it as a metaconcept for understanding worker writers in their publishing contexts. It is a healthy act to create rather than purchase, to build networks of writers, to publish and recognize outside writers, to raise the money, find the time, juggle the tasks, and make the material sacrifices. This is not feel-good New Age–ism for people who can afford masseurs. Rather, this is resistant cultural and political work, crucial foundational work for societal restructuring. It is "firmly planted. Not fallen from on high: sprung up from below" as Octavio Paz writes.[8]

Here I examine some of the agencies of written expression formed outside the academy and on the fringes of capitalistic culture machines in a contemporary context. We have, fortunately, wide-ranging studies of progressive cultural expression at specific historic moments, particularly the1930s, as well as literary histories documenting the struggle for labor representation.[9] I wish to look more narrowly and locally at contexts for worker writings, alternative publishing, and avenues for mutual recognition and inspiration in a collective sense as well as in the accomplishments of individual worker writers.

"One must understand," Antonio Gramsci writes, "the impetus by which workers feel drawn to the contemplation of art, to the creation of art, [and] how deeply they feel offended in their humanity because the slavery of wages and work cuts them off from a world that integrates man's life, that makes it worth living."[10] Gramsci's analysis of the intersection of culture with material circumstances, education, and political struggle usefully frames our understanding of worker writing and working-class cultural formation. Gramsci grounds his thinking in certain critical assumptions: that culture is indigenous, in the sense that human beings are born into a culture; that education should be synthetic, that is, manual and intellectual labor are not separate; indeed, that human beings are thinkers and have an intellectuality, albeit not necessarily organized nor developed; that socialism is a life system of integration rather than compartmentalization; and that all humans beings have aesthetic needs.

> Most people ignore most art because most art ignores most people.
>
> —Joe Smythe, *Come and Get Me*

Let us turn again to the practices of the Federation of Worker Writers and Community Publishers (FWWCP). Formed in 1976, the Feds is a nonprofit umbrella organization for local writers' groups and community publishers located in city neighborhoods and towns throughout Britain and abroad. Founded on the shared belief that writing and publishing should be accessible to all, the FWWCP publishes *Federation Magazine* and a broadsheet, runs the annual Festival of Writing, organizes training sessions, presents writing awards, develops networks, encourages people to express themselves, and performs a witty traveling ensemble piece called "Feds under the Beds."[11] With over fifty independently organized writers' workshops, community publishers, and organizations in Britain and around the world, it is a model of viable alternative space for working-class writing and publishing. The bottom line requirement for membership is that each group must be self-organized (not controlled externally by

Federation Magazine

The magazine of The Federation of Worker Writers and Community Publishers £1.50

Coming Out at Night

Rosie Lugosi's new book reviewed p22

Federation Magazine No.19 Spring 2000

Urgent alert for action - Fed Members arrested in Mauritius

Glasgow Fed Day

Community Writing - views from   Barnsley and Quebec

From Student Newsletter to Community Practice

QueenSpark's Diary Project

Over there, over here

Fritz-Hüser-Institut

Hand-in-Hand Update

issn 1330-8598

FED

Federation Magazine. Courtesy of Tim Diggles.

some agency) and must publish in some form. The word *federation* signifies collective activities and resistances. In the chapter "Disestablishing literature," the editors of *The Republic of Letters* explain:

> By becoming a Federation—by coming into association with each other, sharing and looking at the body of work we have produced between us, making space to reflect on what we do and to bring together our separate reflections—we have put ourselves in a position to challenge Literature as it is dominantly defined. It is a two-fold challenge: we claim both that we are already producing literature, that our books are full and excellent examples of it, rather than provisional statements until we learn the refinements of Craft or Art; and we claim that our practices are on a collision course with Literature.[12]

Collision course is a feisty term; I enjoy it, but it claims too much. Rather than a violent impact, the Feds' project offers conditions for cultural agency. Such agency answers the real violence done to people when their realities, their lived experiences, have no cultural reflection or outlet for expression. Perhaps what is really "disestablished" is the mystification of "the book" as something formed at a distance, an artifact to be purchased, consumed, but not made. The Feds' workshops provide a context where ordinary people can express their lives in writing and have a hand in getting their work published and out to an appreciative audience. (And technology, with the accessibility of desktop publishing, is, for once, on their side.) The Feds provide a space where nonhegemonic social relationships can form, an alternative context to the school, the television, and the mall.[13]

In his essay "Joe Shakespeare: The Contemporary British Worker-Writer Movement," Nicholas Coles estimates that FWWCP members have published roughly one thousand titles, with over a million volumes in distribution in twenty years' time (195).[14] It is important to note the simultaneity of their cultural acts—writing, critiquing, editing, publishing, launching a new publication, distributing, reviewing, reading to local audiences, all the small democratic acts of involvement and participation. The Feds declare that yes, it is possible to write and publish, be read and heard, outside the profit-seeking arena of trade publishing. Federation books, published and written in local communities, have won annual Raymond Williams prizes for reflecting the voices and experiences of people in particular communities. With an elastic definition of *working class* and an absence of any overarching political agenda, the multiple utterances of the Feds still offer a healthy undercurrent of political consciousness and critique forged out of the lived conditions of outsiders to power but insiders to working-class epistemology. Ken Worpole offers this straight-from-the-shoulder definition: "Working-class writing is the literature of the controlled and exploited. It is shot through with a different kind of consciousness from bourgeois writing. Whatever its subject matter, working class writing, when it is any good at all, must contain in its tissues and exude through its pores, working class experience. Politically, the class struggle would be felt and communicated, even if indirectly, even if the writer has no such design on the reader."[15]

Some of the publishing projects include a chronicle of a local football club, documentaries and oral histories of local communities, working-class women's literature, critical memories of working-class school days, survivors' poetry, children's writing, global immigrant writings, the words of asylum seekers, prison poetry—indeed, every variety of human expression including drawings and other visual images.[16] More often than not, the writing groups emerged out of local social actions including literacy projects and rent strikes. The common ground of each location is the face-to-face meetings of the workshop group. From first words written or taped to finished text or book collection to public readings, book launches, and sales in local working-class communities, the process is dialogic, reciprocal, and organic. Ken Worpole explains, "people have not limply received the books as just further products of a monolithic leisure industry. They have discussed what they've read, written letters of praise and criticism, or set about writing their own accounts to complement what they have read. This, we submit, is live culture."[17] These publications also reveal the diversity of working-class self-representation and the complexity of working-class identities.

This healthy process of cultural formation also releases fissures and differences generationally (a dad's nostalgic memory of a place may be a son's geographic prison), racially, and in terms of sexuality, gender, and citizenship. These differences speak to the particular historical circumstances and formative elements of cultural acts. And, I would argue (especially for American cultural critics fixated on the 1930s) it is important to heed the advice of the editors of *The Republic of Letters* and *not* "elevate one particular historical form of working class culture and organisation to a point where it is seen as the fixed standard, the essence of what working class culture has to be" (101). The Feds is a critical model of local ownership of cultural production, a generative, sustaining network that recognizes and affirms human expression and the need for mutuality, outlets, and audience. And, as Tillie Olsen writes in *Silences*, "not to have an audience is a kind of death" (44).

> The word, like the plow, the chisel, the needle, the spindle, is a tool.
>
> —Meridel Le Sueur, *Worker Writers*

Tools are artifacts of design. Placed in the human hand, given particular applications, contexts, and purposes, they alter material existence. The language tools of worker writers cannot function, that is, exert their use value, as solo actions. Meridel Le Sueur's particular words, quoted above, survive in part because of the solidarity of West End Press editor John Crawford who quietly shaped Le Sueur's pamphlet *Worker Writers*. Crawford writes about his intentions in founding West End Press in 1976 as a desire to "publish our people's literature in a more premeditated, permanent way."[18] Crawford and dozens of other small press editors and publishers (including, among others, those of Crossing Press, Arte Publico, Kitchen Table/Women of Color Press, Hanging Loose Press, Thunder's Mouth, White Pine, Singlejack Books, etc.) might be described as pragmatic idealists.[19] They are, as Crawford says, engaged in a continuing struggle of "defin[ing] ourselves all over, finding paths of resistance and a sense of the future." As publisher, editor, bookseller, and writer, John Crawford purposefully illuminates the context for the writing he publishes at West End. From 1977 to 1985 his press produced a newsletter entitled *Worker Writer,* which included documentation on a Writers Congress organized in the 1980s.

Consider what it takes to sustain a small, progressive press in the face of multinational publishing conglomerates and chain bookstores fixated on celebrity. The Feminist Press, now in its third decade of publishing, emerged in the early 1970s with the women's liberation movement and the development of women's studies. Its success is grounded in the mission of recovering "lost" women's voices, notably Rebecca Harding Davis's *Life in the Iron Mills* and Agnes Smedley's *Daughter of Earth.*[20]

Larry Smith, rooted in the Ohio heartland, continues publishing the plain-spoken language of working-class people in his Bottom Dog Press. Partisan Press out of Norfolk, Virginia, publishes the quarterly *Blue Collar Review,* edited by Al Markowitz and Mary Franke. This is but the briefest mention of what could be a substantial list of alternative and small presses, multicultural, feminist, gay and lesbian, independent and nonprofit, continuing and ephemeral, that not only offer opportunities for readers and writers outside the mainstream, but pose critical questions about what constitutes culture and who owns and controls it.

We do not presently have a *federation* of worker writers and community publishers in the United States. Given the geography, diversity, and scale of this country, not to mention the dominance of the market, it is, perhaps, an unlikely formation. But we do have many regional pockets of left-leaning cultural formations—writing and reading circles, labor musicians, documentary films and videos, oral history projects, progressive photographers, labor history associations, zine makers, and who knows how many working-class writers. Individually, Lilliputian; collectively, Brobdingnagian. We have inherited and continue to build, albeit in a fragmentary, multigenerational, cranky, argumentative, and diverse way, a people's culture committed to telling the story of working-class experience and to persisting in the struggle for a just world. As Fred Whitehead writes in *People's Culture,* it's "art for humanity's sake," not art for art's sake.[21]

Douglas Wixson's magisterial *Worker-Writer in America: Jack Conroy and the Tradition of Midwestern Literary Radicalism 1898–1990* traces the formation of class consciousness out of the physical and relational conditions of work for a particular writer at a particular time.[22] Wixson's biography of Jack Conroy, as much a book about working-class cultural process and circumstances as it is a biography, quite usefully offers rubrics and categories of analysis for worker writings.[23] What distinguishes Wixson is his articulate understanding of how class consciousness emerges out of the physicality of work and the material intimacy of home rather than out of received top-down ideology. Wixson presents two organic and theoretical metaphors: the rhizomatous and the arborescent. Rhizomatous structures are horizontal pathways, sturdy weeds, unplanned connections, "movements of deterritorialization and destratification" suggestive of the social relations of workers in mining communities (33–34); *arborescent*, in contrast, signifies the room-and-pillar system of the mines, structurally vertical and hierarchical, a stratified class system headed by the owner (34). One always has to be cautious about such clean bifurcations, but as tools to assess the instrumental and aesthetic elements of worker writings they are useful.

The *Mill Hunk Herald* (1979–1989) released rhizomatous expression in its ten-year life. Emerging out of Pittsburgh, this worker writer magazine series opened space for caustic, sarcastic, humorous, and feeling-full howls in response to closing steel mills, hierarchical unions, and Reagan trickle-down economics. The title itself is a reclamation of the anti-Slovak ethnic slur "Hunky"[24] transformed even from the working-class "hunk" (meaning, at least in my working-class female world, quite a physically attractive guy, a real "hunk") into a powerful and positive reclamation. Workers' lives may be shadowed and shaped by the job or lack of a job, but—as these stories, tributes, poems, songs, cartoons attest—some space and some voices survive to talk back and resist dehumanization. A self-proclaimed "worker rag," the *Mill Hunk Herald* is described by editor Larry Evans as not always a "Class Act" but definitely "an act of class" (xi), and, more seriously, "a microcosm of what an unleashed workers' self-educative movement might look like"(xiii).[25] The *Mill Hunk Herald* offered an exciting, chaotic, participatory, democratic, barely edited alternative to conservative union publications featuring "bowling scores and photos of officials squeezing fleshy palms" (ix). Consider the imaginative strategies Evans and others used to midwife the *Mill Hunk Herald* into existence:

> To swell the ranks of our writers (eventually numbering 741 over ten years), we took on the local press and union publications, boasting that we would be a democratically-run publication for all working people, 'not owned by anyone' or 'operated from the top down' and not 'ass kissing.'. . . We recruited from the rankled ranks of mainstream 'letters-to-the-editor' writers who never seemed to get published frequently enough or in entirety. We clipped their letters and forwarded our invitation to write for us through the local papers. Of 80 folks approached in this way, 63 sent us submissions. Some sent trunk-loads. (xi)

Also, references to the physicality of labor punctuate *Mill Hunk* writings. Mihal Pecio, a Pittsburgh postal worker, writes in "Our Hunk Heritage": "I believe half the kids of my generation growing up in the South Side during the '20s and '30s lost their fathers through work related accidents or diseases. Strong, lusty men who had never returned home from the job or had returned with less of themselves than they had taken. Their still reverberating tragedies traumatized the widow and bent the children with no apparent focus on the crime or the criminals."[26] John Paul Minarik's poem "finisher at duquesne works" begins with an epigram from Thomas Bell's novel *Out of This Furnace* that gives testimony to Pete Casey, "A man with iron forearms" and our shared humanity—"the same carbon that makes iron into steel / is found in all that is organic / in all life and death."[27]

During the same period that *Mill Hunk Herald* published regularly, on the West Coast David Joseph was shaping his small magazine and newsletter, *Working Classics* (1982–1991?). With every issue "free on the picket line," David Joseph was a one-man, working-class publishing band, although not without some donated labor from his friends.[28] In plain language, David Joseph, working out of his San Francisco apartment, defines "Working Classics" in his first issue "as creative work by people who work and for people who work. *Working Classics* is about their working lives and their family ties too. *Working Classics* is interested not only in the work you do for a living, but also in how you managed to produce the creative work you did, and how that fits into your life" (vol. 1, no. 1, 1982). Volumes two and four featured poetry, articles, news items, and drawings from an eclectic collection of working writers including Nellie Wong, Sue Doro (reprinted from *Mill Hunk Herald*), Stan Weir (publisher of Singlejack Books), Sesshu Foster, Julia Stein, Myung-Hee Kim, Carol Tarlen, Donna Langston, lyn lifshin, Ernie Brill, Terri L. Jewell, and Karen Brodine and cartoons by Carol Simpson and Doug Minkler. In his brief introduction to an issue focusing on workers' poetry, Joseph writes, "We've been receiving so much fine work at *Working Classics* from all around the nation that it has been frankly at times a bit overwhelming. There appears to be a renaissance of working class literature happening everywhere at once in a variety of styles and concerns. We didn't know there were so many of you out there" (vol. 2, no. 1: 3).

In referencing these instances of eruptions of rhizomatous working-class culture, I wish to be suggestive, rather than encyclopedic or dogmatic. I do not want to claim too much or too little. Economic conditions, such as the steel mill shutdowns, trigger cultural formations with varied forms of aesthetic expression. As Meridel Le Sueur puts it, "The thing we're talking about really is a continuity of people's culture, a working class culture, and how this bridge can be made. . . . The culture of struggle never ceases. In America, the American people have a guerilla-like skill of going underground and disappearing. . . . This underground guerilla culture has been there all the time, and is coming up in the social necessity of struggle, in the social climate of other communal people who are resonating to that" (3).[29]

Worker Writers

At this juncture, it may be useful to glean some characteristics of worker writers. Almost all are born into the working class; some are educated out of it but maintain allegiance to their class; many are autodidactic and love learning, Gramsci's organic rather than traditional intellectuals. They possess a consciousness of social relationships in relation to economic circumstances. Generally, they cannot support themselves by their writing, do not have sufficient degrees or fame for academic jobs, and must balance work, often quite physical labor, with writing. As a result, their publications may be occasional or fragmented, and they may choose shorter forms such as short stories or poems. Often, but not always, content trumps structure and form. The writing is often instrumental, feisty, and documentary. Worker writing bridges orality and textuality (and, I would argue, physicality), inclusively presenting a multiplicity of voices and forms of idiomatic expression as well as sarcastic humor.[30] Storytelling, perhaps a declining oral art, may be inserted in the frame of a poem or the field of a novel as in the work of Smedley and Olsen.[31] (I have not discussed music, but, obviously, it is an enormous part of working-class cultural expression. Also, more research should focus on the links between traditional forms of people's culture and newer electronic forms and formats.) These subalterns definitely speak. As John Crawford says, "there are many kinds of voices: outcries, condemnation, inspiration, lament, agitation, reflection."[32] Worker writing has a restitutive or reparative character, an antidote perhaps to inadequate recognition of the contributions workers make. Memory and consciousness of generational difference play critical shaping roles as do place, community, and support systems. Lines of distinction between writers and readers may blur; audience matters. Actual events, lived experience are catalysts for the individual writing which generates more writing in response. Experience is respected. Interior subjectivity is linked to other workers and communities and historical patterns; the writer is witness to struggle, personal and political. Writers dialectically probe connective tissue and document alienating circumstances. Worker writing is situated outside mainstream publishing and might be considered economically disengaged writing, that is, not intended as money-making opportunities. (Do I hear a chortle?) It might be likened to outsider art or "art brut," in the sense that it is outside the mainstream—especially of the high-tone, MFA program–driven literary magazines—but it is not necessarily experimental or avant-garde. Indeed, Emmanuel Cooper in *People's Art,* a revelatory history of visual working-class art in Britain, raises concerns about the problematic class assumptions imbedded in such categorizations as low art, alternative art, outsider art, and naïve art, and recommends "people's art" because "it lies outside other definitions, [and] has no already proscribed meaning."[33] Fundamentally, worker writing exudes a particular tension between the necessity of human expression and desire for beauty and the economic conditions and circumstances of work. This is not about a room of one's own (although no one would turn that down) or about a chosen bohemian lifestyle. It is not a life*style*. The leap of difference is its grounding in a communal rather than an individualistic sensibility. On the job, the mutuality of dependence is rarely questioned, although the job itself may be bluntly critiqued. Worker writers insist on a dignity often denied to them on the job and by the larger society. They might work in hierarchical structures, but they have little patience with managerial mindsets and are not impressed by institutional bureaucracies. They write about the claims work makes on our common humanity. They know the fatigue of labor. At its most political, worker writing speaks to the necessity for structural economic and social change. Worker writers document oppression but resist sociological accounts of victimization. Their words offer hope and model struggle.

It is, as Douglas Wixson explains through his study of Jack Conroy, "a literature of commitment that addresses the concerns of working people in a language they understood" (180). He focuses on the hyphenated connection of worker-writer, and the worker's "proletarian night," the lack of sleep from working all day and writing all night (or the reverse depending on the shift),[34] as well as an ambiguous sense of being "joined and divided at the same time" (211). Although Wixson's emphasis is somewhat restricted to the world of men and industry, he does offer a useful distinction between proletarian writing and workers' writing, giving the latter category more elasticity: "The term 'proletarian writer' is ideological, detached from any comprehensible basis in social relations and experience. Worker-writer, on the other hand, has an analyzable basis in the lives and work of individual writers" (207).

Members of the Federation of Worker Writers and Community Publishers also argue the meaning of *worker* in their federation name, much of the debate hinging on politically overt writings versus expressions of the feelings and thoughts of ordinary people. As Feds Coordinator Tim Diggles puts it, "our agenda is to reflect the whole of the lives of working class people, which means their loves and sadness, as well as their striving for equality and a voice. . . . I feel we also have to see that the special interest groups—Survivors, Adult Learners, Asian and Black, Disability—are reflecting in their writing a society which does not value them and use the writing to have a voice. In some ways why should people be ghettoized by having only to write about their issues, problem[s], and so forth; their own lives and views on life are worthwhile, that is what the Fed is about."[35]

Sue Doro's much-anthologized prose poem "Cultural Worker" is a model of contemporary worker writing.[36] Doro, mother of five, worked as a machinist for thirteen years and writes about a midnight shift at the plant. "Cultural Worker" embodies her skill as a machinist, her life juggling job and family, her relationships with other workers—sometimes solidarity, sometimes estrangement—and her labor consciousness about the differences between workers, managers, and owners. "Cultural Worker" brilliantly synthesizes multiple human elements and needs, work and home, poet and skilled worker: "The poem. The woman. The mother. The machinist. All became one" (6). At its center is the thrusting impatience of a poem waiting to be born. As Doro works her midnight shift, another part of her is midwifing a poem, as finely machined as a train wheel, honing image after image. The personified poem waits for the shift to end, waits to be birthed, to erupt in these final celebratory lines:

> I'm a midnight rider
> A cat's eye glider
> A second shift mother goin' home.
>
> I'm a moon rock walker
> A pink bird stalker
> A short tall shadow headin' home.
>
> I'm a cool old river
> A seasoned survivor
> I'm a factory workin' poet goin' home. (6)

From a theoretical and perhaps more doctrinaire perspective outside working-class experience, the celebration of the pleasure of going home after a long shift may seem like a modest political act. Yet, it is unwavering in its clarity about workers' position in the dominant society. Doro accomplishes a Gramscian synthesis of work and culture, taking as much pride in her machinist skills as in her poetic expression, as she determinedly resists the thwarting of her creative expression.

Harvey Swados, as quoted by Jack Conroy at the 1978 Foolkiller conference, expands our understanding of worker writers in relation to the sustaining of a people's culture:

> While political or philosophical conviction may have influenced the Depression writers in terms of subject matter or stylistic manner, at their best they transcended politics. The intensity of their concern sprang from a richer and deeper source: Their desire was to wed their craft not to the examination of the solitary intellectual, but to an interpretation of the bewildering complexities of American life. This radicalism, this humanity, this searching not for the absurdity but for the meaningfulness; not for individual disillusionment but for the profoundest sense of comradeship—this is what animated the best writing of the Depression years and this is what the record of those years by the best of its chroniclers has had to offer.[37]

My intent is not to set politics against culture; indeed, they are inextricably rooted in common ground. Rather, I wish to offer a more expansive understanding of working-class cultural formations, including those that do not necessarily fit into perceived and often prescribed political and theoretical frames.

Articulations: Culture Is Not Negation

Wilma Elizabeth McDaniel: Worker Writer

Thus, in the working-class movement, while the clenched fist is a necessary symbol the clenching ought never to be such that the hand cannot open, and the fingers extend, to discover and give a shape to the newly forming reality.

—Raymond Williams, *Culture and Society: 1780–1950*

I remember walking out of the mill after a graveyard shift with Willie, an older worker who pointed out to me the overnite appearance of 20 red posters plastered across the plant gate wall. It was a cheerful Chairman Mao waving revolutionary greetings. Willie looked disgusted and said to me: "I don't know where that Reverend Moon gets all his money to put up all them posters!"   —Larry Evans, "An Organizer's Odyssey"

Rural and agricultural, rather than urban and industrial, female rather than male, unaffiliated with political or labor movements, Wilma Elizabeth McDaniel is a worker writer who defies orthodox academic assumptions or categorizations. The one category about which there is no debate, especially in McDaniel's sense of herself, is poet. What she writes about one of her characters also characterizes herself: "You might as well realize now that you are different from the other children running around in Big Muddy. You see everything and feel everything. You are a poet, and a poet is bound to get hurt. You will be disappointed so many times."[38] Poet is a large word in McDaniel's cosmos, not out of any sense of self-aggrandizement—in fact, she is extremely reluctant to talk about herself—but rather in the sense that a poet is someone anointed with a capacity to absorb and deeply read the world with all its natural and human complexity. For her, writing (the distinctions between poem and prose blur) is a calling, breath itself: "Nowadays, more people ask me about the origins of my writing; when did it start? These questions always leave me awkward and unprepared to answer them for one reason. I can hardly remember when I was *not* some kind of writer, specifically, a poet. At age four I was so entranced by the sight of tiny silver minnows in a brook that I almost became ill. *I must tell someone* how lovely the minnows were. *No one else knew.* I look at this moment as the awakening of my true calling, and often, my affliction."[39] Because of this gift or what she calls "the creeping disease of poetry," and because she recognizes that she is the one with the capacity, she *must* write. And McDaniel has, literally all of her life—without computer, writers' workshops, academic training, agents, or any of the accoutrements of literary success. Hers is a singular voice that speaks volumes. It is distinctive *and* representative. Collective *and* solitary. Poetry for her is not a hobby or a life*style*. She draws such distinctions in "Obscure Poet at Literary Tea":

Classic hostess with purple hair
wearing a string of pearls
pouring tea from a silver pot
you have figured me

all wrong
Five minutes after we met
in this rarefied room
you fill my cup
and tell me it must be nice
to have a little hobby
something to pick up
when I feel bored
and put down when I please
Exasperating woman
give me an éclair
to close my angry mouth
before I lose control
and tell you
there is no place
where a poet can put it down
just kiss it off
and walk away[40]

It is tempting to compare Wilma Elizabeth McDaniel to fictional characters, perhaps Mazie, Tillie Olsen's child of wonder in *Yonnondio,* or the resourceful mother and wood carver, Gertie Nevels, in Harriette Arnow's *The Dollmaker.* However, that would be almost too literary and too easy an analytical response to McDaniel's work. She challenges critics to recognize her capacity to create believable portraits with minuscule verbal brush strokes. Her subjects, a pantheon of individuals like Orville Kincaid, Buford, Wanda, Vonetta Jones, E. B., Willis Cates, Lila Faye Palmer, and many others, are somewhat reminiscent of the subjects of Edwin Arlington Robinson's Tilbury Town portraits, but these folks are somehow less distant, less studied. Her honed-down style opens to an unexpected interiority. Despite their accessibility, many poems boomerang the reader back to the title for a second look and a deeper understanding. McDaniel's perspective is that of a sympathetic and knowing insider: sometimes it comes through the consciousness of an observant female child growing into an economically narrow adult world, a very distinctive *Kunstlerroman.* Any serious analysis of her work must cautiously avoid the traps of turning her into a red-dirt exotic or, worse, patronizing or colonizing her. We lack theoretical frames that accommodate writing that is so clearly grounded outside the world of canonical literature, the academy, and bourgeois institutions.

I suspect McDaniel's resistance to autobiography comes in part out of working-class hesitation about individual attention (especially for someone of her generation and gender), but also a shrewd caution about having her life's work, her writing, reduced to her life. She, as Douglas Wixson suggests for worker writers generally, "is not content to be viewed as a 'folk character' or eccentric" (216). For that reason, I did not begin with the biographical details, poignant as they are. I wish to suggest that we consider Wilma Elizabeth

Roman Loranc,
Wilma Elizabeth McDaniel.
Courtesy of Wilma Elizabeth McDaniel.

McDaniel as a worker writer, evidencing most if not all the characteristics listed above, particularly a deep well of storytelling, but also something more, something that comes closer to Harvey Swados's vision. In her resistance to the theft of working-class epistemology and culture by consumerism, in her penetrating portraits of human diversity within the working class, and in her capacity to bridge orality and textuality, she practices what I call a *radical humanism.* It is radical in the sense that it is deeply rooted, certainly in Oklahoma and the San Joaquin Valley. But along with the Okie twang in her writing voice is a deeper consciousness of the dual condition of being simultaneously rooted and uprooted.

Nothing is wasted on her. She is also radical in insisting on the validity of the commonplace and ordinary as subjects. She is a poet of the dismissed and forgotten. In her pithy, unsentimental, incisive voice, she recognizes the interior lives of subjects deemed so low as to be unworthy of artistic recognition. In the face of academically stimulated postmodern simulacra, her stories, poems, vignettes (never quite fashioned into the bourgeois form of the novel), challenge the reader to see a complex humanity beneath her vernacular language. In its modest, persistent way, McDaniel's writing steadfastly commits to the struggle for an evolving humanity. The most ordinary thing—perhaps a paper shopping bag with a withered strap—becomes transformed in McDaniel's hands and imagination into a metonymy for human endurance. She challenges big-city intolerance for the seemingly corny and banal. Beneath her reticence, beyond the years of tedious menial jobs picking cotton and fruit and cleaning other people's dirt, is a steadfast insistence on her identity as one tough poet with a great thirst for beauty. Above all, she recognizes her role as a witness for her people, a collective consciousness embodied in an individual voice. Commenting on the word *witnessing*, she writes, "It means a great deal to me. I heard the word from earliest memory, Bible accounts of witnessing 'even to the shedding of blood.' Haven't poor working women always done a lot of that?"[41]

At last count she had published fourteen small press books. She is also the subject of a documentary video, *Down an Old Road: The Poetic Life of Wilma Elizabeth McDaniel.*[42] Her collected works, which she assembled and sorted into three differently colored dishpans, will be published by Heyday Books. She wrote steadily and in isolation for nearly fifty years before her first book was published in 1973. She is well known in the Central Valley of California as the "Okie Bard" and "the Gravy Poet" for her poem expressing trust in gravy to stretch out the meager sausage, and "the dreams from payday / till tomorrow,"[43] and for her newspaper column, "Walking on an Old Road," for the *South Valley Arts.* In 1936, when she was seventeen, she and her family migrated out of the Oklahoma dustbowl into the promise of California. She lived the experience that Steinbeck fictionalized in *The Grapes of Wrath* (1939), and tells the story with less artifice and, in my mind, more attention to the complexity and diversity among the Oklahoma migrants themselves. In "The Journey" she writes of the Okie's sense of alienation and exile in their own land:

> The fifth morning of the trip, we reached the California border. Papa got boiling mad when the officials turned back a truckload of people from Oklahoma.
>
> The big cheese in charge wore shiny riding boots and told these pitiful people they could not enter the state. The woman and children were crying and the two men looked scared and helpless. All they could do was turn back to nowhere.
>
> Papa's eyes turned to blue ice. We knew he wanted badly to cuss, but he held himself, gritted his teeth. "A shame and a scandal," he muttered as we waited our turn for inspection. "American citizens, mind you, right here in the U.S. of A., talk about your Communist State. It can't be worse than this!"[44]

Although a country doctor declared her lost to the vicious influenza epidemic of 1918, Anna McDaniel did survive to give birth to Wilma Elizabeth on December 22, 1918, the fourth of her eight children. Wilma grew up near Stroud, Oklahoma, in a sharecropper family. She describes those early years with her characteristic eye for telling descriptive details combined with a sharp-tongued directness:

> My entire childhood and early adulthood were formed, forged in great rural poverty and hardship. My mother was a devoutly religious woman of heroic

stature. I close my eyes and see her with head tied up in a baby diaper taking down frozen laundry from the clothesline. This sometimes had to be accomplished by hauling water two miles from a neighbor's well. The smell of lye soap assails my nostrils in memory. I see Mama's hands so reddened and raw from the homemade soap. I learned firsthand how caustic it was. I took my turn at the washboard early.

I suppose as far as suffering, ill health, non-existent medical attention for years at a time, and lowered expectations go, I could probably swap horror stories with some of the best whiners, but that would be ridiculous and a waste of energy.

I am simply not a whiner.[45]

About not whining as a cultural trait, Roxanne Dunbar-Ortiz recalls in her memoir, *Red Dirt,* how "Complaining was forbidden. Anything that suggested weakness was forbidden. We took pride in not being gripers and whiners, 'belly-achers.' And that was our image writ large, as in *The Grapes of Wrath,* the stoical, silent-suffering, dignified people of the soil" (32). Of Anglo-Cherokee heritage, Wilma Elizabeth McDaniel doesn't whine, but she also does not let you forgot that she stakes her claims as a poet based on a life of hardship as well as kinship. She knew what it meant to be simultaneously a multigenerational American and a migrant. Reading McDaniel, I understand better why my family, particularly my mother and aunts, resisted, vehemently, any reference to them as poor. Yes, they were materially disadvantaged, but in their own eyes, to say they were poor stripped them of dignity, and besides they measured wealth in terms of the arithmetic of human relationships. However, without creative release, this sense of vivid identity, generating spirited language and confidence within the extended family, dissolves into silences, awkward uncertainties, and resentment in relation to the outside world. And there is a trace of defensive edginess in relation to the dominant culture in McDaniel's work. She claims not to be political, but she has a deeply grounded ethos and does not hesitate to speak truth to power: "Medi-Cal will only pay for one bridge of six teeth. You had better figure on getting along with only your five remaining lower front teeth. How you chew with no lower molars is a secret of the government."[46] And she is not chauvinistic about her own kind. When asked about anti-immigrant sentiment against Mexicans in California, often by descendents of Okies, she answers with a poem: "They forgot so easily, / the same road led / everyone to this place."[47]

Where does Wilma Elizabeth McDaniel fit within the category of worker writer? She is not a darling of the Left nor a labor organizer; she is not sanctioned as a suitable subject for graduate students; she is part of no literary establishment; she definitely is not postmodern chic. She poses a challenge. Either one dismisses or ignores her (which I refuse to do) or tries to wrestle with what is steadfastly there in her copious writings. (She has battled very poor health, but never writer's block.) Without doubt, she wants an audience and wants to write in a way that her audience will expand and hear her voice. In choosing to write about hardship obliquely, from a visual slant, perhaps in keeping with her own stoic sensibility, McDaniel creates a world of surprises and wonder among the least privileged of the human condition. She says, "I don't feel despondent, rather I am hopeful, quite often, full of hilarity with the world."[48]

McDaniel traverses the space between heroics and victimization. She calls herself a "cotton-picking, two-room school house academic" (true), but chooses to emphasize not absence (of education or sustainable work) but presence of human stamina and grit. Her style differs from the literary sophistication of widely known male poets born into the working class but educated out of it like Philip Levine and Jim Daniels, who use much more complicated syntax (especially Levine). Both Levine and Daniels have mined the relatively brief industrial work experiences of their youth even as their material lives in the academy and as celebrated poets have greatly improved. McDaniel, however, largely unrecognized in the academy, has never left the working class, and has never had the opportunity of either highly paid industrial labor or higher education.

Consider Wilma Elizabeth McDaniel as connective tissue, as memory link, and as surviving practitioner of a dying art, storytelling. Each of her poems, stories, vignettes, pungent commentary in letters, stands alone; yet, gathered together as a whole (yet to be done by some discerning critic) they present a cumulative, heteroglossic panorama of human conditions, particularly the Lilliputian and Brobdingnagian of rural, working-class, Okie, Central California lived experience. In his essay "The Storyteller," Walter Benjamin laments the decline of the art of storytelling, "the ability to exchange experiences," and the devaluing of experience.[49] Benjamin views experience as inseparable from storytelling, and great storytellers, Benjamin makes clear, carry orality, the many tellings of the tale, into the written formulation. Acknowledging how traditional storytelling loses ground to the modern flow of information (more true today than ever), Benjamin stresses that every real story contains something useful. "The usefulness may, in one case, consist in a moral; in another, in some practical advice; in a third, in a proverb or maxim" (86). Further, Benjamin claims orality is what distinguishes storytelling from the bourgeois genre of the novel: "The storyteller takes what he tells from experience—his own or that reported by others. And he in turn makes it the experience of those who are listening to his tale. The novelist has isolated himself" (87).[50] I employ Benjamin—whose relationship to labor could not be more different from McDaniel's— here because he offers a useful theoretical frame for locating McDaniel's work within a literary tradition, in his case the European fairy tale and in hers, music, sermons, and daily conversations in the context of work, home, and kinship ties, as well as her inherited Native American tradition of storytelling.[51] Although we cannot literally document the stories told after Sunday dinner or shared with neighbors on the front porch, reading her poems we can see how McDaniel rescues and mines the storytelling tradition of her Okie culture. She acknowledges as much in her one-paragraph "The Storytellers":

> Mr. Crowley is going back to school, to finish his teach [*sic*] credential. He said, "You people from Oklahoma are superb story-tellers. I have never seen your equal. I mean I have never heard your equal. I want my two children to come over and just sit out under the trees and listen to you talk. I am desperately afraid that they will grow up without the touch of magic so many of you possess."[52]

It is ironic that the very European Walter Benjamin, an *homme de lettres* incapable of sustaining himself economically, enables a reading of McDaniel that affirms her traditional and distinct voice and situates her within a very deep and long current. Consider Benjamin's commentary on storytelling in relation to McDaniel's work. First, he identifies storytelling as coming out of the "milieu of work—the rural, the maritime, and the urban—[as] . . . an artisan form of communication" (91). Benjamin recognizes the craftsmanship inherent to the story, as "traces of the storyteller cling to the story the way the handprints of the potter cling to the clay vessel" (92). Next, Benjamin's appreciation for the miniature, the abbreviated, and the aphoristic illuminates McDaniel's honed technique. Further, Benjamin links the authority of the storyteller to an intimacy with death. Wilma Elizabeth McDaniel answers death with memory, story, and speech gestures. In "Roster," a rare commentary on private loss and grief, place embodies death:

> No alternative route
> only one road leads from
> yesterday
>
> and every town
> I pass through
>
> is a place where someone
> I have loved
> died much too young
>
> Merced
> Fresno
> and Malibu, California
> Medford, Oregon
> and El Paso, Texas
>
> heaven forbid that
> I should ever stop in
> Boise, Idaho
>
> Coda:
> This is not a poem.

It is a cold fact.
Five of my brothers.
All young.[53]

Benjamin concludes his analysis by underscoring the artisanal quality of storytelling, linking words with soul, eye, and hand as a practice. The hand especially:

> The role of the hand in production has become more modest, and the place it filled in storytelling lies waste. (After all, storytelling, in its sensory aspect, is by no means a job for the voice alone. Rather, in genuine storytelling the hand plays a part which supports what is expressed in a hundred ways with its gestures trained by work.) . . . In fact, one can go on and ask oneself whether the relationship of the storyteller to his material, human life, is not in itself a craftsman's relationship, whether it is not his very task to fashion the raw material of experience, his own and that of others, in a solid, useful, and unique way. . . . Seen in this way, the storyteller joins the ranks of the teachers and sages. (108)

Storyteller and sage, vestige of another time and world, Wilma Elizabeth McDaniel illuminates and questions what it means to be a human being. "You are absolutely correct that I am not recognizably political in the way the academy would like me to be," she writes. "I am, perhaps even doggedly, holding to the sure hard and sustaining vision which has brought me this far, a quiet justice is no less a justice."[54]

Working-class cultural formations endure: the poem machined like a railroad wheel, the federation's enclaves of readers and writers, the proletarian night of the worker writer, and a surviving Okie poet—our collective Kizaemon Tea-bowl, imperfectly glazed perhaps, but pleasurable to hold, and, oh, so useful.

In the Skin of a Worker

or, What Makes a Text Working Class?

While it is true that there is a long literary history of depictions of the working classes, it is also true that we cannot assume that representations of workers automatically constitute working-class writing. Indeed, working-class writing as a discrete body of writing, grounded outside the academy, but studied within it, is still struggling for name recognition in the academic marketplace. Among the 130 divisions and discussion groups of the Modern Language Association, ranging from the magisterial categories of English and American Literature to the particularities of Old Norse and the more recent Computer Studies and Disability Studies, there is no category for class or labor literature. Perhaps class differences are subsumed within diverse ethnic locations and identities or are displaced by the dominance of other identities. Or, perhaps, this invisibility of class is another indicator of "labor's untold story"[1] and institutional resistance to the recognition of class differences.

In 1993 I sent a proposal to the MLA for a permanent discussion group on working-class literature with a petition signed by 160 members of the MLA. The Program Committee and Executive Council rejected it because it did not offer a definition of working-class literature that would enable the identification of a set of working-class texts, and because there was "no need" for such a discussion group. My intent was less to storm the MLA than to ensure a home by way of two sessions at the annual convention for scholarly explorations of working-class literature. In a book on Shakespeare and the culture wars, Sharon O'Dair reviews this petition and suspects "some disingenuousness" in the MLA's response, drawing the analogy that working-class literature is "literature by or for—or even about—members of the working class,"[2] a definition that would be comparable to describing any number of discussion group categories— Sephardic, Scottish, or Slavic, for example. The obvious sticking point is that un-American and slippery category of class. Neither national nor ethnic group, defying stable definitions, class is named, usually, as the tag category in the trinity of identities and then all but disappears. What seems forgotten is that even though walls may fall, theories are discredited, and liberals turn neoconservative, working-class people themselves still struggle to exist.

I wish to do no more than acknowledge these class-blind spots, not dwell on them. I think it is critically important to include working-class cultural study in any academic setting because such study expands and tests assumptions about all kinds of knowledge and culture. The very fact that insecurities about class definitions and identities exist strikes me as a claim for deeper and further self-reflective study.

It is more useful to begin from a different starting point, one that better fits working-class literature than a priori definitional approaches. First, a few caveats. I am not concerned here with writing produced for working-class consumption such as romance or dime novels, but I do take into account the many forms (journals, songs, novels, memoirs, poetry, plays, speeches, pamphlets, oral testimony, sketches, etc.) of working-class writing, and the long, albeit fragmented, lineage of working-class literature. Also, I certainly acknowledge the extraordinary scholarship on proletarian literature of the thirties, but I do not want to limit our considerations to a particular period of time.[3] The working class(es) are not stable nor are they necessarily accommodating to any political ideology or agenda. Further, I do not want to essentialize the authorship of working-class writing. Certainly, writers born into middle-class circumstances—with the appropriate imaginative and class-conscious leap—can and do write working-class texts. Alexander Saxton (*The Great Midland*) and Harriette Arnow (*The Dollmaker*) are two of many examples.[4] Finally, as an anthologizer of working-class writing, I am cautious about corralling working-class writing inside categories constructed under highly privileged class circumstances, as well as cognizant of the importance of discerning class differences in literary production and representation.[5]

How do we recognize a working-class text? If we focus on process rather than category, it is possible to move from the static "what *is* a working-class text?" to the more dynamic and active "what *makes* a text working class?" In other words, we can begin to discern the indicators that enable a reader to recognize a working-class text and to identify strategic elements, those external shaping forces, as well as those internal traces, residual and emergent, that shape working-class writings.

In his essay "The Writer: Commitment and Alignment," Raymond Williams makes an important case for grounding the self in a social context without reducing an individual to an essentialized identity.[6] Williams calls for a commitment to "social reality" and a consciousness of "our own real alignments" (86). Recognition of these alignments, located as they are in a matrix of social relationships, creates (rather than thwarts) artistic openings. Williams is identifying and affirming a deep alignment (not obligation or submission) that, paradoxically perhaps, liberates writing: "But when it really happens, in the many different ways that are possible, its sound is usually unmistakable: the sound of that voice which in speaking as itself, is speaking, necessarily, for more than itself" (87).

Williams's emphasis on relationality and active cultural formation provides a frame for recognizing working-class writing. His focus on voice, particularly the voice that speaks "for more than itself" is critical to understanding motive and catalyst for working-class writing. The working-class writer has a heightened consciousness of the multiple "we" inside the writer's "I." It is both a burdened consciousness, because working-class writers are conduits, mediators, pipelines for those (usually) silenced multiple voices, and a liberated consciousness, because attending to these collective voices enables the writer to speak (Williams's notion of heightened artistic freedom). It is a reciprocal process, a complex matrix inseparable from lived economic and cultural material realities. What I am suggesting is a discursive and literary relationality. It is a different paradigm than that of the individual figure emerging out of a social milieu to explore the isolated, dangling, and usually damaged self. This is not the *bildung* of up and out, of discard and disregard, but of traveling with, that is, of carrying working-class experience, history, knowledge, language, values (with all their contradictions and complexities) out and into the world. Or as Williams puts it in another essay, "we must emphasize not the ladder but the common highway."[7]

Also, using Bakhtin's concept of "answerability," Peter Hitchcock describes working-class writing as "structured from within by a potential answerability to a variety of community interests"(27).[8] Hitchcock, in his interpretation of Bakhtin, provides a theoretical frame for naming those moments of encounter and recognition between working-class-aligned writers and readers. "In general," Hitchcock writes, "answerability is a form of social responsibility that allows workers to 'speak' to one another across a range of discourses, discourses of memory, of experience, of alienation, of solidarity" (28). Conceptually, answerability, like Williams's alignment, allows us to penetrate some of the dynamics of relationship within working-class texts as they affect readers. This approach is distinct from discussions of audience in the context of market forces.

Further, I am not suggesting that one can draw a hard-and-fast line between working-class and bourgeois literatures. Rather, through comparative readings, one can understand better how a text works to centralize working-class lived experiences. For example, consider how textual space is utilized for descriptions of material conditions—the food, clothing, possessions, homes of working-class people—and for representations of relationships and multiple voices within working-class communities (not that these voices are always consistent or monologic). Next, notice whether the relationship between workers and their employers/bosses is foregrounded or backgrounded. Then ask what effect that relationship has on the bodies of workers. While it is true that class is a relationship and not a thing, to evoke E. P. Thompson's famous and frequently quoted preface,[9] it is also true that class oppression can turn human beings into things. Working-class writing recognizes and resists the transformation of the human I/we into an it—a thing, a commodity, a working unit, a disembodied hand. Working-class writing may or may not have an overt political consciousness, but it does have a recognition of class disparities—understanding class not as an abstraction but as a set of lived human relationships shaped by economic forces and a shared materiality and relationship to work at particular historical moments. This historicity of class experience is inseparable from an understanding of working-class literature. Finally, one recognizes a working-class text by the way it invites, cajoles, even insists, that the reader step into the skin of a worker.

Outside and Inside the Skin of a Worker

Michael Ondaatje's *In the Skin of a Lion* (1987) is a highly intertextual postmodern novel that parallels the coming of age of the male protagonist, Patrick Lewis, with Canada's transformation from a largely rural society to a country of industrialized and booming urban centers fueled by capital and built largely by cheap, immigrant labor during the first three decades of the twentieth century.[10] It is a fine novel of great verve and style and language play. It is certainly sympathetic to workers, a novel committed to recognizing the invisible workers who built cities but were excluded from official records, and certainly from literary canons, but it is not a working-class novel.

Ondaatje raises the question that is pivotal. Describing one of the central characters, Ondaatje writes: "He was one of those who have a fury or a sadness of only being described by someone else. A tarrer of roads, a housebuilder, a painter, a thief—yet he was invisible to all around him" (199). What does it feel like to be described by other people and erased by them at the same time? Or, to look at it another way, what spaces are created within a text for workers to represent themselves? And, what are the political and economic implications of those representations?

Ondaatje presents us with a series of worker tableaus. In the first, Patrick Lewis is a young boy who rises early to watch a group of workers pass by his farmhouse. They are thirty loggers, "wrapped up dark, carrying axes and small packages of food" who already "seem exhausted" (7, 8). Notice the perspective. The boy Patrick moves from window to window; each window serves as a frame temporarily freezing the men as if they were a detail in a movie or the background in a photograph or a scene etched on a Grecian urn. We see the loggers through the boy's eyes. The men step aside to let some cows (that they do not own) pass. The men politely steal warmth from the flanks of the animals. The reader does not get to listen in and overhear the loggers speak to each other; they are as mute as the cows.

There are several other tableaus, of bridge builders, tunnelers, slaughterhouse workers, leather dyers and cutters. Ondaatje describes the physicality of their labor. Each carefully wrought episode is moved to the foreground of the novel, observed, noted by the reader, and then submerged again into the background, the latent, silent landscape of labor. These are dioramas, well-intended but ultimately static representations of labor. We never see the relationship between paid and domestic labor; we are not privy to the conversations between the workers; nor can we know their interior and subjective differences. Instead, the author provides a comfort zone, a peripheral awareness of the plight of labor without the costs of political engagement. The novel evokes history and resists it at the same time. In the end, the novel is like a darkened theater where the reader, as sympathetic spectator, watches scene after scene advance on the screen. But the writer never asks too much of the reader. We do not have to break the line of demarcation and step into the skin of a worker, and move beyond compassion into solidarity.

We could contrast Ondaatje's novel with many working-class novels to see the differences of interiority and subjectivity and to measure what the reader learns about working-class life. Consider, as a short list, Thomas Bell's *Out of This Furnace,* Agnes Smedley's *Daughter of Earth,* Pietro di Donato's *Christ in Concrete* or works by more contemporary writers such as Carolyn Chute's *The Beans of Egypt, Maine,* Dorothy Allison's *Bastard Out of Carolina,* or Helena María Viramontes's *Under the Feet of Jesus.* I want to single out, however, Tillie Olsen's (unfinished) novel *Yonnondio* (1975) as an undisputed working-class text in contrast to Ondaatje's *In the Skin of a Lion.*

If we put aside the material class differences of the two authors, differences of circumstances and conditions for writing, differences of nationality and age, and differences of gender and location (huge differences, I agree), that is, if we look at the novels apart from the biographies of the authors, what do we notice as distinctive about working-class representation in *Yonnondio* as compared to the sympathetic treatment of labor in *In the Skin of a Lion?*

Unlike the depiction of work in Ondaatje's postmodern, magical-realist novel, there is no comfort zone in *Yonnondio.*[11] Olsen demands a lot from her readers. From the first words, Olsen plunges us into the interiority of working-class lives: the exhausting rhythms of reproductive and productive labor; the cadences, dialects, curtailed responses, directness of working-class speech; the meager clothes and household furnishings; the making do; the starchy, inadequate food; the simple pleasures of songs and stories shared in good times; and always the graphic description of the physicality of labor, the risks on the job, the costs to the body of too much work, too frequent births, and the stamp of work on the begrudged play and abbreviated childhoods of children. The novel is dominated by the struggle for breath (in the slaughterhouse the women working in Casings, where the men won't work, breathe with open mouths). Breath symbolizes Olsen's persistent themes: humanity thwarted and crushed because of unjust work and yet still resisting, enduring.

Olsen begins her story about ten years after Ondaatje's fictional Patrick Lewis gazes from his farmhouse window at the immigrant laborers walking to their logging jobs in the cold and the dark. Like Ondaatje, Olsen uses the mind, eyes, and ears of a child as the introductory consciousness of the novel. But unlike Patrick who gazes from inside the early morning quiet of his farmhouse, Mazie

Holbrook awakes to an assault of sound. Whistles pierce her sleep like "some guttural-voiced metal beast" (9). This is the benign morning whistle; those that shriek during the day mean death—"somebody's poppa or brother, perhaps her own—in that fearsome place below the ground, the mine" (9).

The instances of death and injury on the job are distanced in *In the Skin of a Lion*. The reader learns that Patrick Lewis's father is a dynamiter and that he is killed on the job. But the reader is not privy to the details or circumstances. Ondaatje prefers to engage his poetic imagination with the extraordinary and the magical: the bridge builder swaying out in space on a dark night who reaches out and catches a nun swept away by the wind. In contrast, the physicality of labor—the risks and dangers of work—are immediately centered in *Yonnondio*. A thirteen-year-old boy, his father killed in the mines, must descend into the mines, give up his education, and replace his father's body at work. Olsen describes the transformation of miners from white to black as they enter the "bowels of the earth"; the imaginative child Mazie wonders if the earth is a "stummy [bowel, stomach] and maybe she eats the men that come down. . . . Earth black, and pop's face and hands black, and he spits from his mouth black" (12).

Olsen's readers are assaulted by sensory detail: the shriek of machines, the stench of the packinghouse, the cutting of corn stubble into bare feet. Olsen rejects the aesthetic tableau. She addresses the bourgeois reader with the caustic question, "And could you not make a cameo of this and pin it onto your aesthetic hearts?" (30). Class identity and consciousness forge Olsen's aesthetic. She seeks to reclaim the humanity of the "grotesques, this thing with the foot missing, this gargoyle with half the face gone and the arm" (30) and rejects the cameo(d) carving out, the separated, examined, and then submerged artifact of human labor. Olsen does not allow the reader to avert her eyes. Also, Olsen rejects not only the static moment of observation, but the framing and posing of work in isolation and stillness. She comes as close as any writer can to the movement, motion, rhythm, pounding beat, repetitions of labor: the mother holding the screaming baby in one arm and with her free hand pouring and capping and sealing the boiling jelly. "Skim, stir; sprinkle Bess; pit, peel and cut; sponge; skim, stir" (149). And in the slaughterhouse the awful parallel scene in Casings, the temperature 110 degrees: "over and over, the one constant motion—ruffle fat pullers, pluck separators, bladder, kidney, bung, small and middle gut cutters, cleaners, trimmers, slimers, flooders, inflators—meshed, geared" (134).

Attentive readers of *Yonnondio* are likely to experience an emotional discomfiture. Olsen creates what Raymond Williams calls "structures of feeling or experience," not only in the text, but quite literally because of the graphic power of her sensory detail, through the reader's necessary intimacy with the text. (Williams describes "structures of feeling" as "meanings and values as they are actively lived and felt . . . affective elements of consciousness and relationships."[12]) *Yonnondio,* because of its insistence on an affective and experiential relationship between the reader and the text, is a much more emotionally unsettling book to read, and, I believe, a more difficult book to teach than *In the Skin of a Lion.*

I want to suggest that parallel readings of comparable texts about work, such as this abridged highlighting of Ondaatje and Olsen, offer opportunities to discern differences in class consciousness in writers and in readers and to discern better what makes a text working class. Olsen's writing asks readers to reflect on their own expectations from a text and perhaps their own resistance to confronting and internalizing the physicality of labor.

What Makes a Text Working Class?

How do we move from the particularities of textual observation to larger considerations of those elements that distinguish working-class literature? What are the forces that shape a working-class text? What patterns can we identify in a reliable way? I suggest we build theoretical models out of attentive observation of the texts themselves. This may involve quieting the theoretical and interpretive voice and *listening* to the voices of working-class people themselves, those voices, as Williams suggests, speaking, necessarily, for more than themselves. I offer these observations of working-class writings as a modest beginning.

- A working-class text centers the lived, material experiences of working-class people. Working-class texts take up the burden of an embodied representation. We see the (thinking) body at work (both productive and reproductive labor) and the effects of work on the human body. The working-class subject is taken seriously: here is a mind, a voice, a body. Working-class texts contest the dehumanization of the working mind/body.
- The writer of working-class literature (who may be living a middle-class life) creates imaginatively or realistically (often through intertextual materials) a space for working-class people to represent themselves. This is a humble witnessing, not hegemonic ventriloquism. This representation frequently has politically strategic as well as pragmatic value. Working-class representation usually includes the idioms, dialects, syntax, curses, blessings, and direct tones of working-class speech in particular regions and accented by ethnic and racial identities. Perhaps this is the most challenging aspect of writing the working class.
- Working-class literature is not a solo, solitary act. This is not so much collective writing, but rather communal sensibility. The writer is conscious of his or her ghosts, of the multiple, competing, contradictory, and demanding voices that inhabit the "we" inside the individual writer's "I." The fictional or autobiographical working-class *bildung* leads not to separation and alienation but to a consciousness of connective tissue and multiple histories and lives that comprise the self.

- Readers who are of the working class have the opportunity to recognize themselves in working-class writing, a rarity in an economy that uses working people and simultaneously erases and denies their existence as cultural citizens. Published writing by workers not only affirms working-class experience, but also gives permission for working-class readers to become writers of their own experience. Working-class texts offer readers an opportunity to recover their personal as well as regional and national submerged labor histories. On the other hand, the class-privileged reader who ordinarily sees himself reflected in other texts, both literary and nonliterary, is displaced and de-centered in working-class writing and is challenged to make an imaginative leap into another class world.

- Working-class writing is not "White" writing. Many texts ordinarily categorized as ethnic or African American can also be read as working-class texts. This is not a privileging of class over race or gender or sexual identities, but rather an insistence that any analysis of race, gender, sexuality, even disability, cannot be complete if class is excluded.

- Working-class texts give language to human suffering and grief. This suffering comes from economic forces weighing on the lives of working people, not from free-floating anxiety or alienation. Working-class writers are particularly attentive to the physicality of suffering. This is a validation of the physical conditions that separate working-class life from bourgeois existence. It is a validation not only of a "structure of feeling," but also of the depth of feeling and the relationship of feeling to thought that is so ignored by the dominant culture.

- Conversely, working-class humor, wit, and language play have to be decoded in working-class texts. The working-class voices are not always so silent; sometimes they mouth back, or have "smart mouths," at the expense of the dominant culture. Working-class humor often takes the form of in-your-face sarcasm, ridicule, and irony.

- Any serious study of working-class writing must concern itself with cultural formation. The formation of working-class cultural expression often parallels the opportunities for writing workshops, community gatherings, and publishing, such as the Federation of Worker Writers and Community Publishers, a network of local writers located in large and small communities throughout Britain.[13] Also, the formation of working-class writing often depends on antecedents different from those in bourgeois texts. Writing by workers is often based on actual events such as strikes or industrial accidents, or writing is composed in response to and in dialogue with other working-class expressions, such as the worker's correspondence that is the source for Tillie Olsen's poem "I Want You Women Up North to Know."[14] This process of formation is not about the death of the author, but rather the grounding of individual writers in larger histories and untold stories.

- Working-class texts are intended to be useful, to have agency in the world. Many writers link writing to survival, not to intellectual property. Working-class texts are less concerned with postmodern linguistic play for its own ends (although they may be deeply inventive, lyrical, and funny), and more interested in the forces of history on human relationships over time and generations, that is, in the continuous, larger struggle for economic justice.

■ Working-class texts question and challenge dominant assumptions about aesthetics. They contextualize aesthetics, insisting on the contingent nature of aesthetic form and practice, and the complexities of local knowledge, and other circumstances.

■ Working-class texts have consciousness of class oppression. Many texts present the formation of consciousness, the coming into class knowledge (Agnes Smedley's *Daughter of Earth* may be the classic example[15]). Class oppression is evident on several levels—in the backgrounded landscape of an economic system of exploited labor, and in the more foregrounded subjective landscape of working-class characters (voices) as they interact with others inside or outside their own class. Some working-class texts bring the structural background into sharper focus and the "class war" becomes the subject of the text without losing the subjective element (Denise Giardina's *Storming Heaven*).[16] Other working-class texts illuminate that deeper structure through the intensely felt and lived class circumstances of the characters (*Yonnondio*).

■ Many working-class writers, especially those writing in more pronounced historic moments of class struggle, take sides. Florence Reece's famous song, written on an old calendar as an organizing tool for southern Appalachian miners, starkly asks: "Which side are you on? Which side are you on?"[17]

■ Pride rather than shame is a characteristic of some working-class writing. It is an insistence on human dignity despite economic hardship. Consider Mary Casey's feisty poem "The Class Game" with its in-your-face attitude, rhymes and rhythms, and direct address to an unnamed "you" whose assumptions about class identity she challenges:

> How can you tell what class I'm from?
> Have I a label on me head, and another on me bum?
> Or is it because my hands are stained with toil,
> Instead of soft lily-white with perfume and oil?
> Don't I crook me little finger when I drink me tea,
> Say toilet instead of bog when I want to pee?
> Why do you care what class I'm from?
> Does it stick in your gullet, like a sour plum?
> Well mate! A cleaner is me mother,
> A docker is me brother,
> Bread pudding is wet nelly,
> And me stomach is me belly,
> And I'm proud of the class that I come from.[18]

These categories and characteristics *should* be contested and debated. Offered as empirical framework, not rigid criteria or working-class manifesto, they draw class-based cultural distinctions and query literary assumptions. "The America of the working class is practically undiscovered. It is like a lost continent": Mike Gold's observations in the *New Masses* of 1929 still apply (although not necessarily only to his young, masculine worker).[19] American working-class literature is more than the occasional story about shopping at K-Mart. It has discernable history, complicated aesthetics, and representational power awaiting further critical exploration—if not at the MLA, then elsewhere.[20]

No way is a good way to lose your job.   —*Doris McKinney*, Portraits in Steel

Jude began to be impressed with the isolation of his own personality, as with a self-spectre, the sensation being that of one who walked but could not make himself seen or heard. He drew his breath pensively, and, seeming thus almost his own ghost . . .
         —*Thomas Hardy*, Jude the Obscure

MAD AVE: 40,000 protesting construction workers bring midtown to a standstill.
         —New York Daily News, *1 July 1998*

Worker Ghosts

I. Ghosted Work

Benign or malevolent, ghosts are signs of unfinished business—lives abruptly ended, stolen, or shortened. Felt, but rarely seen, ghosts hover between presence and absence, invisibility and visibility, trailing the residue of life, of relationships, of labor performed, a history buried but not completely lost. The ghosts that concern us here are not the constructions of popular culture, the dead manifesting themselves to the living; rather, they are emblems of a particular reversal, workers who have been *ghosted*, living human beings turned into dead workers.

In *Jude the Obscure* (1896), Jude Fawley, Thomas Hardy's intellectual and sensitive stonemason, wanders down the aged alleys of Christminster and converses with imagined sages. Longing for higher education, thwarted by the meager choices of his class, he seeks kinship and a "common mental life" (132). In this setting of decaying medieval buildings, he realizes not kinship, but his own invisibility, and senses "his own ghost" (125–126). Hardy's Jude-ghost, an embodied disembodiment, a reversal of the dead body manifesting its presence to the living, becomes a "self-spectre" (126).[1]

One hundred years later, far away in time and place from the dim, lonely lanes of Hardy's Christminster, tens of thousands of angry New York City construction workers disrupt midtown Manhattan. Incensed by city officials awarding a major transportation construction project to a nonunion firm, they put aside their differences long enough to fight the erosion of all their union jobs. On June 30, 1998, union ironworkers, carpenters, truckers, laborers, roofers, and electricians brought Manhattan's "midtown to a standstill" as they demonstrated in front of the nonunion job site and rallied around a "15-foot-tall inflatable rat that . . . symbolize[d] the nonunion workers nibbling away at their livelihoods."[2] The raised fists, angry clashes with authority, and determination to have their presence felt and seen suggests not only a resistance to Jude-like individual disembodiment, but, more pertinent to the pattern of U.S. deindustrialization, a resistance to the erosion of adequately paying union jobs. In a spirit of collective solidarity (at least temporarily) not individual pathos, these workers evoke an ancient etymology of *ghost* meaning, "fury, anger." The fury of these workers is a refusal to be "ghosted" in the Jude sense, but also in an early sense of *ghost,* "to wound, tear, pull to pieces."[3] To have one's job torn away is to become ghosted, wounded, and, perhaps, "pulled to pieces."

In the last twenty years, the jobs of millions of workers have ended because of deindustrialization (so-called), mergers, automation, capital mobility, and corporate cost cutting. These jobs were not "lost" or misplaced; they were cut and severed. Left behind are work sites as ghosted spaces, echoing a presence, revealing an absence. These spaces emerge from within two separate but parallel and overlapping structures. One is the structure of corporations, of buyouts and mergers, of outsourcing and automation. The other is the structure of feelings[4] and experience: of workers rising to go to work, facing the job, sustaining relationships, anticipating payday, all the rhythms of work and life in a complex, textured way. This is an individual and communal structure and rhythm, often described as "just like a family."

"The worker is out of the picture now," says former furniture maker Robert Riley.[5] What happens when the structure of work abruptly disappears, when the plant closes and all that is left are the ghosts of the women and men who worked there, without their machines and tools? How do these workers carry on? Who hears their voices and bears witness to their lived experiences? In other words, the space that is created when the plant closes may be, in a literal sense, emptied out space, but the workers left behind are not empty space. They are living, breathing human beings, not ghosts. "Worker Ghosts" is a trope, a way of framing textual processes that simultaneously document visibility and invisibility, presence and absence, ways of putting workers back into the picture. It is a metacommentary on efforts to foreground blue-collar workers in the United States who are caught in an historical shift not of their own making.

"You were a damn fine machinist, Rudy."

— Kurt Vonnegut, *Player Piano*

In *Player Piano*, Kurt Vonnegut's 1952 prescient, postwar dystopia, work as we know it—as anyone knows it—is obsolete.[6] Located in the fictional Ilium, New York, a hub of managed no-work, *Player Piano* is economically segregated: managers, civil servants, a few professionals and the machines tucked in one corner, and across the river, Homestead, "where almost all of the people live" (1). Vonnegut describes a familiar world where managers and engineers controlled by a tiny business elite regulate the machines that regulate everyone else. And this elite corps is fanatical about the possibility of resistance and sabotage. The real saboteur, from the perspective of workers, however, is management combined with advanced technology. Vonnegut's imagined workers live in a relatively benign dictatorship where citizenship, is, in effect, defunct. This is a condition not so different from today's political and economic landscape of ghosted workers up against the expanded corporeality of corporations, what E. L. Doctorow calls the "supracitizenship of conglomerates."[7]

Technology is the Trojan horse in this novel, distilling the very essence of human "know-how" (a 1950s description of worker knowledge) from human hand to machine. Every detail of the hand movements of Rudy Hertz, master machinist, was recorded: "Here was Rudy as Rudy had been to his machine. . . . Rudy, the turner-on of power, the setter of speeds, the controller of the cutting, too. . . . This was the essence of Rudy, . . . the small, polite man with the big hands and black fingernails" (9). Rudy Hertz, the fine machinist with the big hands, at least got to retire with the memory of work. The younger generation of the fictional Ilium, however, have no living memory of industrial work or the pride and satisfaction of skilled labor. For those who don't measure up, as literally determined by elaborately economically-biased tests, there are few choices (for men that is; Vonnegut cannot really imagine women in the work force): either the army or the "Reeks and Wrecks," the Reconstruction and Reclamation Corps (21–22). The older craft workers have become ghosts, like the invisible hand on the player piano: "Makes you feel kind of creepy, don't it . . . watching them keys go up and down? You can almost see a ghost sitting there playing his heart out" (28).

With mock-heroic flourish, Vonnegut sets in motion the eventual battle between two secretive societies: the engineers/managers who gather together at the Meadows, a kind of summer camp for overgrown business boys, and the underground band of displaced workers, neo-Luddites who form the Ghost Shirt Society. Shirts figure prominently at the Meadows also, but these are competing T-shirts which each team of engineers wears as they grovel, jockey, and bond through physical competition, pep songs, slogans, and pageantry. The culminating moment is the induction of the "young braves," unseasoned engineers and wannabe managers, into the "spirit of the Meadows." Led by "the Indian," an aging professional actor in a beaded G-string, the braves pledge obedience to the "wise commands" of their chiefs (193) and so the week ends in nauseatingly sentimental splendor in tribute to the sacred religion of profit, business, and control.

In contrast to the co-option of Indian history into business lore at the Meadows, the underground Ghost Shirt Society tries to reclaim a lost history of Native American resistance:

> Toward the end of the nineteenth century . . . a new religious movement swept the Indians in this country. . . . The white man had broken promise after promise to the Indians, killed off most of the game, taken most of the Indians' land, and handed the Indians bad beatings every time they'd offered any resistance. . . . With the game and land and ability to defend themselves gone . . . the

Indians found out that all the things they used to take pride in doing, all the things that had made them feel important, all the things that used to gain them prestige, all the ways in which they used to justify their existence—they found that all those things were going or gone. . . .

And the Ghost Dance religion . . . was that last desperate defense of the old values. . . . [S]ome of the more warlike tribes that still had a little physical fight left in them added a flourish of their own—the Ghost Shirt . . . . They were going to ride into battle one last time . . . in magic shirts that white men's bullets couldn't go through. (249–250)[8]

The displacement of workers by machines and the resistance of the Ghost Shirt Society (while not literally comparable to the expropriation of Native American lands) are historically significant narrative links. Embedded in Vonnegut's easily accessible satire is a historical line of resistance to the forces that turn people into ghosts, from the early nineteenth-century Luddites to the "mad" Manhattan construction workers.[9] What is at stake in these diverse movements and events is more than opposition to a particular technology as thing, tool, or artifact; rather, it is the realization by those who resist that what is being lost is a culture, a way of life, and a self-determining future.

Kurt Vonnegut is too jaundiced a writer, even as early as 1952, to treat such revolts seriously for very long. After the revolt and pending capture of the Ghost Shirt Society's leaders, the workers poke through the debris of the machines they recently destroyed to find the parts to repair them, starting with the Orange-O machine, the dispenser of a soft drink concoction universally despised (292). Suggesting that "the People" are complicitous in their own making and unmaking, Vonnegut sabotages the plot of resistance and ends the novel in his usual indeterminate, ideologically distrustful, oddly postmodern fashion, with an ambiguous shrug and the final words, "Forward March" (295). The managers once again gain control and are advancing toward their own imaginary of progress (for them)—what will become fifty years later the new millennium's superhighway, transnationalism, and restructured globalization. As Vonnegut would say, "So it goes."

Some people got free furniture, and some people got bubonic plague.

—Kurt Vonnegut, *Cat's Cradle*

In early 1995, at the start of the first massive layoffs at Eastman Kodak Company, employees were handed a manila envelope by their supervisors. Each envelope contained one of three messages: your job has been retained; your job has been terminated but you may seek another job within the company; or your job has been terminated (note that jobs are terminated, not people). Whether the news was good or bad, the envelope also contained a little booklet, similar to those simple cartoon pamphlets found in doctors' offices. The multicolored booklet, entitled "Coping with CHANGE: How to Manage the Stress of Change," features on the cover a multicultural cluster of stressed men and women in a sinking little boat called USS *Uncertainty* which is about to be engulfed by the big wave of CHANGE, spelled out on white foam.[10] The contents feature cartoons of workers in different stages of "solving" their problems by learning "coping skills." After learning how to cope, the same cluster of now-smiling workers reappears on the back cover, securely tucked into a boat called USS *Confidence* under the heading "Steering Your Own Course."[11] Faced with the possibility of the devastation of termination, workers were handed this grim/happy comic book with the clear message that change just "happens" and you must cope individually by changing yourself. It is reminiscent of a little narrative embedded in Vonnegut's *Cat's Cradle* in which, after a mutiny and shipwreck, everybody drowns except the rats on board the ship. The rats, carrying bubonic plague, land on one island; the ship's cargo of wicker furniture lands on another. And Vonnegut can shrug and say, "so it goes."

Despite severance pay and the chance for early retirement for a lucky few, deindustrialized and downsized workers have had little choice but to learn new skills or retrain, take two jobs that pay less than the former one, or, for some with fewer choices, either go to prison, guard prisoners, or sink. The deciders of their fates, answerable not to workers but to investors and the stock market, are secure behind their fenced houses, don't desire cheap wicker furniture, and are not likely to catch the bubonic plague of unemployment. In the last thirty years, and especially since 1989, the cosmic shrug that is Vonnegut's signature has morphed into TINA, that is, "there is no alternative" to multinational capitalism.[12] And this is a sink-or-swim capitalism—learn the new technology or drop into the sea of redundancy or of low wages, accept the huge wage gap between workers and CEOs, haves and have-nots, smile, smile, smile in the face of compassionate conservatism, and keep consuming those cheap sweatshop goods. Civility has replaced conscience and justice. And the worker has paid.

Workers' secure jobs have been stampeded by what the Labor Institute calls the "Four Horsemen of the [Apocalyptic?] Workplace": downsizing, globalization, automation, and the increased use of temporary or contracted labor.[13] Manning Marable, in his prescient 1983 book, *How Capitalism Underdeveloped Black America,* and William Julius Wilson, writing *When Work Disappears* thirteen years later (albeit from different political standpoints) demonstrate how the combination of institutional racism (within the labor movement as well) and deindustrialization have economically damaged black communities particularly.[14] Labor lawyer Thomas Geoghegan, in his poignant *Which Side Are You On?* describes the loss of seventy thousand steelworker jobs in the Reagan years: "It was as if, once, the whole industry was part of the village commons. Then came the barbed wire, the security guards. Then the mills, which had been there for seventy-five years, which were half as old as the city of Chicago, were suddenly gone. I think of it like the enclosure movement in England, in the 1400s, when the nobles started to enclose the village commons."[15] Geoghegan astutely suggests that we not talk in terms of the American economy in the singular, but rather see the economic contradictions of different, even polar economies where downsizing for some means stock-price increases for others, and he insists, "[t]here's no other country (outside the Third World) where it's tougher legally to organize a union" (256).

We now have a mini- industry in academia of studies documenting the radical loss of millions of jobs in the last thirty years.[16] The problem is not a dearth of information but a crisis in economic justice and with it sustainable democracy.

II. Embodied Workers

"They say people who die sudden, violent deaths are most likely to become ghosts and haunt the earth. On March 28, 1980, all the workers died a sudden violent death, [when the steel mill closed] no time to say goodbye."

—Thomas Geoghegan, *Which Side Are You On?*

In response to the deconstruction of industrial work a significant number of writers, historians, photographers, and essayists have constructed books that witness the impact of job elimination on working people. Any representation of people who are not imagined characters, composites, or constructions faces enormous challenges, risks, responsibilities, even dangers.[17] This is especially true when borders of class and circumstance are crossed. In his preface to *Let Us Now Praise Famous Men*, James Agee speaks to this problem in describing the intentions of his project with Walker Evans: "Actually, the effort is to recognize the stature of a portion of unimagined existence, and to contrive techniques proper to its recording, communication, analysis and defense" (xiv).[18] Agee develops his concerns about the partiality and limitations of representation in his agonizingly self-conscious preamble: "I am liable seriously, perhaps irretrievably, to obscure what would at best be hard enough to give its appropriate clarity and intensity; and what seems to me most important of all: namely, that these I will write of are human beings, living in this world" (12–13).

Although Agee is describing his nominal subject, three white tenant families, he is also commenting on the impossibility of a book *containing* his subject, "This is a *book* only by necessity. More seriously, it is an effort in human actuality" (xvi). In this essay I examine books that take up the burden of representing human actuality: Sue Doro's *Blue Collar Goodbyes*,[19] Milton Rogovin and Michael Frisch's *Portraits in Steel*,[20] Bill Bamberger and Cathy Davidson's *Closing: The Life and Death of an American Factory*,[21] and Stephen Cole, Cedric Chatterley, and Alicia Rouverol's *"I Was Content and Not Content": The Story of Linda Lord and the Closing of Penobscot Poultry*.[22] All center, through language and photographs, the lives of human beings abruptly denied their livelihoods, their shared worlds of work. With the exception of Sue Doro's *Blue Collar Goodbyes*, all were composed from outside the experience of their subjects and began as photography projects.

In examining these books individually and specifically, I am concerned with questions about representing worker subjectivities. I also wish to illuminate the particular tectonics of each book, the "techniques proper" of how they were assembled, and the relationship of voices to images. I am asking how books in this new genre about job closures resist, mediate, mute, or meliorate the ghosting of workers. I probe the intentionality of these books, the interests they serve, the uses they make of their subjects, and whether the authors construct a "collective answerability," a way, as Peter Hitchcock suggests, "of taking others into account without dominating them."[23] How do workers recognize themselves in these books? Even though their jobs may have ended, their sense of themselves as workers, of the particular skills they still own, has not necessarily ended. To put it in a more working-class way, how do these workers say, "Hey, I'm not dead. I'm not a damned ghost. Don't erase me"? To say it more academically, I am asking, "What space exists in these texts for workers to represent themselves, indeed, to resist their own ghosting?"

> The air compressor blasts. Cranes clatter. Engine lathes, boring-bars, mills, drills, and forklifts rumble and growl, till the football-field-sized factory is a comforting roar, loud enough to silence the sound of our futures, subject to change.
>
> —Sue Doro, "Subject to Change"

Sue Doro's *Blue Collar Goodbyes* is a pivotal reference and ur-text for any study of representations of plant closures and ghosted workers. For thirteen years, Doro was the only female machinist at the former Milwaukee Road Railway and Allis Chalmers Tractor Shop. Author of several other poetry collections, Doro is a Gramscian organic intellectual who in this collection of prose and poetry constructs a "knowable community" for herself and her co-workers.[24] What seems to be a loose collection of poems and stories, *Blue Collar Goodbyes* becomes, with closer inspection, a historically informed chronology from the worker's perspective of the sale of the railway company, the actions of the new owners, and the uncertainties of the workers: They "rob us of our weekends / worry bites holes into Friday night plans" ("White Collar Crime," 24); "One day at a time they tell us / well that's fine for a TV comedy show but no way to plan a life" ("Hard Times in the Valley," 23). Doro offers poetic portraits of her co-workers—those who are lucky to retire, those not so lucky, those who resettle in Minnesota (jobs lasting only a few years, as it turned out) —and the ultimate dispersal of her work "family" and her own move to California and search for another job.

Doro's is an indigenous voice, a worker writer who moves beyond privatized loss to construct a location and "idiom of collective experience."[25] It is easy for the reader to forget that *Blue Collar Goodbyes* is very much a one-woman operation with Doro's collective sensibilities creating convincing portraits of individual workers—as sympathetic co-worker, not outsider looking in—as well as documenting, with sarcasm and working-class humor, the phony assurances of the new owners, the ineffectiveness of the union, and the relationships that make going to work more than a job. Doro thanks all those who helped her "machine" the book, insisting that these are "real people living and working in the heartland of this country" and "their lives created the words of the poems and, stories of the book" (xi). Doro's writing has the reciprocal quality of much working-class literature, a relationship between subject and writer, freely given, not exploitative. The one who can write, writes, and so tells the collective story.

One of Doro's portraits is of "Doc" who supplies her with "floor dry, not because he thinks I can't carry it myself, but because he knows how difficult a job I have just being here. Knows from years of being 'one-of-a-kind' himself, starting back in '43 when he was the railroad's only African-American laborer. Seventeen he was, when the foreman wisecracked, 'They'd rather have a white boy for the job, but they were all at war.' Doc didn't laugh, he just worked, and his paycheck came every two weeks just like everybody else's" ("Floor Dry," 13). Floor dry, Doro explains, is "the factory worker's indispensable ally, . . . absorb[ing] oil spills with thousands of tiny, rocky sponges" (13). Doc's anticipation of Doro's need for floor dry, "not among his assigned laborers' duties," may seem like a small gesture but is indicative of a deeper and larger ethos of community, a worker neighborliness that Doro reciprocates when she helps him sweep up at night and (perhaps in a mutual masking of his illiteracy) reads "notices off the bulletin board. (He claims his glasses won't let him see)" (13).[26]

Doro also situates the individual worker within a personal and public historical context. She introduces the reader to Verona, who started at the railroad in Milwaukee at the end of World War II and became a waitress in the cafeteria and then a laborer: "You raised your kids on railroad wages, / grew your muscles strong as the sturdy plants / on your Wisconsin window sill" ("Verona, Your Life," 20). The only women in the plant, Verona "came to work a little early. / [Doro] stayed a little late, and / our shifts meshed like a set of perfect gear teeth" (20). The railroad is sold and Verona, "with less than a year to go till retirement," is not allowed to work her remaining days because the new owners wanted only one laborer, who had "more whiskers in the union, / and he was a he" (21).

Doro writes with a machinist's precision, cutting away at hypocrisy and managerial platitudes. The reader meets Mickey, "the kid on second shift / who kept on saying / 'at least we got a job'/ over and over / until the night / he read his name / on the layoff list / and his mouth / clamped shut / tight / as the guard house gate / closing behind him" ("May 22, 1985," 8).

Doro's snapshots complement her poetic portraits. They breathe an ease and familiarity into the regimen of the shop floor, evident in the still life of Doro's hardhat, work gloves, and shiny, machined railroad wheel. These are not images of defeated workers. Doro documents the climate of uncertainty and closure without presenting her co-workers as victims. These seemingly casual

Sue Doro, *Soo Line Bought the Bankrupt Milwaukee Road Railway,* 1985. Courtesy of the photographer.

snapshots (often dismissed by my professional photography students) suggest wider narratives of individual lives—Verona's broken arm with the graffiti humor of "Carol was here!" sprawled on the cast, expressive hands and face mugging for the camera, and two old buddies squinting into the lunchtime sun, feeling lucky, perhaps, that they are close to retirement. These images look and feel like a family album and behind them we can imagine the kind of conversations people have who know each other well and face hard times together. Doro's own commentary on these photos credits and dignifies the people behind the images: "They represent not only themselves and their unique personalities, but also the music of the working class. I was able to take most of the photos the last few days before the railroad shut down. They are a piece of history" (xi).

Doro is unsentimentally critical of the forces that take jobs from workers, "the people [who] own it all / still smiling dollar signs" ("TWO Conversations," 31), as she pays tribute to her co-workers, with blue collar goodbyes like "a jumpstart / on a frozen battery midnight parking lot" ("Blue Collar Goodbyes" 64). The poem is the essential pipeline, an aesthetic, relational, and *material* connector: "blue collar goodbyes report Wisconsin to California / on lined school notebook paper stark and strong / THERE'S BACK PAY COMING. . . . YOU BETTER CALL" (65). Doro's people are "survivors / that corporate minds

Sue Doro, *My Hardhat and Gloves*, 1985.
Courtesy of the photographer.

Sue Doro, *Verona with Arm
Broken in Three Places from
Falling in Wheel Shop*, 1984.
Courtesy of the photographer.

will never know" (65). Scattered across the country, maybe without the work they were trained to do, Doro's "work friends like family"(66) are not pitiful and surely they are not ghosts.

The authors of *Portraits in Steel, Closing,* and *"I Was Content and Not Content,"* composing their books from locations *outside* the lived experiences of their subjects, must address critical questions of representation quite differently from the worker writer Sue Doro. Also, their books, published by presses with access to media and marketing and costing $30 or more, may find their way onto coffee tables. Sue Doro, on the other hand, producing a more economically accessible kitchen table book, faces problems of distribution and staying in print. Unlike the other authors, her work may encounter a particular kind of cultural elitism, a disbelief that workers can and do produce their own culture.

> The world don't owe us a living. A world should put a place there for us to make a living and we should go out and get it. I think that's important, that you got to go out there and do your share if you want a living. That's what I believe on.
>
> —Benjamin Boofer, *Portraits in Steel*

In *Portraits in Steel,* historian Michael Frisch is particularly sensitive to academics' propensity toward over-interpreting their subjects, and, in so doing (unintentionally) colonizing them. Frisch places great weight on the book's intention as *portraiture,* not analysis or investigation (20), even deciding not to annotate or define the technical terms and work processes described by the chippers, burners, riggers, molders, cast makers, grinders, and cinder snappers in the steel and foundry plants in the Buffalo region. Worker epistemologies (and I use the plural deliberately) are privileged; academic readers are disprivileged and must make the necessary intellectual and imaginative leap into the world of steel production. At the same time, Frisch also reveals the production process of the book, the conversion of thousands of pages of taped conversation into narrative portraits. He had documented the editing process, line by line, in a revealing and useful earlier essay in his 1990 book *A Shared Authority.*[27]

Photographer Milton Rogovin quotes Bertolt Brecht's poem "A Worker Reads History" as a kind of orchestral prelude to the symphony of portraits which are presented in *Portraits in Steel* without textual commentary. Rogovin, a political activist and former Buffalo optometrist, was hounded by the House Committee on un-American Activities (HUAC) in the 1950s, and became a documentary photographer in the Lewis Hine tradition. Rogovin used a waist-level reflex camera so he is always looking up to his subjects (Doherty, xix). The camera, Rogovin's tool, is used in a particular manner so that the subjects, presenting themselves, as Frisch describes, *give* their portraits to Rogovin rather than have them *taken* (3).The resulting documentary portraiture opens expanded possibilities of eye/I contact between the subject and the viewer/reader.

Steel production in the Buffalo region was an interrelated system, and so when the big mills went down, the smaller plants fell, domino-like. Between

1975 and 1978 Rogovin photographed workers in the smaller plants but also made portraits of workers in the larger Bethlehem and Republic mills outside of Buffalo. He photographed workers on the job and then visited them at home, where he photographed them with their families. These portraits attest to the relationality between home and work and, unbeknown to photographer and subjects at the time, document a world of work that ended with the shutdown in 1983 of the Bethlehem Steel complex in Lackawanna and the ripple effect of that closing on Republic Steel and numerous small industrial plants. In the mid 1980s Rogovin rephotographed these former steel workers at home and invited Frisch to conduct interviews with them in order to create a portraiture in narrative form, a "textual parallel" (2) to the photographic portraits. The oral histories, printed in question/answer format, are framed by miniatures of the larger Rogovin portraits at work and at home. Frisch used both sets of photographs as a way of building trust for his interviews and shaping the published oral histories. Would the interviews have been different without the workers' relationship with Rogovin and the photographs? Probably.

Frisch's introduction outlines the process of his and Rogovin's work and traces the complex industrial history of Buffalo. Although he likens his work process to steelmaking itself, seeing it as pushing raw tapes "through a variety

Milton Rogovin,
Mary Daniels, 1976.
Photo © Milton Rogovin.

Milton Rogovin,
Mary Daniels, 1976.
Photo © Milton Rogovin.

Milton Rogovin,
Mary Daniels, 1987.
Photo © Milton Rogovin.

of oral-historical mills" (x), I wonder if that is stretching the analogy too much. Crafting books is still clean and safe work, and, perhaps, in this case, closer to the craft and labor of sculpting, a skilled and necessary cutting away to reveal the submerged subject. Frisch critiques the use of the word "deindustrialization" as misleading and antiseptic (2), hiding more than it reveals, yet finds it difficult to avoid using the term in describing the patterns of work in Buffalo's important industrial history. Unlike the small company towns in other studies (for example, *Closing*), Buffalo is and has been a "complex, metropolitan community" (14) and Frisch's job as urban historian is both to evoke the web of deeply rooted community experiences in a Williamsian sense and to record the patterns of industrial, technical, and corporate changes, a complexity beyond urban "descriptive homogeneity" (5). Mostly the introduction attempts to sketch a landscape, with a very useful map of work and home sites, for the visual and textual portraits that follow.

The reader begins with the gallery of photos of workers on the job and at home before and after the closings. (Most of these paired portraits became part of a "Working People" exhibit in a 1992 one-man show at the Smithsonian's Museum of American History). In his prefatory, brief history of documentary photography, Robert Doherty claims that Rogovin uses his "greatest artistic skill in capturing his images to endow his subjects with dignity" (xix). While Doherty is obviously paying tribute to Rogovin, his language reveals a limited view of Rogovin's subjects. It is a misreading of Rogovin's relationship with these workers to say that the images were *captured* or that Rogovin *endows* them with dignity. These workers are not still lives; they have dignity—quite apart from the visual and textual portraits.

In *Portraits in Steel* we hear the voices of twelve former steelworkers (nine men and three women, eight whites and four blacks). They begin by describing the process of their work, their tools, craft, the physicality and dangers of their jobs, the rhythms of overtime, layoffs, and swing shifts, and then add larger observations about their families, communities, working relationships, industrial changes, foreign competition, unions, and the nature of work itself. Certain patterns emerge, but not without contradictions and differences. Dick Hughes claims that "the union got too powerful, they didn't know when to stop . . . the union just showed strength all the way to the end, and they just died with it" (106). Mary Daniels claims that the "union really tried; the international itself has given up concessions like crazy" (219). To label these workers victims or heroes is simplistic and reductive, although from a working-class perspective, having a job cut when you are six months from a pension is a crime and not giving up in the face of repeated rejections is heroic. One consistent refrain in all the narratives is struggle: the struggle to carry on when your health deteriorates, when you are harassed as a woman for supposedly taking a job away from a man, when you face dangerous working conditions every day, and when, one day, you have to face no work.

And there's ghosted space. At the time of his interview with Frisch, Ralph Wils was working for $3.35 an hour as a Pinkerton guard, protecting an empty mill where he used to make $16 an hour: "An empty plant. On the graveyard shift. Just walking around, checking, make sure everything's all right. Turnkeys. Empty buildings. It's really weird. Stop and think of one time how many guys were working there and what was actually going on. It's really kind of spooky. Get out the turnkeys and sometimes you turn around and you think you hear something. There's nothing there" (127).

Resisting ghosting is a collective effort. Mary Daniels, a rigger's helper at Republic Steel, is an undaunted, multivoiced storyteller: "And you know, if you don't have the security of a job, you really need the people around to give you that sense of security, people that care about you, can give you a sense of security about yourself. When the newspaper article came out about us and the plant closing down—it sounded desperate. People that we know, just friendly neighbors—'Hello,' and 'How's your garden,' and stuff like that—they called us up and said, 'Is there anything we can do? Can we lend you some money, can we drive you here, can we do this for you—if you ever need us, we're here'" (223).[28]

There are several occasions in *Portraits* in which the interviewer and the interviewee are overtly conscious of a larger audience "listening in" on the conversation. Frisch asks Frank Andrzjewski: "Do you have any final things to say to whomever you might imagine might be reading all these things?" Andrzjewski responds: "Well, our times are hard, but we are still proud, we still have our own private life and we still, no matter how hard times get, if you have a family and you stick together you can make the best of it. . . . But as long as you have a little something to hold onto. You don't want people to feel sorry for you, but you want people to know the truth—you don't want the government to come along and say everything is hunky-dory, yeah we never had it so good. Bull! That's bull! I mean, tell the truth, because people are getting fed up now" (291–292).

The last interview, with cinder snapper Joseph Kemp, is remarkable for the power of Kemp's language as well as his analysis of the steel industry and its refusal (as seems to be true of downsizing in general) to see "the people's side of view" (312). Frisch, the astute dramatist, restrains his own commentary, and lets Kemp have the last word, a lyrical resistance to worker ghosting:

And all the people that had those jobs in the plants—really, if they wasn't old enough to come out and retire, they should work on them training programs, just whatever you can cram into your brain. You might have to relocate but sometimes it be worth it, too, you know. Got to keep a family together. Keep a dude and his wife together and slowing down a lot of the heartaches, you know. Trying. That's the only thing I can tell you to do now is *try* to do the best you can. And that's it. . . .That's it. Do the *best* you can! The best! That's it. Do the *best*! When you know that you done did the best, you going to lay on down and go to sleep then. That's it. That's you know. But I can tell them don't anybody give up. You can't give up. You know. You can't give up. (316)

Joseph Kemp died at the age of fifty-three on April 6, 1995.

In concluding his introduction, Frisch underscores the dialogic intention of the book. That potentially rich dialogue is repeated with each careful reader. But who are the readers? When Frisch mentions "the implicit dialogue across the boundaries of class" (20) is he, perhaps rightly, assuming that the reader will not be a working-class industrial worker? We do not know the responses of the subjects of the book to reading their own words and those of the other workers. But we can acknowledge the efforts of the relatively more class-privileged photographer and historian in placing themselves in a position vis-à-vis the workers that I call "respectful not knowing" and, despite the acknowledged and necessary editing of the text, creating space for these workers to speak and to represent themselves, to establish a standpoint position that cannot be easily colonized—or ghosted.

> White Furniture Company will never be dead so long as we have children who have children. You take my son. A lot of things I do at home when I'm working around in my little shop, I do as he's around. I'll show him whether it's a different kind of wood or whether it's maybe boring a hole in cherry that's very brittle and will break unless you bore a hole before you put a screw in it. That my son learns. He knows how to sand with the grain of the wood, and so long as he's alive he can pass that on to his children. White's will always be alive so long as there are people around in this area. Where we go, whatever we do, White's will never be dead.
>
> —Ronnie Sykes, *Closing*

Closing: The Life and Death of an American Factory chronicles the closing in 1993 of White Furniture Company and the subsequent ending of 203 jobs in Mebane, North Carolina. White was an 111-year-old family firm that manufactured ornate, highly-priced reproduction antiques, furniture out of the financial range of the workers who made it.[29] Before it was sold to Hickory Manufacturing Company in 1985, White was emblematic of a successful paternalistic company. The workers traded higher wages for job security, most saw themselves as skilled artisans who valued the products of their labor, even if they were out of their own reach, and all spoke of the familial environment on the plant floor. But the familial environment of the owning White family disintegrated when majority stockholders, worried about future earnings and their inheritance, voted to sell the company. White company workers went from an artisanal environment of self-regulatory autonomy and quality production to Tayloristic monitoring, regulating, and quantity production—and better pay and benefits (68). Until the sale, White Furniture Company might have been seen as an antique itself when measured against the ethos of 1990s corporate practices.

Also, the particularized skill of woodworking is presented as a distinctive shaping force. (Is it more so than machining or pouring steel?) One worker,

Robert Riley, says, "Isn't it amazing what you can do with a tree?" (162). A plant supervisor, Don McCall, comments, "I've been in textile mills and a lot of other kinds of factories. You don't get that sense of family in those other places. . . . I never have been in a wood working plant that the people didn't bond close" (106). In the final days of the closing, the workers were asked to destroy the furniture patterns and templates, a painfully symbolic end to a craft history and whole structure of experience and work life.

Like *Portraits in Steel*, *Closing* began as a photography project. Bill Bamberger, a professional photographer and teacher at the University of North Carolina at Chapel Hill, lives in Mebane, five blocks from the White Furniture Company. The CEO of the merged Hickory-White Corporation gave him permission to photograph the final months and days of the plant. Before any text appears, the book opens with black-and-white images of White furniture employees at work, followed by an image of workers being informed of layoffs and then a shot of an empty cabinet room on the final day of operation. This cluster offers a kind of précis of the images that follow. Given the bad news, the workers are still; some have the glazed eye look of animals in headlights. As a cluster, the images suggest a narrative of circumstances, perhaps beyond anyone's control.

Bill Bamberger, *Layoff Meeting, Cabinet Room.*
From *Closing: The Life and Death of an American Factory*
(Doubletake/Norton, 1998).

Bill Bamberger, *Avery Sweeping the Cabinet Room Floor on His Final Day of Work.*
From *Closing: The Life and Death of an American Factory* (Doubletake/Norton, 1998).

Well-designed, with heavy, glossy paper and wide margins, *Closing* is quite a handsome book. Bill Bamberger's black-and-white photographs of workers at various stages of the production process—from "feeding the hog" in the rough mill to machining, sanding, and rubbing the finished product—reveal the craft and tradition of fine furniture making and hint at the unmaking of workers as department after department closed as each step of production was completed (41). Images of workers getting the terrible news and reading their official severance papers underscore the pain of economic uncertainty rather than reveal the hidden corporate hands producing the official documents from afar. The photographic narrative segues into scenes of equipment in operation followed by scenes of equipment waiting to be auctioned, and then the empty space after the closing. The final section, of beautifully photographed color portraits of the plant, of equipment, and of workers at work and then at home after the closing, is visually stunning, but narratively ambiguous. In the last two color images we see the downcast eyes of Robert Wynn the summer after the closing followed by a portrait of sections of ornately carved eighteenth-century-replica poster beds. Are we to conclude that the workers, like the destroyed templates, are finished—just so many embodied disembodiments and so much ghosted space?

One worker, Ivey Jones, a cabinetmaker, remarks on his initial resentment at the intrusive photographer/stranger documenting the final days: "It tee-totally pissed me off. . . . It's humiliating enough to lose our jobs. We are already frustrated. We don't know where our next paycheck is coming from and we don't know where we will find a job and here this guy is looking at everybody's face and taking pictures, taking pictures, taking pictures. . . . I looked at him [Bamberger] just like I did management, just one more vulture in here trying to pick the bones of the employees" (21). Later, according to Cathy Davidson's description, Jones changes his mind, convinced of the commitment of the photographer to document the closing so "it's not totally forgotten," so "[s]omebody will remember" (21).

Closing contains more interpreted than direct commentary from workers. Cathy Davidson, a widely recognized literary scholar, author, and Ruth F. DeVarney Professor of English at Duke University, entered the book project after the factory was closed, at the invitation of editors at the Center for Documentary Studies at Duke. Her writing includes a preface that sets the elegiac tone of the book, a lengthy and useful history of White Furniture Company in the context of mergers and national trends in downsizing, and five crafted portraits of former White employees, all of whom held some kind of supervisory position, except for Annette Patterson, an African American woman who worked in the physically intense rough mill. Davidson visited the now-closed plant with Bamberger and had informal conversations with her subjects, but it appears that most of the quotations are excerpted from oral histories (housed at the Southern Historical Collection, University of North Carolina, Chapel Hill) that were done some time earlier by trained oral historians and their graduate students. She concludes with a description of a postclosing show of Bamberger's photographs in Mebane and an epilogue. The epilogue, "Does Anybody in America *Make* Anything Anymore?" is a critical commentary on the human costs of corporate downsizing, deindustrialization, and mergers.

The textual portraits describe Margaret (with Steve), James, Don, Annette, and Robert. Margaret Holmes White, company loyalist, executive assistant to various company presidents, and, ultimately, wife to the former, now-disabled president, Steve White, chronicles, through Davidson's interpretation, the death of the century-old company. On a last tour of the plant in 1993 Margaret described the ghosted space: "It was really weird to go through—and you could about hear the voices and see the men working, playing, laughing" (71). Master upholsterer James Gilland, who grew up during the Depression and built his own home by hand, survived the closing because of his lifelong frugality and eligibility for retirement. He stayed with the company despite the low pay because he "enjoyed his work" (79). Don McCall, a middle manager brought in by the new owners, but sympathetic to the older workers and the artisanal nature of furniture making, was in a straddling position, having to tell workers their jobs were finished and watch them "feather out" of the plant (104). He left Mebane and managerial employment, taking a production line job elsewhere, below his experience and education, saying, "I was in Vietnam. I closed a factory. I don't ever want to be a manager again" (119). Annette Patterson, divorced mother of three, was one of two women hired in the labor-intensive, male-dominated rough mill. Despite the noise, the harsh and dangerous working conditions, even the increasing speed-up in the rough mill, Patterson's comments reflect an unalienated sense of connection to the finished product: "I felt like I was part of cutting the wood to make this furniture. I cut the length of the wood and made sure the wood was good-quality wood, planed it down to make it smooth, made sure is was glued together right, and all this. See, I was all a part of this, right from a piece of lumber to a piece of furniture, you know, going up the line. I was a big part of that" (124–125). Like many deindustrialized workers too young to retire, Robert Riley has had to work two jobs to earn less than he made after thirty years at White's, where he was the first African American supervisor in the Hillsborough plant. At the end he was one of the last workers to leave, dismantling the machinery and sweeping the empty floor: "It was like they were tearing us apart inside and selling us off in pieces," he said (135).

Between this image of a loyal worker being torn to pieces by a capitalist lion and the highly refined visual and textual final product of the book lies the problematic of worker self-representation. Unlike in *Portraits,* with Frisch's emphasis on the production process of his own book, in *Closing* the reader has to read the fine print in the acknowledgments section at the end of the book to learn the identities of some of the oral historians. (Bill Bamberger thanks interviewers Pat Huber and Jeff Cowie and transcriber Jackie Gorman. In Davidson's profiles it is difficult to discern where the oral histories are spliced in and where the text represents casual conversation between Davidson and her subjects. Rather than creating space for self-representation, Davidson, *characterizes* each of her subjects in a literary, descriptive style allowing little room for readers to encounter and dialogue with workers on their own terms. We learn that Margaret and Steve have a "cozy" living room and Margaret has "clear eyes, lovely smooth skin" (62), Don is "a sensitive man, attuned to . . . his own inner life" (104), and Annette has the "aura of someone who knows what she likes and doesn't like" (123). It is as if readers are reading a novel where the writer overly describes the characters leaving little space for the reader to interpret and negotiate identities.

The least mediated section is "Reunion," which describes the involvement of former White employees in arranging for the opening of a show of Bill Bamberger's photographs in a former department store in Mebane after the closing. Over 130 workers attended and several testified to their life at the plant, beginning by stating their names and the number of years they worked at White Furniture Company. Davidson describes the event as a "memorial service for the company, the town and the workers" (161). But the workers are not dead, not ghosted Judes; they continue: "We have regrouped"; "We have to accept it and make the best of it" (161); and as Ronnie Sykes says in the epigraph above, "White Furniture Company will never be dead so long as we have children who have children" (162).

When I first went to work there, my hands were awful sore. They would swell up. You'd go home and you'd soak them and try to get so you could move them. And about when you got up in the morning so you could move your hands, you were back in there and you had to go through it again. Oh, it might take two or three months, and finally your hands get used to it. But it was a job. It was a fairly good paying job for around this area at the time. So, in many ways, I was content and not content.

—Linda Lord, *"I Was Content and Not Content"*

On February 24, 1988, Penobscot Poultry, a broiler-processing plant in Belfast, Maine, closed down. With the plant went the jobs of twenty-year employee Linda Lord and about four hundred other workers. *"I Was Content and Not Content": The Story of Linda Lord and the Closing of Penobscot Poultry* is an ensemble text, presenting the story through interviews by oral historians Stephen A. Cole and Alicia J. Rouverol and in the images of workplace, homeplace, and community by photographer Cedric N. Chatterley. Recognizing the impact of the closing of Penobscot Poultry on the local community, Cole, although himself a new resident of Maine with a commitment to another oral history project, contacted Alicia Rouverol at the Northeast Archives of Folklore and Oral History at the University of Maine to inquire about sponsoring a photo documentary on Penobscot's closing. Cole invited Chatterley, a visiting photographer, to document poultry processing at Penobscot before it closed. The book evolved out of this early collaboration between Chatterley and Cole and their accidental meeting with Linda Lord in a coffee shop near the plant. Chatterley photographed the grain mills, hatchery, poultry barns, and plant, and he and Cole later interviewed Lord about her job at the plant and her search for employment. This became the traveling exhibit, "One Year Later: The Closing of Penobscot Poultry and the Transition of a Veteran Employee" and the starting point for the expanded text *"I Was Content and Not Content"* and oral historian Rouverol's interviews with Lord. The photography exhibit, which opened a year after the plant's closing, was attended by over two hundred people, some who applauded the closing of the smelly plant and some who opposed the shutdown. This is a multivoiced, heteroglossic collaboration between Chatterley, Cole, and Rouverol, who also provides contextual essays on the history of Maine's poultry industry, on the problematic (indifferent?) relationship between companies and communities, on the context of Lord's life and her struggle to find a decent job, and on the complexities of doing oral history. In her introduction, Rouverol describes the tone and perhaps the intent of the book: "Partly Linda's story, partly our own, it might be said that this book is not only about work and community but also about *home*: about those who choose to stay and those who leave" (xix). This carefully edited, polished, but not overly aestheticized book includes an astute preface by Michael Frisch and the written text of a lecture presented at the photography exhibit in Belfast by Carolyn Chute, which is the most incisive, blunt, and pungent analysis of contemporary class differences one could find anywhere.

Chatterley's black-and-white photographs, reminiscent of Sue Doro's last day snapshots, suggest rather than document the stench, blood, pace, heat, and noise of the labor of slaughtering and processing poultry.[30] The photographer seems to realize that this is not a work site that can be "captured" on film; rather, the images offer surface, fleeting representations of the grueling labor behind the packaged meat we purchase. Chatterley comments about the shock of witnessing this kind of labor and his initial glimpse of Linda Lord in the "blood tunnel" as "she quickly took her knife to what would be the last chickens to go through Penobscot Poultry" (xv).

Lord may be out of a job, but she clearly has a life after the poultry factory and Chatterley photographs her in a variety of settings—applying for unemployment benefits, trying to retrain, as a volunteer firefighter, as a drummer in a band, in her new job at Belfast Rope, at home, and on her three-wheel motorcycle. There is a quiet, respectful, and modest distance to the photographer's

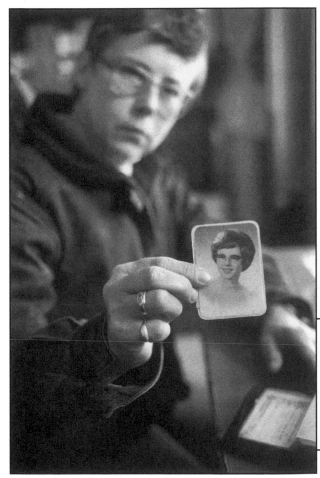

Cedric N. Chatterley, *Linda Lord Holding Her High School Graduation Photograph—Rollie's Café, Belfast, Maine, March 15, 1988*.
From *"I Was Content and Not Content"* by Linda J. Lord (Southern Illinois University Press, 2000). Photo © C. N. Chatterley.

Cedric N. Chatterley, *Linda Lord at Work in the "Blood Tunnel"*—
The Final Day of Penobscot Poultry, Belfast, Maine, February 24, 1988.
From *"I Was Content and Not Content"* by Linda J. Lord
(Southern Illinois University Press, 2000). Photo © C. N. Chatterley.

work; he allows the potential aesthetics of an image to be trumped by the
strength and resilience of a human being. He frequently photographs Lord in
motion—talking, hanging laundry, standing on top of a fire truck pulling on a
cigarette, and working. She is not anyone's ghost.

The center of the book is the life of Linda Lord as told over a period of time
to Chatterley, Cole, and Rouverol. Anyone committed to the idea of the multiplicity and multivocality of working-class representation might be skeptical of
a text that attempts to tell a larger story through a single life. But because of its
collaborative construction and mostly because of the respect the authors give to
Lord's own epistemology, *"I Was Content and Not Content"* offers a persuasive
case for Raymond Williams's observation that "the most uneventful life would
take a library of books to transcribe."[31] Besides, the authors make no claims that
Linda Lord is a stand-in for all workers.

There are six sequenced interviews in a period of about a year beginning
shortly after the closing in 1988 when the thirty-nine-year-old Lord sets about
the process of retraining and finding another job, and then a final follow-up
interview in 1994.

This text successfully creates a space that simultaneously acknowledges the
corporate body in global search for the cheapest hands *and* insists that ordi-

nary workers are more than slaughtered chickens or rendered byproducts. This is accomplished because of the complexity, stamina, and resilience of Linda Lord. First of all, there are multiple Lords: caretaker to aged parents, skilled worker who "sticks" half-killed birds (slices the neck vein), helpful neighbor, the only female lifting 100-pound bobbins at Belfast Rope, volunteer fire-fighter, drummer in a band, motorcyclist, gardener, union steward and nego-tiator, certified EMT (Emergency Medical Technician), restaurant helper, fisher and hunter, lover of nature and dogs, single self-supporting divorcee, and one-eyed worker.

Linda Lord lost the sight of her right eye in an accident at Penobscot Poul-try, an incident that she initially "mentions" after the tape recorder has been shut off: "It [a hose like a huge rubber band] pitched me right into the guard that they had go over the foot cutter, pitched my head right—and I hit right through here and it broke the skin. I still have scars. It was two or three days later that I started seeing bright light in this eye. . . . In another three or four days, I was in the hospital. Stayed there a month and a half, and had three oper-ations on that eye. They got the retina fused on, but they couldn't get it to lay down so I could see anything" (36). Three years later Linda got a $13,000 settle-ment for an industrial accident that would affect her future work life. She used her accident to educate other workers about workers' comp, brought a workers' comp lawyer into the plant, and shook up the union to pay better attention to worker safety. But as Lord rightly concludes: "Yeah, they made a settlement and stuff; but it wasn't enough to pay for—you know, when it interfered in your try-ing to get a better job. I looked around for other jobs when I was working down there at Penobscot, but a lot of places they wouldn't even talk to you if they knew that you had one eye, because they didn't want someone like that around" (37).

The authors wisely allow Lord's own low-key descriptions of the physicality of her laboring life to claim epistemological center stage: "I de-beaked chick-ens, sexed them, injected them, de-toed them . . . you name it I did it" (1). One of her most poignant and powerful commentaries is in her description of the effect of chicken processing on workers' hands: "that infection . . . would set in, even though you'd try washing your hands good. And eventually it would get into your blood system and pretty soon, if you didn't take antibiotics or something, you'd have red streamers going right up your arm. And you'd take what helped to cut the feathers so they would pick better—the solution they added with the water . . . and you'd take it with the grease and stuff, and that would cause you more trouble and make your skin peel right off your hands, too" (2). And, as is her inclination, Lord situates her problems within a larger context of work and connects to similar struggles of other workers: "A lot of people have had warts come out on their hands because of handling chickens. A lot of people have tendinitis. . . . And they've had blood poisoning, you name it" (5).

Linda Lord's work ethic certainly belies sociologist Stanley Aronowitz's announcement that "the great impulse of the working class . . . is to do as little work as they can."[32] Arriving at the poultry plant at 4:00 a.m. to set up a production line that started at 7:00 a.m., checking the machinery, hooking up pipes, coming in on weekends to do maintenance and painting, Lord seems incapable of shirking; besides, she needed the overtime pay. Whether in the blood tunnel or as the only woman lifting 100-pound extruder bobbins loaded with poly-pro, Linda says, "I'm one that I won't *half* do anything" (75).

When pressed by her interviewers on why she stayed at the poultry plant, Linda responded that she never really cared for Penobscot, but the pay was pretty good and it was "close to home." "Close to home" for Linda Lord is not just a geographic reference; it is also an idiomatic, symbolic utterance that evokes "homeplace," a whole set of relationships and meanings. Home is where she cares for her elderly and ill parents (even though she has two college-educated siblings nearby), where she plays in a band, where she volunteers for the fire department, where her memories and favorite hunting spots are, where her house is and her parents' home is, where she feels *at home*. For industrial workers, particularly women, home and capital mobility are incompatible and deindustrialization with its often disastrous effect on communities is a betrayal of home. Like Verona in Sue Doro's *Blue Collar Goodbyes*, Lord weighs the possibility of moving for the sake of a job and decides to hang on and try to find something "close to home." When, after six months of unemployment, she gets a job at Belfast Rope where she is paid partly by piecework and where she has no breaks and eats her lunch watching spools of rope, she says, "the only reason I tried this Belfast Rope company was it was close to home, you know" (63).

It is important not to read Linda Lord as a docile worker. While we are told little about the edited process, the reader has the strong impression that the interviewers constructed a text where Linda Lord could represent herself without external characterization. There are elisions, however. On several occasions, Linda refers to an operation that she had to have right out of high school which kept her from going to college. Either the interviewers knew the details and decided to protect her privacy or they did not probe one of the most pivotal moments of her life more deeply.

More problematic is the interpretative thread of ambivalence. Cole asked her if she was "discontent . . . during the years you worked at Penobscot." Lord's response is telling: "I really wasn't happy." She continues by explaining the physical toll on her hands and concludes with "it was a job" (21). She took the job because the pay was "fairly good for around this area at the time." At that time, twenty years earlier, fresh out of high school and recovering from her operation, she was also concerned about her mother who had had several heart attacks and was later paralyzed by a stroke. "I stuck it out for that reason—to be close to home for my father. But now I regret that I haven't furthered myself as far as education," Lord says (21). This is not ambivalence; rather, it is a clarity about the repercussions of life's trade-offs. As is true for many working-class women with a strong sense of family responsibility but few financial resources, life's circumstances limited Linda's choices. The word "discontent" is the interviewer's word, not hers. Ambivalence suggests a middle-class sense of choice. Accepting responsibility for the circumstances of your life is a working-class value, coming as it does out of a recognition that there may not be an official backup support system, no private trust fund, only the extension (and sometimes sacrifice) of self to sustain others. This is a material reality rather than innate nobility, although Linda Lord certainly demonstrates the steadfast, invisible, and unnamed heroism of many working-class people. What characterizes Lord's life more than ambivalence is struggle: "Life is one hard struggle," she says in a phone conversation to Alicia Rouverol in 1994 (79). When Rouverol asks her again if she is "content or not content," Lord responds, "Well, the only thing is, you'd like to find a good paying job, where you haven't got to struggle to make ends meet. But of course, that's what life is all about" (81). She answers the specific language of Rouverol's question, "In a lot of ways, I'm content. I mean, I've got the place up here now [her deceased parents' home]. And I'm out of town. But it isn't much fun living by yourself either. But otherwise I'm getting by. That's the main thing. Been lucky. I've got a job, which a lot of people don't" (81). Her final remarks echo Joseph Kemp's soliloquy in *Portraits in Steel* of continuing, doing the best, the best you can do with the circumstances you face.

Carolyn Chute's brilliant commentary, "Faces in the Hands," is on one level an unintended dialectical response to Lord's more conservative comments about big business, government, and welfare, and on another level a stunning narrative of re-embodiment, of reading the working hands of her own people in answer to the "pastel"-shirted engineer she meets at a party who describes machine operators as "just a pair of hands" (85). "Just a pair of hands. Yep. How about just a stomach?" (86) In a meandering voice that insists on its own unhurried pace, Chute challenges assumptions and stereotypes about the poor and working class. Laboring on the bridge of a potato harvester or at the conveyer belt in a chicken factory was not for the sake of the "great, grand Maine work ethic," but to feed a hungry stomach. The essay is a call for a democracy of work and a democracy of recognition of the value of all work. It underscores Lord's comments about struggle, about circumstances rather than choice: "You hear it these days . . . a lot of talk about choices . . . good choices, bad choices. You are shepherds of your own destiny, they say. There are how-to books on making the right choices. There are high-priced counselors you can go sit with to help you pick the right life. Doesn't luck play into the game somewhere? Like having the great big good luck of having what you are naturally good at be marketable, highly paid, highly respected" (91). Chute remembers her child, Reuben, whose death she attributes to government cuts which took away her welfare medical card and the medical care that might have saved her dehydrated, breech-birth son. Reuben, who might have lived a life where his skills, like his father Michael's, were deemed "unmarketable," is the ghosted worker no one should forget.

To not forget, to create cultural artifacts (published books, photographs, exhibits, archived oral histories) that function in time as witnesses to the enormous industrial and economic shifts affecting the lives of ordinary workers, is the common intention and success of this cluster of texts and others like them.[33] Each book within its own terms and frames is concerned with "architectonics," an unstable Bakhtinian concept best understood, according to Michael Holquist, as involving "questions of building, of the way something is put together."[34] As Holquist explains, Bakhtin viewed architectonics as similar to architecture "insofar as it is about building wholes through the manipulation of relations between parts" (xxiii), but architectonics is distinct from architecture in that it describes an *activity* and not just an edifice or inert thing: "wholes are never *given*, but always *achieved*; work—the struggle to effect a whole out of the potential chaos of parts—is precisely what, in fact, architectonics theorizes" (xxiii). That activity involves a physical thing (the published book) but also sets of relationships that are in motion and also in tension. This relationality constitutes a kind of aesthetics that is not exclusively about the construction of beautiful things, but rather seeks "a form of embodying lived experience" (xl).

Answerability for Bakhtin is the intense dialogism between art and life that is created through the human agency implicit in architectonics. What each of these texts *builds* is a context where a set of relationships (between writer and audience, between speaker and oral historian, between co-workers, between workers and their jobs and communities and families) emerges with a history and a hoped-for future. And the great challenge of this work is that it must construct its parts, negotiate its voices and images in the foreground, and, at the same time, document the deconstruction of the embodied, lived experience of work that no longer exists, in the background.

Consider again Thomas Hardy's obscure Jude entering Christminster City and coming upon a medieval college with its decaying buildings. It is not the architecture of the buildings that interests the stonemason Jude as much as how their physical presence evokes the ghosts of the thinkers, the "worthies" who once lived in and now haunt these ancient buildings. It is only in the light of day that Jude sees the renovation work on the buildings and temporarily recognizes the skill and knowledge involved in regenerating them: "that here in the stone yard was a centre of effort as worthy as that dignified by the name of scholarly study within the noblest of colleges" (131). This realization suggests possibilities for other kinds of work, dialogic rather than polarized, between such scholars and working-class worthies who in collaboration document and perhaps resist the transformation of workers into ghosts.

Blue Collar Goodbyes, Portraits in Steel, Closing, and *"I Was Content and Not Content"* share the good intentions of resisting the ghosting of workers. But what larger architectonics is built out of the juxtaposition of these books, especially as we study them as a genre of worker representation? What active, tense, continuing sets of relationships and discourses emerge? How do these texts dialogue with each other and with present and future generations of readers? Whether speaking as Sue Doro does from inside working-class experience, or from outside as the academic authors and professional photographers do, all engage, with varying degrees of success, the problematic of "shared authority."[35] This is an explicit and implicit collaboration between interviewer and subject that depends for its existence on the situated knowledge of the subject, particularly his or her epistemology of work.

In juxtaposing and examining these texts it is important to recognize the imaginative leap that takes a photographer, writer, or oral historian into the discomfort zone of another's life and work. But it is also necessary to see how bourgeois assumptions and attitudes can unintentionally frame questions and shape characterizations. Two class lines that are not easily crossed are the psychological rupture of a job ending and the physicality of hard work. Would Mark Cieslica have had a longer life if the steel mills had not gone down (*Portraits in Steel,* 317)? Maybe. Do the authors recognize the physical, corporal differences between their work and that of their subjects? Mary Daniels *reminds* them/us: "Industry is not exactly the same as sitting behind a book. I mean there's a difference! I'm not saying that it's not mentally much more taxing to work behind a book, but your physical hazards of constantly looking at potential disaster is much greater in a physical kind of job" (*Portraits in Steel,* 220). Joseph Kemp *instructs:* "The worse thing is the cinders, cinder burn is a burn that will last five or six days. It's not like an iron burn, iron will hit you and pop right off you" (*Portraits in Steel,* 296).

My deepest concern in constructing this essay about ghosted work and worker ghosts is with the possibilities for worker self-representation and how writers and photographers create *aesthetic circumstances* that enable self-representation. That representation, I realize, is always unfinished and incomplete (but not indeterminate in a postmodern sense). At the very least there is the centering of workers' presence and not their negation or victimization. But assumptions about what can be known should not come easily, because as former steelworker Doris McKinney reminds us, "Some people do come with various attitudes. You have to clear the air. They know nothing about you, nothing whatsoever" (*Portraits in Steel,* 185).

It is in the recognition of not knowing, and in the respectful spirit of seeking to know, that these books have purpose in resisting the ghosting of workers.[36]

ZONED
FOR
SLAVERY
THE CHILD BEHIND THE LABEL

SCHOOL BUS

GITANO

Illegal Immigrant Death Rate

Social class
linked with
health, say
researchers

TRIANGLE SHIRTWAIST FACTO
(ASCH BUILDING)

HAS BEEN DESIGNATED A

NATIONAL HISTORIC LANDMA

THE TRIANGLE SHIRTWAIST FACTORY FIRE,
IN WHICH 146 WORKERS DIED,
OCCURRED HERE ON MARCH 25, 1911.

THIS BUILDING POSSESSES NATIONAL SIGNIFIC
IN COMMEMORATING THE HISTORY OF THE
UNITED STATES OF AMERICA

1991

NATIONAL PARK SERVICE
UNITED STATES DEPARTMENT OF THE INTE

OH, LET THE GIRLS SIT DOWN
By J.R.S.

I tell you that 'tis very wrong.
It is cruel and not right,
To keep the girls upon their feet
From morning until night,

1876.

Recoveries

Useable Pasts

ncidents that affect the lives of working people in one generation often become historical and cultural antecedents for future generations. These recovery narratives may take the form of poetry, plays, memoir, or even paintings. The silenced, oppressed, or forgotten are reclaimed and reimagined. This is a process of cultural formation that is reciprocal: the dead give inspiration to a new generation of storytellers and the writers and artists witness for those who can no longer tell their own stories.

Traditional humanistic approaches concerned with literary lineage emphasize the anxious influence of extraordinary figures—a Milton or an Emerson—over succeeding generations. This textual tradition, while not completely exclusionary to working-class cultural formation, is policed, regulated, and controlled within academic institutions. What is problematic is the latent assumption that everything outside of that learned tradition is less worthy. Cultural representations linked to the working-class body, if they are not completely ignored, face unacknowledged Cartesian mind/body-split assumptions. It is possible, though, to resist that split and to claim processes of cultural formation that are grounded in actual events, lived experiences, community, history, and reciprocal relationships. This is not solo-voice thinking, as Toni Cade Bambara observed, but cultures stemming out of collective and historical sensibilities, dependent, as she said, "on so many views, on so many people's productions."[1]

"Fire Poetry on the Triangle Shirtwaist Company Fire of March 25, 1911" documents the circumstances of the fire that took the lives of 146 workers, mostly young immigrant women, and analyzes the powerful poetic responses to the fire at the time and later by working-class women poets. "Stillness, Motion, Bodies, and Possibilities for Working-Class Studies" not only recognizes the collective sensibility within individual texts, but also offers a connective model of reading multicultural literature as working-class literature through the frame of unsafe labor and the search for sustaining work. It speaks to the necessity for recognizing a continuum of labor oppressions that steal childhood, wear bodies down, and deprive workers of stable homes. In highlighting the writing of Leslie Marmon Silko, Helena María Viramontes, and Cherríe Moraga, I wish to position working-class studies as space for reciprocal cultural visibility grounded in the shared experience of labor. Lastly, the paintings of self-taught working-class artist Ralph Fasanella tell a complex, epical story of working-class people's lives, struggles, jobs, politics, heroes, and pasttimes, all within the context of his beloved New York City.

The lesson of the hour is that while property is good, life is better, that while possessions are valuable, life is priceless. The meaning of the hour is that the life of the lowliest worker in the nation is sacred and inviolable. —Rabbi Stephen S. Wise

I would be a traitor to those poor burned bodies if I were to come here to talk good fellowship. We have tried you good people of the public—and we have found you wanting.
—Rose Schneiderman

Fire Poetry on the Triangle Shirtwaist Company Fire of March 25, 1911

It was March 25, 1911, a late Saturday afternoon, and nearly spring. One short block from Washington Square Park in New York's Greenwich Village a fire raged on the eighth, ninth, and tenth floors of a building occupied by the Triangle Shirtwaist Company. A passerby at a busy corner of Washington Place and Greene Street noticed a "bale of dark dress goods" come out of a top-floor window. He thought that someone was trying to save expensive cloth. But then another bale came down, and another. One caught the wind and opened. It was not a bale of goods; it was a young woman.[1]

The Triangle Shirtwaist factory fire took the lives of 146 workers, 20 men and 126 women; the average age was nineteen. Most of the workers were Italian and Jewish immigrant women whose families depended on their wages. Many were involved in the famous shirtwaist workers strike of 1909 to 1910. They died because their working conditions were unsafe.

That this event is part of the useable past of some Americans, forgotten by others, and absent from the historical consciousness of most, is indicative of the contested and suppressed labor history of this country. It is not listed in E. D. Hirsch's best-selling *Cultural Literacy: What Every American Needs to Know,* nor, for that matter, is it included in *Multi-Cultural Literacy,* the Graywolf Annual alternative list.[2]

However, for many working people, especially garment workers, and for many contemporary working-class women poets, the Triangle fire is not forgotten. In 1991 David Melman, then assistant to the president of the ILGWU (International Ladies' Garment Workers Union), said that he got twenty to thirty phone calls about the fire a year and that the fire "hits a psychic chord in people."[3] The Triangle fire has evoked a range of cultural responses: paintings, photographs, plays, dances, songs, novels, and a full-length television movie.

Perhaps because of the injustices it embodies, the Triangle fire, as historical location and as symbol, has not yet been appropriated as a commodity for popular consumption. It exists in the present as a site of subjugated historical memory, as a source of inspiration, and as a symbolic link to the tragedies of lives lost and stunted because of unsafe working conditions and economic oppression. The use of the Triangle fire as a subject for literary expression is an example of a nearly lost understanding of popular culture, what Gramsci recognized as culture produced *within and out of* the circumstances of lived experience, rather than what is imposed *on* people from sites of power and cultural production.[4]

U.S. working-class literature is often labor and site specific; Colorado miners' poetry, the Lowell mill girls' *Offering,* and the automobile assembly-line poetry coming out of Detroit are but a few examples.[5] Poetry about the Triangle fire presents a different vein of working-class literature, one that, although located in a specific historical place and time, involves writers who are from varying regions of the country, are of different races and ethnicities, and do not necessarily come from a family background of garment workers. What these poets have in common is a sense of kinship with the women who lost their young lives and a sense of outrage over the injustice done to them. In researching and collecting writing by working-class women for my anthology *Calling Home: Working-Class Women's Writings,* I received or found at least a half dozen different poems about the fire.[6] As one poet put it in a letter to me, "everyone writes about the fire; here's my version." I realized that I was not unique or alone in my private interest in this fire. Others have taken it personally too. Others have been compelled to read the old newspaper accounts, look at the photographs, and stand at the corner of Greene Street and Washington Place, shut out the hubbub of New York University, and—reconstructing the event in imagination and historical memory—hear the screams and see the falling bodies.

How do working-class people generate their own literature? That is the larger question behind this examination of the "fire poems." For working-class writers, literary antecedents often come from material existence and what I call "the texts of trouble" which document worker oppression, rather than canonized texts. I am suggesting that the Triangle Shirtwaist factory fire of March 25, 1911, and the newspaper accounts, photographs, and narratives contemporaneous with the fire, tap a collective memory of class oppression and injustice—especially for women.

This fire poetry is not an expression of individualistic angst; nor is it an effort to "make it new." Rather, it evolves in response to the enormity and palpability of the violence done to workers. It is a history and consciousness reclaimed. These writers compose out of familiar working-class values of thrift and repair, of salvaging and restoring, and of abhorring waste—especially here, the deprivation and waste of all those young lives. This poetry is more than a tribute to dead sisters and workers across time. In writing about the fire, and struggling against an aphasia imposed by privileged-class domination of culture, these contemporary poets—Chris Llewellyn, Mary Fell, Carol Tarlen, Julia Stein, Safiya Henderson-Holmes, and who knows how many others?—are engaging in a reciprocal cultural practice and joining a larger conversation about class oppression. In drawing from this collective tragedy and witnessing for the dead, these "fire poets" release their own poetic voices.

Through these "fire poems" we see the interplay of historical reality, public language, and cultural expression. In describing the Triangle fire and presenting reportage, poetry, and narratives contemporaneous with the fire, I trace the process of cultural production for working-class writers from event to text to audience (and from text to event for readers?) and call attention to these particular antecedents—literary and historical—as providing a different cultural context and self-critical stance for working-class poets. The fire poems are not commodities to be consumed by readers who can then feel satisfied that class oppression has been "covered." The context of creation and historical antecedents are as crucial to a proper reading of these poems as the Old Testament is to reading Milton or decoding metaphysical conceits is to parsing a Donne sonnet.

Although these contemporary fire poets are not self-referential, their individual selves are not displaced or lost, either. The self of the poet is *expanded* because of dialogue with and kinship for the fallen workers. While it is not requisite to know every detail of the Triangle fire to read these contemporary poems—all are historically centered and, to some degree, narrative—it is necessary to recognize that a strictly autotelic reading of them is inappropriate—and perhaps impossible. Ultimately, and collectively, these poems lead back to the *event* rather than to the poet or other texts.

It is not news to say that American literature, as it has been academically shaped for generations of students, allies itself with a white, Anglo-Saxon, male—and class-privileged—paradigm. The scholarship on gender, race, and ethnicity has disrupted the old canon to a degree. But class is another matter. Class is often evoked as essential to this new critical formulation, but, in actual practice, the gritty, difficult differences of class relations are often suppressed and subjugated in the study of cultural productions and representation. We need hybrid theoretical models which take into account the circumstances of class differences not only in the creation of literature, but in the critical act as well.[7] While many canonical writers have noticed workers—for example, Robert Frost in "Two Tramps in Mudtime," or Hawthorne in "Ethan Brand"— the critical interpretative emphasis is not on workers. Rather, it derives from a cultural context where manual work is at a distance—perhaps literally unnoticed and invisible—and an incubated intellectuality of abstractions and structure is privileged.

The Fire

The "uprising of the 20,000" of 1909 and 1910, a general strike led by thousands of immigrant women garment workers, began at the Triangle Shirtwaist Company. The Triangle Company resisted the five-month strike with violence, lockouts, and scabs, and was the exception to a general victory by the shirtwaist makers. The Triangle workers won a small pay raise and a slight decrease in their work week, but they lost the strike on the big issues: the right to organize their own union, not a company union, an end to the exploitative subcontracting system involving two layers of bosses and no fixed rates, and improved sanitary and safety conditions. News accounts of the fire note the ironic coincidence that the same police who had arrested and clubbed striking waistmakers the previous winter were now piling their bodies into city coffins.

Rose Safran, one of the Triangle strikers, said, "If the union had won we would have been safe. Two of our demands were for adequate fire escapes and for open doors from the factories to the street. But the bosses defeated us and we didn't get the open doors or the better fire escapes. So our friends are dead" (quoted in Stein, 168).

The police in charge of the bodies of the dead.
Courtesy of the Tamiment Library, New York University.

More victims. Courtesy of the
Tamiment Library, New York University.

By every account it was a horrific fire. The contemporary poet Chris
Llewellyn describes it as the "day it rained children." It was not caused by an
act of God or Nature; it was caused by the privileging of products over people.
The clarity of opposing interests—the greed of the owners and the victimization
of the workers—the swiftness of the deaths—young women having to choose
between succumbing to the flames or plunging from ninth-floor windows—the
series of ironic details and the great weight of the tragedy on hundreds of immigrant families attest to what is the underside of the American economic success
story, that is, the expendability of workers.

Leon Stein's *The Triangle Fire* is a compelling narrative as well as an essential
account of the fire. Stein interviewed survivors, combed newspaper and journal
accounts, and studied court records. Each chapter of *The Triangle Fire* is headed
with an epigraph from Dante's *Inferno* and Dante's lowest circle becomes in the
real events of the fire the ninth-floor inferno of trapped workers.

Stein begins his book with an observation of the season: "The first touch of
spring warmed the air" (11). It was *almost* spring, almost Passover and Easter.
Holidays, with their promise of special foods, maybe a new hat, a celebration
with relatives, are important occasions for working people because they are
color in the gray of daily lives focused on survival and burdened by human concerns. Fifteen minutes made all the difference. The workers had their Saturday
paychecks. In fifteen minutes they would have vacated the building. From the

Plunged through pavement. Courtesy of
the Tamiment Library, New York University.

first fire alarm to the last body falling took about fifteen minutes. Sixty-seven
people plunged; all perished.

The circumstances and details of the fire are tragically ironic: the ten-story
Asch Building, located at the corner of Greene Street and Washington Place, was
technically considered "fireproof"; the fire-fighting equipment available at that
location was "state of the art"; the builder met every detail of the "letter" of the
law. Indeed, the building, with its steel structure, an emblem of the new urban
landscape, survived—and today is part of the New York University campus—but
146 workers died. Workers died because they were trapped on the eighth, ninth,
and tenth floors and fire hoses could reach only up to the seventh floor. There
were no fire drills, there was no sprinkler system. Heavy metal doors opened
inward rather than outward; one was kept locked so that management could
"keep track of the girls"; the one inside narrow fire escape reached only to the
second floor, and collapsed under the weight of the escaping workers, dumping
its human load to the concrete backyard with its spiked fence.[8]

The Triangle Shirtwaist Company was the largest manufacturer of women's
shirtwaists. Produced by the thousands, in imitation of Charles Dana Gibson's
"Gibson Girls," these sheer blouses were signs, representations, of a freer, more
independent—and, of course, class-privileged—American woman. They were

also clever contradictions. Topped at the neck by a mannish collar, they blossomed like peonies tapered to fitted waist stems by tailored darts and pleats. They were lovely deceptions, simultaneously concealing and enhancing the female figure, presenting a "clean" look with a fabric "more combustible than paper" (Stein, 160). They are ironic metaphors for the traps and deceptions of waistmakers' work.

The New York factory law required 250 cubic feet of air for each worker. Since the loft ceilings were higher than the old tenement or railroad flats the owners could "get away" with crowding more workers into less space (Stein, 161). The company employed subcontractors who hired immigrant women to sew separate pieces of the garments. The rate was fixed between the owners and the contractors; the women never knew how much their work was worth. The payroll listed only the contractors; the company never knew exactly how many workers it employed (Stein, 161). In that way, the women who produced the shirtwaists were both figuratively and literally invisible to the owners who profited from them.

Isaac Harris and Max Blanck, the owners of Triangle, escaped the fire. Socialist lawyer Morris Hillquit noted how they didn't go down with their workers; "What a tremendous difference between the captains of ships and the captains of industry!" (quoted in Stein, 140). Harris and Blanck had seven fires before the

Parade in memoriam. Courtesy of the Tamiment Library, New York University.

Triangle disaster. Backed by a powerful brokerage firm, not only had they had no difficulty maintaining coverage or acquiring new policies, but at the time of the fire they carried the greatest allowable amount of fire insurance (Stein, 173). Leon Stein notes that that "the proprietors of the Triangle Shirtwaist Company collected in indemnity $64,925 in excess of any claim for which they could furnish legal or convincing proof of loss." They "cleared" $445 for each dead Triangle worker (Stein, 176). They were indicted on charges of first- and second-degree manslaughter and acquitted by a jury of their peers.

The material effect on the families of the victims and the survivors presents a very different attitude about the value of money in relation to kinship and community. There was no question that economic need was great and that families counted on the Triangle wages to survive. The Red Cross raised substantial emergency funds for immediate distribution on the Monday after the fire. But, as Stein reports, no one came to claim the aid. The workers who died were from recently immigrated Italian and Jewish families accustomed to surviving by the collective struggle of the family, not by government or organizational handouts. Rose Schneiderman, with colleagues from the Women's Trade Union League and volunteers from the Red Cross, went into the tenements on the Lower East Side and found the victims' families, "who in this moment of great sorrow had become oblivious to their own [economic] needs" (quoted in Stein, 124).

Elizabeth Dutcher, a member of the joint Red Cross and union relief committee, speaks of the "searching investigations" made by the relief committee and the reports that were subsequently issued. By detailing the family circumstances, the number of dependents, and the income of the victims, these reports show how necessary victims' wages were to the support of their families, and debunk middle-class stereotypes of "working girls" holding jobs merely for fun or furs.[9]

The Language of the Fire

The trial of Harris and Blanck presents a telling case study of the interpenetration of power and language. According to Bertha Rembaugh, a lawyer for the Women's Trade Union League of New York, Judge Crain's charge to the jury was worded in such a way as to assure acquittal. The women who managed to survive the fire were defeated by language in court. The defense lawyer, Max D. Steuer, came from the Lower East Side and used this subjugated knowledge against his own people; he was what Gramsci might consider a functionary rather than an organic intellectual. The witnesses for the prosecution were young women dressed in their best clothes, struggling with a language not their own and the trappings of officialdom. When Celia Walker described how she escaped by jumping from machine table to machine table, Steuer asked, "Was your skirt as tight as the skirt you've got on now?" In cross-examining sixteen-year-old Ethel Monick, Steuer commented, "You do like to argue some, don't you, little girl?" (quoted in Stein, 180). The perceptions of the representative of the people, Assistant District Attorney Charles S. Bostwick, hardly served the victims better: he described the witnesses as "of tender years—most of them not able to speak the language, not of great intelligence . . . working at their machines, working and working with no time to look up" (quoted in Stein, 181). Steuer tried to discredit testimony by survivors by suggesting to the jury that it was coached and contrived. Writing in *Life and Labor* about a year after the fire, Bertha Rembaugh says of the girls who testified: "while they were confused occasionally, their statements were not substantially broken."[10]

One of the jurors who acquitted Harris and Blanck was a shirt manufacturer, another was an importer; both felt there was no one responsible for the fire, one claiming that "the girls who worked there were not as intelligent as those in other walks of life and were therefore the more susceptible to panic" (quoted in Stein, 199). Protection of the owners' property, demonstrated by the staged presentation of a large woman's handbag big enough to hold four waists, was a language the jurors could understand. Never mind that the value of the goods pilfered from Triangle never exceeded $25, the door was locked and the workers were trapped (Stein, 203). A young worker describes the frisking of workers: "When leaving work they have men at the Greene Street door searching all the girls. We were made to open our pocketbooks, and when a girl didn't do it she was made to come up two or three flights and show that she didn't have a piece of lace or anything else. A girl could not carry a waist in her pocketbook, and all one could steal was a piece of lace or embroidery worth two or three cents. Leaving work we were treated worse than criminals."[11] Emma Goldman in her predictably blunt style wrote in *Mother Earth* that "the acquittal of Harris and Blank [*sic*] signifies the legalization, the justification, of industrial murder as an established economic fact."[12]

Writing about the fire for the *International Socialist Review,* Louis Duchez raises questions about truth and reality that should interest contemporary theorists who may be convinced that reality waits for those who construct it. He begins, "Truth is indeed, stranger than fiction. As I write this story of the bold, brutal and cold-blooded murder of one hundred and twenty-five girls [*sic*] averaging nineteen years of age, and twenty men, here in New York, I wonder if what I have seen and heard and felt is real." Duchez does not spare the squeamish reader as he piles detail on detail of dismembered bodies and shredded, blackened flesh. He concludes by blaming organizing labor for "the Triangle slaughter," for not striking "as one man when the girls struggled so desperately in 1910 against the Triangle," and chides the unions for not calling a general strike the Monday after the fire.[13]

Inherent to the struggle for economic justice is the struggle for language dominance—for control of the circulation of meaning and judgment in the public forum. Harris and Blanck invested in an advertising campaign on their own behalf in the New York City newspapers. The socialist newspaper the *New York Call,* whose masthead proclaimed, "Devoted to the Interests of the Working People," photographed their check and returned it, printing the whole transaction in its next editions (Stein, 159). The *Call* grouped individual portraits and the names of dead workers. The outrage and anguish of the workers were visualized on the front pages of New York daily newspapers in editorial cartoons by Crosby, Tad, Boardman Robinson, and John Sloan. The triangle became a symbol of avarice and slaughter. The language of the news accounts, particularly in the *Call,* is figurative, laden with literary tropes. Neither bloodless abstraction nor exaggerated sentiment, this is figurative language as appropriate tool to express intensity of emotion. For example, the news stories incorporate simile and metaphor (a "spider's web fire escape") and irony ("every care was taken to insure death of girls" piled deep behind an "iron door of profit") to create images worthy of the gravity of the event.

Literary discourse does not and did not construct this event; the tragedy of the fire evoked poetic response—and still does. Notice the chiaroscuro effect in this front-page report by Carrie W. Allen in the *Call,* which might be subtitled "tenderness for the dead, brutality for the living." I have determined the poetic line and made minor omissions from the news account, but my "poem" is essentially the text of the front-page article:

A hideous little bundle
slowly lowered
from a ninth floor window
swirled and flapped
grotesquely
in the wind
as it made
its lone journey
to the street.
Huge search lights
cast their white rays
into every nook and corner
of the desolated building.
The Triangle blazed forth
in shining letters
above the three-sided
trademark
of the waist company.
One by one
the bundles
started their journey
to the street
casting fantastic
shadows

as they swirled
about
and traveled slowly
down.
One—a very little one—
made its way
falteringly and reluctantly
clinging to each ledge
as the feet tarried
the specter face would turn
upward
as if to seek
the answer
to the tragedy
in the cold black sky.[14]

Early Fire Poetry

The first published Triangle fire poem appeared four days after the fire on the front page of the *Jewish Daily Forward*. It was composed by the Yiddish poet Morris Rosenfeld, the "poet laureate of the slum and the sweatshop" (Stein, 145). It is a formal threnody, a five-part dirge, in which the poet takes the persona of bard or spokesman for the inarticulate and outraged workers. In elevated language, Rosenfeld strains to convey the weight of the event. He locates the sorrow of the city not with "battle nor fiendish pogrom," nor with natural forces—earthquakes or lightning—but with the unnaturalness of greed personified as "Mammon" devouring "our sons and daughters" like a capitalistic Minotaur (Stein, 145–146).

The elevated tone is sustained in the next stanza even though the poet speaks more directly of "my sorrow," as he urges the reader to look and "see where the dead are hidden in dark corners." The poet's task is to illuminate the horror and to vent the collective anger: "Damned be the rich! / Damned be the system! / Damned be the world!" Rosenfeld's approach is sweeping and generalized—unlike the particularization of names we see in contemporary women's poetry. He "weep[s] for them all." His penultimate stanza is highly evocative as the dead women metaphorically become "beautiful, beautiful flowers destroyed," and foreshadows the particularized flower imagery in Safiya Henderson-Holmes's contemporary fire poem, "rituals of spring." Rosenfeld turns from the epic to the ordinary as he encloses his audience in a familiar Jewish ritual, "Now let us light the holy candles / And mark the sorrow." This invitation of connection with his audience/reader enables the poem to become itself a ritual, a recitation of history and an incantation of memory. We will see this evocation of ritual again in the writing of other contemporary fire poets. For example, Mary Fell's "Havdallah" acknowledges ritual, but urges "strike" for justice. Rosenfeld concludes his poem with a threatening reminder—"There will come a time" when the guilty will face the oblivion of death. In the meantime the guilty will be cursed with the memory, "Until time erases you," of "daughters in flame" and "this red avalanche" that will destroy their sleep and mar their joyous celebrations with their own children. Avalanche here is powerfully connotative of the trapped and falling bodies, of the gushing, futile hoses, and of the guilty remembrance that cannot be stopped.

In examining journals, newspapers, labor periodicals, poetry collections both contemporaneous with the fire and on anniversaries of the fire, I was looking for a continuous line of literary expression, particularly in poetry, about the fire. My findings indicate a fragmentary poetry line beginning with Rosenfeld and including poems by women in labor journals shortly after the fire. And then, eclipsed by two world wars and a global depression, there is very little about the fire until after the publication (1962) and republication (1985) of Stein's book and the commemorative events he helped organize. Stein's research and the resurgent scholarship on women's literature and history converge to provide an impetus and context for contemporary fire poetry.

However, a few contemporaneous literary responses to the fire mingle Rosenfeld's elevated outrage with imagined views of the subjectivities of the working girls and critiques of the social order. Writing about a year after the fire, Alice Henry, in "The Way Out," dramatizes how the system of justice advances the interests of the powerful at the expense of the poor by using puns, tropes, and literary allusions to deconstruct criminality.[15] She prefaces her polemic with an excerpt from the Norse poem "The Edda" in which Thor is challenged to lift a certain Gray Cat. Thor can barely move the Gray Cat and succeeds in lifting only one paw, under which is Midgrard, the serpent whose tail and mouth gird the world. Henry sees the simple morality of right and wrong of ordinary people as situated within a hidden, powerful, new, "lawless" business and industrial world "so complex and so complicated . . . that we had no time to grow the corresponding moral code to fit its conditions." Until this shadowy world of power is evident to the sensibilities of the bourgeois, there will be "no strong public opinion to move the Gray Cat." She concludes by urging working people to organize themselves to press for new laws and their enforcement, safer working conditions, adequate fire escapes, and a genuine "Way Out."

Appearing in the same issue of *Life and Labor* as Henry's essay is a two-part poem by Violet Pike, "New World Lessons for Old World Peoples."[16] Didactic and dialectical, this straightforward poem contrasts the theory of lesson seven, "Factory Laws," with the reality of lesson eight, "Fire." The immediate lesson to the reader of the poem is not to assume, naively, that laws, even adequate ones, are enough. They can be "obeyed" the day the inspector visits, and ignored the rest of the time. Immigrants learn quickly that for them the "new world" is no more safe than the "old world." The poem concludes with the question: "Who can . . . make the bosses keep the law?" The answer lies not in despair, but in the context of the poem, that is, unionization and solidarity across class and ethnic lines.

This same call for solidarity—"Each for all be our call, / Without class, without caste, without clan"—is in the quietly rousing poem "The Future" by Constance Lounsberry."[17] She alludes to the Triangle fire, "like a beast at the feast / They have stricken the least," but hope rather than tragedy is her focus. Published two months after the fire, this simple anthem is a call for the dignity of good, safe work: "And let no man be idle and vain, / And let no one be crippled with toil." She calls for a future in which divisions between manual and intellectual labor —"For the head shall not war with the hand" —and between sexes—"Nor the women do battle with man"—shall disappear so that *everyone* can claim a "birthright of joy," "[a]nd the word of the world shall be work" and "our work be in joy, not in pain."

Contemporary Fire Poetry

The fire poetry of Chris Llewellyn, Mary Fell, Safiya Henderson-Holmes, Julia Stein, and Carol Tarlen is a genuine vein of contemporary working-class women's literature. This poetry offers an opportunity to study class differences in the writing of women's poetry and an occasion to test theoretical practices. I want to begin not with theory, but with the words of the poets themselves in response to my question: "Why write about the Triangle fire?"[18]

Mary Fell says, "It dealt with both women and the working class, so it met my hunger to affirm my joint identities. At the time I wrote 'Triangle Fire' I didn't know any one else had written about it. I felt I'd recreated it. For me, the experience was completely satisfying. It allowed me to reclaim and disseminate some of my own history, and to blend both my own and other's voices. . . . It allowed me to express both love and loyalty to my history and anger at its attempted destruction [and] eradication."

"I always say this subject chose me rather than I chose 'it'," says Chris Llewellyn. "Being so moved by these real-life stories, I needed to retell the Triangle Fire in my own way as a poet, not as an historian or scholar. I aspired toward the emotional truth in this retelling of the stories of the victims, witnesses, and survivors. It has been a privilege to share this work with reading and listening audiences around the country."

The West Coast poet Julia Stein says, "I wrote about the Triangle Fire twice. A few years before I wrote the first poem, I had a bad burn where my nightgown caught on fire, and about 1/4 of my body was burned—my hands and back. . . . I was discovering Yiddish poets at the time, and wrote my poem 'The Flame' about the Triangle Fire. In a way, my first Triangle poem was a female answer to Rosenfeld's poem. I wrote the second Triangle poem, 'The Triangle Fire,' [because] there seemed to be parts of the story that demanded to be told. The event still seemed to be invisible, not recognized. I was struck by how most writers on the fire always stressed the women's victimization, but never talked about the organizing afterward. At first the second poem had a sorrowful ending; when I read it to a trade union audience, I realized that the poem needed a different ending. The trade union audience taught me what the ending was— not in a catalogue of suffering but in the victory of the safety legislation. When I read this version, it seemed right. I guess that the second poem had a new look at the Triangle Fire that demanded to be told."

Carol Tarlen, also from California, says, "despite the tragedy, [the Triangle fire] represents solidarity and resistance. I am also moved by the youth and courage of the women. I wanted to emphasize [in my poem] sisterhood, courage and solidarity, and in a personal non academic way. . . . I have always been moved by the fact that the women embraced each other and jumped together. Some people find this too much a celebration of death (not me) and others think I am too Luddite about the sewing machines that the women worked on. I don't find these contradictions. I guess because I am not Jewish or Italian, I get nervous that some women will think I am stealing their heritage, but I think the fire belongs to all women's histories." And, as an afterthought, Tarlen writes, "my handwriting is terrible because I suffer from carpal tunnel syndrome. No wonder I respond to that fire. Work maims and kills."

Safiya Henderson-Holmes, Julia Stein, and Carol Tarlen are all published writers who have written individual poems about the fire; Mary Fell's chapbook "Triangle Fire" is republished in her collection *The Persistence of Memory,* and Chris Llewellyn's book of poems *Fragments from the Fire,* winner of the Walt Whitman poetry prize, is a collection of poems about the Triangle fire.[19]

How do these fire poems speak?

First, they are written out of affiliation rather than just filiation.[20] That is, each poet moves beyond her personal identity of race and ethnicity, her own geography, and her own employment, to embrace—metaphorically—the women of the Triangle fire. This embrace is both imaginative (a sense of kinship with the fallen workers) and historical (a willingness to research and grasp the historic evidence). These poets are symbolically orphaned by the fire. Their poems offer shifting and different perspectives, not so much fragmented, dangling and disconnected selves, but a multivocality and a complex perspectivity. There is no apology for anger in these poems. There is rage rather than quiet weeping. These poets write not just for themselves, but in solidarity with the women who died. What is at stake is a common struggle for economic justice. In the language of strikes and unions, these poets "hold the [picket] line." Some of these writers are activists and have literally placed their bodies on picket lines, but here I refer to poetic lines, those demarcations of language, that engage in resistance to class oppression.

Situated at the intersection of class and gender, this poetry is intentionally oppositional; there is no phony claim to neutrality or objectivity. They are not ambiguous; they ask, "whose side are you on?" and invite the reader to choose. For the critic to assume that these poems are merely propagandistic, and hence easily dismissed, is to reveal a privileged condition where sides have been chosen but not acknowledged.

This fire poetry is not protest or victim poetry. James Scully in *Line Break* offers a distinction between protest and dissident poetry that is useful in perceiving the collective and dialogic nature of this poetry. Scully writes, "the telltale characteristic of protest poetry is that it seldom speaks the active rage or resolution of [oppressed and exploited] people on the receiving end. . . . The real subject is the poet's own tender sensibilities, not what is actually *systemically* going on. Dissident poetry, however, does not respect boundaries between private and public, self and other . . . it breaks silences: speaking for, or at best *with*, the silenced; opening poetry up, putting it in the middle of life rather than shunting it off into a corner. It is poetry that talks back, that would act as part of the world, not simply a mirror of it."[21]

This sense of talking back, of dialogism, and reciprocity is characteristic of this poetry and distinct from Alicia Ostriker's categorization in *Stealing the Language* of [white middle-class] women's poetry as concerned with "autonomous self definition."[22] All of these contemporary fire poets are common readers. They have all returned to the same "texts of trouble": historical documents, newspapers and journals, photographs, earlier poetry, Stein's *The Triangle Fire*, women's labor history, even the small plaque on the Asch building commemorating the fire. They engage intertextually with these materials, transforming newspaper articles, courtroom testimony, investigators' reports, religious liturgy, testimonials, speeches, eyewitness accounts, police reports, even articles of clothing—the charred contents of handbags, remnants of jewelry, and hair combs—all into poetry. In other words, these materials are both the stuff of the writing and the means to the writing—subject and agency for new poetic subjectivities.

Chris Llewellyn's collection, *Fragments from the Fire,* is a multivocal conversation. Entering her text, the reader joins the poet on a historical journey, beginning with the historical memory of the Asch building in March 1911 and ending with the poet standing at the same site (what is now NYU's Brown Building), in the pouring rain ("Soaked to skin"), eye through the lens of her camera, looking at "Eighth, Ninth, Tenth. So this / is where they worked." Llewellyn's fire poetry is particularly crowded with voices: Police Captain Henry, Fire Battalion Chief Worth, café owner Lena Goldman, a derelict, the lost poet Sonya, New York Governor Dix, the 'heroic elevator man,' even the police captain's horse, Yale, give poetic testimony to the event. Llewellyn's collection builds text on text, conversations within conversations. In "Sear" she speaks of process and poetic responsibility: "I plant *direct quotations* on the page, / arranging line-breaks, versification. . . .To write about *them* / yet not interfere, . . ." The "searing" pun is earned; the event is burnished into the consciousness of the poet whose task is to see rightly, to use her poet's eye as window into the Triangle.

And almost always in the fire poetry, there are the conversations with dead sisters across time, naming their names, reconstituting their faces and voices. The emphasis is not on a polemic solidarity, but on human relationships described in terms of imagined physicality. In Carol Tarlen's "Sisters in the Flames" the poet becomes another sister worker, "together we sewed / fine linen shirtwaists / for fine ladies." Tarlen takes the hand of her sister with "hair a mess of red curls" and holds her "in the cradle / of my billowing skirt" and "*together* now fly / the sky is an unlocked door / and the machines are burning" (my emphasis).

Julia Stein's poem "The Triangle Fire" has a broader sweep, including naming the union organizer, Rose Schneiderman, and the fire commission member Frances Perkins, who led the investigation into "canneries where five-year-olds snipped beans," and factories where machinery "scalped women."

Safiya Henderson-Holmes's "rituals of spring" becomes a tragic spring dance, a rite commemorating the spring that was denied to "hundreds of flowering girls tucking spring into sleeves, / tucking and tugging at spring to stay alive." And as if to control the rush and beauty of her own language, to warn herself and her reader, she says, "*and the girls* / were girls not angels jumping, / not goddesses flying or hovering / they smashed, they broke into / large pieces, smell them in the rain."

As daughters in working-class families, as workers themselves, these fire poets share a common economic epistemology and a knowledge of bodies at risk because of the work that they do. It is more than textual knowledge; it is body knowledge. The poets also know the risks of cultural production, how as working-class women poets their subjects and their voices are so easily dismissed, as Llewellyn says, as "schmaltz, soap-opera- / Sentiment" or unacknowledged, tossed away, unfashionable. They also know the risks of appropriation—of, as Rose Schneiderman put it, "becoming a traitor to these burned bodies" by speaking "good fellowship" to those responsible for economic oppression.[23] These poets are conscious of the possibility of betrayal, of their responsibility not to dishonor the dead. They are not voyeurs. To plunge into the details of the fire is to plunge into hell. In writing about the fire, they assume the responsibility of the survivor to be a voice, a mediator, a conduit, for the silenced many. But the relationship is mutual and reciprocal: what is received back from the *giving* of testimony for these dead workers is a release of public, poetic language. The fire becomes the means for claiming working-class subjectivity at a historical moment that is even more hostile to class consciousness than 1911 because class knowledge is suppressed and unnamed.

Contemporary interpretations of women's poetry tend to emphasize sites of domestic and ideological enclosure. But the doors were locked at the Triangle

Shirtwaist Company and for these women workers entrapment was not metaphoric. In terms of the class-conscious poetry that has evolved out of the fire, the theme of entrapment is more than a literary trope; it takes on a heightened, historical meaning. When survival is the subject, separations between the intellectual and the physical dissolve. "The sweatshop is a state of mind as well as a physical fact," Leon Stein reminds us.[24] Contemporary fire poetry by working-class women is neither exclusively private nor public, neither exclusively about work nor about home, but, rather, is situated in the fragmented, double work lives of women workers, in the cross-currents of work and home, as Safiya Henderson-Holmes writes,

> crowded, hard, fast, too fast, closed windows,
> locked doors, smell of piss, of sweat,
> of wishes being cut to bits,
> needle stabs, electric shocks, miscarriages over silk,
> fading paisley, fading magenta,
> falling in love will get you fired, forever old,
> never fast enough, buying flowers is wasteful
> so hurry, hurry grind your teeth and soul
> six dollars a week send to grandfather,
> four dollars a week send to aunt ruth, sleep over the
> machine and you're done for, way before you open your
> eyes man'm, madam, miss, mrs. mother girlie
>
> ("rituals of spring," 31)

Elaine Hedges notes the problem of using the "tropology of women's textile work [as] a useful language for critical discourse" (340), emphasizing how, historically, the relationship between woman and needle and text was more often negative and adversarial.[25] The negativity stems from the "invasive reality of sewing," prior to the mass production of clothing. Consuming needlework usurped time that might have been spent on literary expression. While the Industrial Revolution and the availability of mass-produced clothing freed some women from laborious tasks, it presented new conditions of entrapped labor for other women. The sewing at Triangle was not privatized; rather it is an apt example of a shift in the conditions of women's concrete labor practices to an abstracted labor system of exploitation of the many for the profit of the few. Sweatshop women sewers lost both leisure time and control over their own labor. The possibility of women's needlework as a means to liberation, celebrated, for example, in Alice Walker's *The Color Purple,* is valid, but it should not be assumed that it is universally representative of women's work. Those textile tropes that emerge, perhaps too conveniently, out of the study of women's texts, need to be tested against the realities of the sweatshop and the lives of the women and children who produce the clothing we can so cheaply and readily buy. These contemporary fire poems offer critics an opportunity to examine class differences in delineating metaphors of women's lives. By insisting on relationality rather than autonomy, complexity rather than essentialism, one can see how machines which liberate some from tedious work enslave others.

Out of the darkness of the sweatshop these poems exist. Although spirituality and workers' consciousness are not often juxtaposed, I want to recognize the interplay of secular and religious literary tropes as evidence of a secular spirituality calling for economic justice. Consider the element of ritual in these poems. This fire poetry calls to the reader as the events called to the writers to engage in a ceremony of mourning, remembrance, and continued struggle. I imagine these poets—however diasporically situated—as conveying a women's minyan—individual voices coming together to engage in a ceremony of definition.[26] Each poem is a midrash on the event, a commentary on and dialogue with other voices across time. These poets do not attempt to compensate for the fire, or replicate the event. They take on the burden of mourning and memory, and the poems become a kind of Kaddish, a secular prayer evoked out of class and gender memory, and of shared knowledge of the dangers of unprivileged work. The poems are a symbolic action and a public utterance by the survivors, all the symbolic daughters of the Triangle workers. Their poetry is not a praise song to death or to God, but a way to use language (replete with religious allusions) as a force against historical oblivion. Mary Fell begins her beautiful seven-part fire poem with "Havdallah":

This is the great divide
by which God split
the world:
on the Sabbath side
he granted rest,
eternal toiling
on the workday side.

But even one
revolution of the world
is an empty promise
where bosses
where bills to pay
respect no heavenly bargains.
Until each day is ours

let us pour
darkness in a dish
and set it on fire,
bless those who labor
as we pray, praise God
his holy name,
strike for the rest. (3)

The language of Jewish ritual is useful to describe the ceremonial quality of this poetry. But, as in any good ritual the action is not linear; it is reciprocal.

There is call and response. The Triangle fire becomes an occasion for communal writing and communal experience in a political context that prizes individual achievement. In this writing, the dead make claims on the living, but also the living make claims on the dead. The fire poetry is one answer to my own earlier question of how working-class writers generate their own literature. The event—because it is a profound tragedy inflicted on common people—becomes the catalyst for breaking silence. The restoration of the event in the poets' consciousness and in the poem is an antidote to the aphasia caused by class hegemony over culture.

As I read and reread these fire poems, I hear an urgency in the writing, a clarity about the difference between "texts" and human *lives* and a desire for language honed so well that it might snap these bodies back to life.[27]

It was always a question of work, and work depended on the harvest, the car running, their health, the conditions of the road, how long the money held out, and the weather, which meant they could depend on nothing.

                                    —Helena María Viramontes, Under the Feet of Jesus

Stillness, Motion, Bodies, and Possibilities for Working-Class Studies

Workers migrate in response to the stillness of their economic lives, to the stasis of poverty or the threat of poverty. Nominally free, but linked in a continuum of economic unfreedom, workers are in the global circuitry of producing wealth. Their marginal improvement depends on luck, circumstances, opportunity, determination, collective support, unionization, and continual struggle. The lowest workers—those without family connections, white-skin privilege, training, language, and literacy—do the lowest jobs. Their bodies may wear out faster than their hopes. Their bodies are stuck in the consumer pipeline. They are consumed by dangerous, repetitive work even as they produce more items for consumption. They are consumed by the exigencies of need, of sustaining others, of sending money home. They are connected through the goods they produce to more privileged workers who themselves are caught up in the trap of identity formation based on consumption.

All workers are joined to each other. But stuck in the pipeline, they cannot see those before or behind, or the advantages of such sight. And it can be risky to see too much. In the film *Bread and Roses,* Rosa, an illegal Mexican immigrant, turns Justice for Janitors union organizer Sam Shapiro out of her house, shouting: "I trust nobody. One mistake I'm on the blacklist. . . . You know what? We may be at the bottom of the shit hole, but we are doing our best." When Shapiro tries to argue that "we" can't let them get away with it, Rosa explodes: "WE. WE. When was the last time you got a cleaning job? Don't ever say *we.* No. I believe in nothing, nobody, *nada,* nothing, but this [*she spreads her hands*]. You hear me wise guy? Now get out."[1] But Rosa does have beliefs. She believes in duty, in struggle, in family love, in the small pleasures of food and housekeeping, as she practices sacrifice. She prostitutes herself with her Mexican American manager in order to get a janitor job for her sister. She betrays her coworkers because she needs health care for her husband. She will not join the strike and sing "solidarity forever." She cannot allow herself a political "we," only a familial one.

Contrast Rosa to the politically romanticized and heroic Esperanza in the 1954 film *Salt of the Earth*.[2] Esperanza is the madonna to Rosa's whore. Also, fiercely protective of her family, her political consciousness comes not so much out of her resistance to her chauvinistic husband, but out of her realization—indicative of the political intentions of the filmmakers—that hope lies only through an embrace of the "we" as workers—men and women, Mexican and Anglo—in the zinc mines of Grant County, New Mexico. The male miners cannot win the strike or sustain their lives without the women. But Esperanza imagines something larger than the private needs of her family or even the immediate success of the strike in the still-poignant words, "Whose neck shall I stand on, to make me feel superior? And what will I get out of it? I don't want anything lower than I am. I'm low enough already. I want to rise. And push everything up with me as I go."[3]

If Rosa is stuck in a low-visibility pipeline, Esperanza, fifty years earlier, stands joined with others in a circle of mutual visibility. How do we measure the distance between Esperanza's collective imaginary and Rosa's individual survivalism? I believe a working-class studies that is grounded in multiracial and multiethnic recognitions enables a sharper understanding of the powerful, political, and racist impediments to worker solidarity and Esperanza's imaginary. This is not class against race or economics against culture, but rather a pedagogical practice and political intention in solidarity with the lowest human condition. This is action that comes out of belief in a fundamental entitlement: the right of all humans to be, to exist as human beings. This is the potentially radical intention of working-class studies.

> The demons don't believe this is a human body. This is a chinaman's body.
>
> —Maxine Hong Kingston, *China Men*

Working-class studies is resistance against human fragmentation and the acceptance of inequality as normative. It positions itself against the control of wealth by the few in relation to the continuum of labor of the many. Its pedagogical strategy is to address the exclusion of worker epistemology from academic institutions, to recognize the colonization of our (Western) minds by consumption and capitalism, to provide a historically conscious standpoint from which to build alliances with others, and to see the struggle for justice as a deliberate, creative, and necessarily collective action. As we witness the negative impact of undemocratic globalization on all workers and see the challenge to progressive movements in the wake of the "war on terrorism," we must resist academic theoretical fatigue as well as the easy and perhaps cynical dismissal of these objectives as naïve idealizations.[4]

What I propose is a new attentiveness to how our literary and pedagogical work is grounded. *Grounded* is the operative word. Ground is the solid stuff of the earth as well as what is unstable and open to cultivation and destruction. To grind is to reduce to small particles, to roughen. Any kind of work can be a grind. Metaphorically, ground is capacious, especially as linked to verbs. One *holds* one's ground, or *gives* ground, or *breaks* ground. But, whose ground? And what is the relationship between that grounded materiality and systems of thought, that is, to theory? I write not in opposition to theory as ideas, but to theory as a kind of enclosure act where academicians become groundkeepers. This project is not about the theoretical well-being of the academic, but about academics' (and hence their students') willing exposure to ambiguity, imprecision, and contradiction in confronting definitions of the working class and simultaneously recognizing the common working-class ground of *struggle*, a visceral and material and psychic state not easily or theoretically translatable. In an autobiographical essay, David Joseph illuminates meanings of struggle:

> The idea of struggle, the very word "struggle," had a profound effect on me. It was like a mantra. All I had to do was say it and apply it to whatever was at hand. It meant I could fight back. It meant I could solve problems a little at a time. It was a word, the possibility for personal power in my own life. It meant that everything was not always the same. Things changed, and I could have something to do with it. I did not have to just take everything lying down. I could actively have some say. Even within my own thoughts and feelings, I could struggle with an idea. I could replace a bad thought-pattern with a better one. Struggle saved me.[5]

I share political philosopher Marla Brettschneider's recognition of the importance of "democratic theorizing from the margins," as a way of negotiating the perceived binaries of identity politics versus postmodern fragmentation in relation to political struggle.[6] However, I question the conceptual frame of the margin. Working-class studies, as a flexible and inclusive field, offers an alternative frame and a way out of the impasse of identity politics and identity fragmentation. By drawing a web of connections based on multiple forms of labor, working-class studies demonstrates how the margins are, indeed, the masses, quite literally, the hands that sustain the materiality of the world. This is not a new, or particularly American, historical story. Working-class studies provides an alternative, and, perhaps, new way to narrate it.

I wish to turn theoretical practice toward very specific, physical, tactile, human conditions such as how the body is worn down by work, how childhood is stolen from some children, how homeplace is threatened, displaced, or lost (as a literal and imaginary home), how migrating workers are without citizenship, how the poor and working class are more subject to violence, and how workers are forced to live in temporary stasis, as if they were prisoners doing time.[7] In other words, to choose to recognize the perspective of a continuum of labor (the variegated conditions of workers) where the lowest are intrinsically important to the formation of knowledge. At the same time, to formulate a praxis, a way to use our cultural spaces (whatever our disciplinary training) to do alternative ground work in the academy, in our pedagogical practices and in the books we write, for the emergence of the epistemologies of the least privileged—*in relation to each other.*

In *Remnants of Nation,* Roxanne Rimstead probes the relationship of materiality to subjectivity: "Instead of throwing up our hands and concluding that the subaltern cannot speak, cultural critics should allow the possibility that poor subjects have special knowledge and can and do speak as cultural subjects in ways that academic criticism has somehow been overlooking or devaluing."[8] Rimstead's critical and important work on the "poverty of theory" in relation to the "complexity of everyday experiences, especially among muted subjects" (4) raises pertinent questions about the permeable borders of working-class studies. As we simultaneously make a persuasive case for the institutionalization of this field, we must also acknowledge the vast differences among workers. This consciousness of difference is not about constructing a hierarchy of struggle or suffering. But it is about acknowledging degrees of physical difference, and consequent struggle and suffering. All workers must sell their labor, but they do not all face the same physical costs. Physicality knives through theory; narratives of the least privileged embody history; oppression trumps academic categorization.

Working-class studies must balance a consciousness of difference among workers and simultaneously build a network of connections to reveal common ground. The physics of intimate and distant knowledge is a constant and necessary tension. In his 1975 poetic study of East European male migrant workers, *A Seventh Man,* John Berger (with photographs by Jean Mohr) demonstrates a way of framing and understanding this working-class project. Berger achieves an earned intimacy by imagining a composite subjectivity of migrant workers while situating the daily and private within a larger, global, structural context. Berger's insights about colonialism as labyrinthine offer a more nuanced structural analysis of the old "divide and rule" management tactic, especially regarding the Right's attempts to bolster workers' antiglobalization resentments:

> Only in relation to what men are in their entirety can a social system be judged just or unjust: otherwise it can be merely assessed as relatively efficient or inefficient. The principle of equality is the revolutionary principle, not only because it challenges hierarchies, but also because it asserts that all men are equally whole. And the converse is just as true; to accept inequality as natural is to become fragmented, is to see oneself as no more than the sum of a set of capacities and needs.
>
> This is why the working class, if it accepts the natural inferiority of the migrants, is likely to reduce its own demands to economic ones, to fragment itself and to lose its own political identity. When the indigenous worker accepts inequality as the principle to sustain his own self-esteem, he reinforces and completes the fragmentation which society is already imposing upon him.
>
> That this will continue happening is the calculation of the ruling class.[9]

The great challenge of working-class studies is to build a pedagogical and cultural structure and space of reciprocal and democratic visibility. This large statement comes out of a recognition of the limitations as well as the potential of educational practices and textual readings. To be sure, textual resistance is no stand-in for political struggle. And yet, as James Baldwin reminds us, "the root function of language is to control the universe by describing it."[10] As a daughter of the working class, I distrust language *and* embrace it. Perhaps through an articulation and recognition of the language of the laboring body, language itself can be redeemed as a transformative tool.

Breaking Up the Pipeline

And the hands—I cut off the hands in my poems. But not in conversation; still the hands could not be kept down. Still they insisted on moving.

—Cherríe Moraga, *Loving in the War Years*

Consider reading the writing of Leslie Marmon Silko, Helena María Viramontes, and Cherríe Moraga as working-class texts, particularly in relation to the physicality of labor in a particular historical context. To suggest a working-class reading is not to slight the specific history of the deracination of Indian children in U.S. boarding schools, or the terrorism that targeted women and children in Central America, or the pesticide-poisoned living conditions of Mexican/American farm workers. Rather, it is to see the commonality of their physical labor, their limited choices (so counter to the be-all-you-can-be individualist mantra), the loss or disruption of their homes, the threats to their children, the necessity of fleeing or fighting, and to see how, like prisoners or the colonized, their sense of the present is stolen from them so that their minds must dwell in the past or in a hoped-for future. And yet, Silko, Viramontes, and Moraga shape acts of resistance, especially in the agency of their female characters as they face the enormity of the oppressions lined up against them.

It took a great deal of energy to be a human being.

—Leslie Marmon Silko, *Ceremony*

In her luminous story "Lullaby," Leslie Marmon Silko offers a lament for loss: the loss of children to the U.S. government through forced schooling and war, the loss of ownership of land, and the loss of the means of economic sustenance, the loss of one's body to physical injury and alcoholism. It is the mother's story. Ayah sweeps up her children and tries to hide them from the uniformed, car-driving, watch-wearing authority figures who succeed in taking the seemingly healthy children away to a sanatorium. She blames the children's father, Chato, for teaching her partial literacy—signing her name, something she was once proud of—and unknowingly signs away the children to white authority.[11] But, what do we know about Chato? He speaks once in the story, when he hears the news of their son Jimmie's death in an army helicopter crash, which he reports to Ayah. Otherwise, Chato is mute. We see him in the present as a forgetful drunk. For many years he was a ranch hand. We learn that he broke his leg when the horse he was riding fell. Not only was he not compensated for this on-the-job injury, but "[t]he white rancher told them he wouldn't pay Chato until he could work again" (45).[12] Chato, speaker and reader of English, straighter than a white man, becomes a ghosted worker, discarded by the rancher as too old to work for him anymore, and told to vacate the boxcar shack where he and Ayah and the children lived. The sickness (alcoholism, despair, powerlessness, white oppression), caused by unjust treatment, descends on Chato. In the final movement of the story, Ayah walks in the snow toward the bar to find him, and we see Chato through the inscription of work on his body: "his hands, scarred by ropes and the barbed wire of all those years" (48). It is Ayah, though, who is the conscious, sentient survivor. Her children stolen and gone, her Navajo future robbed, she draws on the deep grief inside her and retrieves a psychic strength: "she felt satisfied that the men in the bar feared her" (49). She finds Chato, limping on the leg that was crushed long ago, smelling of "woodsmoke and urine" and suggests they "rest awhile" (50). Curled beside her, sharing Jimmie's blanket, Chato "in the light from the stars and the moon . . . looked young again" (51). And feeling the rush and memory and unspeakable anguish of mother loss, she sings a lullaby and awaits the advancing "icy stillness" and death (51).

Silko links cultural loss to sustainable work also in her novel *Ceremony*.[13] Economic sustainability without cultural betrayal is crucial, literally and literarily. A special breed of cattle, not the "weak, soft Herefords that grew thin and died from eating thistle and burned-off cactus during the drought," but tough, wild cattle, "descendents of generations of desert cattle, born in dry sand and scrubby mesquite" (77) will provide an economic base for Tayo and his family. These cattle, survivors who adapted to drought and scarce food, are in motion, and are the answer to the family's economic stasis. They do not fit textbook definitions of scientific cattle breeding that do not consider the dryness of Indian land: "The problem was the books were written by white people who did not think about drought or winter blizzards or dry thistles, which the cattle had to live with" (78). The wild, thin-legged cattle are not the ideal beef cow. "I guess we will have to get along without these books," Tayo's Uncle Josiah remarks. "Maybe we'll even write our own book, *Cattle Raising on Indian Land,* or how to raise cattle that don't eat grass or drink water" (78). This book joke is not appreciated by Rocky, the son who valorizes the scientific knowledge in the standard books and does not see the potential of another kind of knowledge, an epistemology of survival and struggle. And Rocky, with his "someday" individualistic ambitions (76), does not survive. The wild cattle represent a differently centered economic strategy connected to a consciousness of collective survival. The cure for Tayo's postwar sickness and Chato's alcoholism cannot be solely individualistic.

In theorizing an aesthetic for Indian women's writing, Paula Gunn Allen underscores the importance of "commonalities of consciousness" for Indian people, and why "individualism (as distinct from autonomy or self-responsibility) becomes a negatively valued trait."[14] This sense of relationality, I aver, has much in common with Raymond Williams, who, coming out of a vastly different geography and relationship to production, recognizes how writing is embedded in social formations and how the writer's voice "which in speaking as itself, is speaking, necessarily, for more than itself."[15] In the hands of Williams, this sense of the writer's commitment and alignment is not Marxism against identity, nor materiality against language, but rather a theoretical bridge linking labor and culture.

Let us consider a wider imaginary for working-class texts, one that recognizes distinct cultural differences, histories, and geographies and yet sees ways of forging radical linkages across cultural boundaries based on the common need for sustainable work inseparable from an ethos of collective well-being. Working-class studies, never intended as white studies, needs the imaginative expansion of writers like Silko to see the commonality between Chato's final state and unemployed postindustrial workers in cities like Detroit and Youngstown. The ethos in Silko's writing speaks to the best values of the working classes about the possibilities and advantages of a shared consciousness whatever their personal identities. This, it should be understood, is not an appropriation of Indian-ness in some New Age way, nor is it a denial of the specificity of labor conditions. Rather, it is a way to construct, architecturally, a set of relationships within the academy between labor and culture. This is the political, theoretical, and pedagogical work ahead of us in working-class studies.

> Kids' bodies are so vulnerable. They pick up stuff way before adults. They got no buffer zone. "The canary in the mine shaft". . . that's exactly what they are.
>
> —Cherríe Moraga, *Heroes and Saints*

Like the lost, sturdy cattle in *Ceremony*, animals and humans are in motion in Helena María Viramontes' brilliant story "The Cariboo Café."[16] From the start, Viramontes makes terrific demands on her readers. Changing perspectives and shifting time zones and zones of consciousness, she gives readers a small sense of what it feels like to be lost in a strange place. Just as the children Macky and Sonya, without their protective latchkey, stumble into the night toward the Cariboo Café, readers must stumble into meaning. Viramontes begins with a "they" without antecedent. "They" are those in motion, "displaced people" arriving "in the secrecy of night," undocumented workers who impose strict rules of survival on their children, including avoiding the "polie," police who may be La Migra in disguise (65). Viramontes centers what is normally de-centered or insignificant to the dominant eye: undocumented workers, forced to run out of a factory to hide from immigration police "like roaches when the lightswitch goes on" (71), a washerwoman whose son Geraldo is snatched in an unnamed Central American country where the military terrorize citizens, and lost children—Macky, Sonya, Geraldo, and JoJo, the café owner's son, "all crumbled up" somewhere in Vietnam. These lost children symbolize, collectively and metaphorically, all the lost and stolen children whose parents—because of the political and economic circumstances of their lives—and not their bourgeois "parenting skills"—cannot keep them safe and alive.

Food, as comfort and necessity, compels motion: the five-year-old Geraldo sent to fetch a mango for his mother brutally disappears—it was just a mango; Macky dragged/bribed by his sister using the global signifier and his only English word, "Coke"; the Cariboo Café itself, whose peeling sign, a double zero (00) is refuge for "the kinda business that moves" (70), and in the symbolic distance, the grazing caribou without borders. Work is the invisible common denominator in this story. Sonya's latchkey is sacred because her parents must work. The children in the detainers with eyes like "cut glass" are made to work for their food by sorting the bodies of the dead disappeared, "as if they were salvaging cans from a heap of trash" (72). The café owner, stirring chili, cleaning crud, claims to run an honest business as he betrays the illegal workers to the police. Many students are drawn to the perspective of the small business owner and fail to acknowledge, never mind identify with, the central worker of the story: the washerwoman. Viramontes' description is prayer and plea not only to "the Lord" but to the reader to see the most marginal: "I am a washerwoman, Lord. My mother was one, and hers, too. We have lived as best we can, washing other people's laundry, rinsing off other people's dirt until our hands crust and chap. When my son wanted to hold my hand, I held soap instead. When he wanted to play, my feet were in pools of water. It takes such little courage, being a washerwoman" (74). But even an illiterate washerwoman must have some little ground to call home. That is stolen from her when Geraldo is snatched by men who are not human, but "babes farted out from the Devil's ass" (75). The story culminates in a scene of utter unrecognition. The police see the screaming woman as a deranged kidnapper of Macky and Sonya. And she sees them as the soldiers come again to take her recovered Geraldo/Macky, and she refuses to let go. In a physically graphic scene, using her hands, arms, and body, she fights the police whose guns are "steel erections" (78) and, importantly, screams not just for her loss, but "for all the women of murdered children, screaming, pleading for help from the people outside, and she pushes an open hand against an officer's nose, because no one will stop them and he pushes the gun barrel to her face" (78). And as the gun explodes, "crunching like broken glass against [her] forehead," and "blinded by the liquid darkness," she refuses to release the hand of her son (78–79) and claims the courage of resistance.

Literary critics of various persuasions and iterations address the problematic of representing the physicality of labor in ways distinct from commentary on the inexpressibility of love and desire.[17] To be sure, a text is still a text and not a stand-in for lived experience, whether it is about ennui, alienation, passion, or insecticide poisoning. However, it matters what texts one studies in arguing against the inexpressibility of physical labor. What makes working-class litera-ture so challenging to teach and read is that it allows little space for the reader to avert the eye. That is, the best working-class writers *succeed* in surfacing an encounter with physicality that is a no-comfort zone for the reader and the critic. And Helena María Viramontes is one of the best.

In her potent and underappreciated novel *Under the Feet of Jesus*, Viramontes focuses on a family of Mexican migrant workers barely surviving in one more labor camp on the margins of the lush fields and fertile gardens of California.[18] It is a life of stasis and motion: the stasis of poverty against the constant motion of picking, harvesting, stooping under the savage sun, and then moving once again to the next field and two-room shack. They are seven, the mother, Petra, her five children, and Perfecto, a man nearly forty years older. Petra was aban-doned by her husband and is now pregnant by Perfecto, who befriended her and now longs to return home to Mexico.

Estrella, the daughter on the cusp of womanhood, is the novel's metaphoric star and center. Reminiscent of Tillie Olsen's Mazie in *Yonnondio*, Estrella inher-its her mother's capacity for *communitas*, an "intense camaraderie," a sense of lives intertwined, of collective responsibility and action crucial for definition and survival.[19] Petra takes in and cares for Alejo, poisoned by insecticides, and Estrella insists that they go to the clinic and then the hospital when it is evident that Alejo is dying. They enact what Brecht calls "the world's one hope," the indispensable "compassion of the oppressed for the oppressed."[20] Not only does Estrella emulate her mother's capacity for solidarity and compassion—"It's not good to leave people behind" (96)—she also claims another identity, a space beyond her mother's religious rituals and fear of authority. When she picks up a crowbar and commands an unsympathetic nurse in the clinic to return their money, she becomes a different Estrella. The obedient daughter acquiescing to her mother's superstitions falls away, and what emerges is another, warrior Estrella, fed up with the unheard and unseen condition of the working poor: "You talk and talk and talk to them and they ignore you. But you pick up a crowbar and break the pictures of their children, and all of a sudden they listen real fast" (151). Estrella acquires a consciousness grounded in a recognition of connection that is as profound as it is geologically deep: "She remembered the tar pits. Energy money, the fossilized bones of energy matter. How bones made oil and oil made gasoline. The oil was made from their bones, and it was their bones that kept the nurse's car from not halting on some highway, kept her on her way to Daisyfield to pick up her boys at six. It was their bones that kept the air conditioning in the cars humming, that kept them moving on the long dot-ted line on the map. Their bones. Why couldn't the nurse see that? Estrella had figured it out: the nurse owed *them* as much as they owed her" (148). Estrella's actions and words are a counterpoint and answer to Ayah's silence and the washerwoman's wrenching screaming. She demands reciprocal visibility. She is transformed not through the magic realism of the comic-book superwoman or the religious miracles of the virgin Mary, but through harnessing the power to act out of a consciousness of their collective condition.

Viramontes links a lyrical English and blunt Spanish to the language of the body, especially hands and feet. Hands are everywhere in this novel. Mother and daughter sleep "like two hands pressed together in prayer" (125). Perfecto's huge hands had veins like "swollen roots" (73). Hands signify commands, respect, authority, refusal, shame, affection, and the insistence on human connection despite the costs of brutal labor: "The twins ran to him, grabbed a thick hand each, their hands fleshy and moist. At first Perfecto recoiled his hands because he no longer liked the feel of the warm little knots of fingers tying into his; but they anchored a hand each anyway, clamping their grasp and laughing" (102).

Working-class bodies know weight intimately. They take up the burden of carrying, literally and symbolically. Perfecto could sense Alejo's imminent death "under his bare feet as he carried him" (101). Estrella carries the twins across the highway. They carry on, balancing on the tightrope of survival. Feet and legs have particular, poignant articulation: the mouth of a bottle pressed on the boil on the sole of Perfecto's foot, the relentlessly throbbing varicose veins in Petra's legs, Alejo's inverted toes from ill-fitting shoes. What lies under the feet of the mother's statute of Jesucristo are the children's essential papers, their birth certificates, testimony to their citizenship.[21] But the hands of the statue are removable, and the head breaks, and it is, in Viramontes' treatment, only a statue, not a protector. Under the feet of Jesus, the lowest of the low, they claim the epistemology that comes out of physical work and the use value of tools. Perfecto teaches Estrella the names and uses of the tools in his box: "She lifted the pry bar in her hand, felt the coolness of iron and power of function, weighted the significance it awarded her, and soon she came to understand how essential it was to know these things. That was when she began to read" (26). And Estrella responds later in the novel with the words Perfecto in his lifetime of labor had never heard: "Thank you" (155). In a barn's loft, the softened shakes crunching "beneath her bare feet like the serpent under the feet of Jesus" (175), Estrella reclaims "the soles of her feet, her hands, the shovel of her back, and the pounding bells of her heart" to call home her own people.

The dialectics of self and others, individual and community, acquiescence and resistance collide in the writing of Cherríe Moraga. Tools and bodies are inseparable from desire and the erotic. In the persona of Moraga's poem "The Welder," one can imagine Viramontes' Estrella and even young Sonya grown up and transformed not into alchemists or master builders, but into women whose sparks, though uncontrolled and unpredictable, mold and shape sturdy structures "that can support us / without fear / of trembling."[22] Self is not denied and community is not ignored. This is a working-class *bildung,* an alternative to capitalistic and individualistic "making it" on one hand, and a particularly gendered submission to authority and tradition on the other hand. It is a trajectory driven by Moraga's transformative vision of linkage between ontology and epistemology. She is the artist/welder taking up a torch that is restorative and liberatory.

Heroes and Saints, Moraga's riveting play about farm workers in the San Joaquin Valley, premiered in 1992.[23] In her notes to the script, Moraga explains that she was inspired by several 1988 events involving the expansion of regional struggles into national concerns: the grape boycott by the United Farm Workers (UFW), Cesar Chavez's hunger campaign, the brutal beating of Dolores Huerta, the recognition of a cancer cluster in the town of McFarland that particularly affected children, and the subsequent UFW documentary about the effects of pesticide poisoning, *The Wrath of Grapes* (89). The core of the play is a disembodied, brilliant, pink, talking head—Cerezita (little cherry). Imagine a head resting on a draped platform, on rollers, whose mobility is controlled by the head's chin. What is perhaps harder to imagine is this head as more than a talking symbol, a choral commentator, talisman, or emblem. This head whose body was stolen in the womb because her mother picked fruit in pesticide-drenched fields is the intellectual center of the play. Cerezita is an organic intellectual with desires, sight, and insight. She seeks engagement and exposure, not concealment. She insists on visibility and the labor epistemology of her missing, phantom body. Knowledge of how the fruit we enjoy is connected to the deformed and stolen bodies of children should *discomfort* us. She refuses to be tongue-tied; using her tongue, her "most faithful organ" (108), she wants to be seen and heard: "The trick is to be noticed" (114).

Moraga mixes moments of purposeful discomfort, of eye-averting unease, with the mundane. In scene 1 it is nearly dawn in a vineyard, and the audience watches as a group of skull-masked children in the distance erect a small crucifix upon which is draped the dead body of an insecticide-poisoned child. This tableau is immediately juxtaposed with a news report titled "Hispanic California" from an airheaded Channel 5 reporter whose first words are "Bob, is my hair okay?" The Hispanic reporter, herself a token, who barely understands Spanish, comments on the "crime" of displaying the children's bodies, not the causal conditions of their deaths. She blocks criticism of the growers with a trivializing question about Cerezita's name. Moraga insists on a militant visibility: "If you put the children in the ground, the world forgets them. Who's gointu see them, buried in the dirt?" (92–95).

Moraga's play both resists and reclaims representations of the California landscape as edenic. She works into her text the crucial connection, articulated in Don Mitchell's important *The Lie of the Land,* of landscape to labor.[24] Describing the California setting in relation to the cheaply assembled "casas de carton" built in Love Canal style on a waste dump (103),[25] Moraga draws distinctions between land and dirt: "What was once land has become dirt, over-worked dirt, overirrigated dirt, injected with deadly doses of chemicals and vio-lated by every manner of ground- and back-breaking machinery" (91). As Mitchell makes clear, this is not the chic postmodern Baudrillardian "hypermo-bility" of privileged California, but an economic stasis, even bondage, of labor to land.[26] Poison is what is held in common—poisoned houses, water, children, and hope.

Moraga also illuminates a dialectic between the conservative Dolores (single mother of Cerezita, Yolanda, and Mario and grandmother of the dying baby, Evalina), and her neighbor, the activist Amparo. Dolores, like Rosa in the film *Bread and Roses,* wants to conserve and preserve what she has left. Although Roman Catholic, she is drawn to the sensuous Pentecostal storefront church, and wants to elevate Cerezita as an unseen saint. Rather than let her be the canary in the mine signaling imminent danger, Dolores wants to put a cloth over Cerezita's cage and hide her from public gaze (125).[27] As she is intolerant of her son's homosexuality, she honors a familial heterosexuality that has failed her. In contrast, Amparo, an extroverted version of *Salt of the Earth*'s Esperanza, embraces a collective motherhood independent of biological reproduction. Modeled on two organizers against pesticide poisoning, Marta Salinas and Dolores Huerta, Amparo summons her courage to address a crowd of protestors. She gives a lengthy speech worthy of serious study. Moraga shows the recipro-cal relationship between speaker and crowd, how each draws courage from the other. Amparo uses the language of entrapment and prisons[28] to argue that they are less protected in their poisoned homes than when, as migrant workers' chil-dren, they slept "under the pertection de las estrellas" (111). Doña Amparo's speech illuminates how the community's children are the canaries in the mine: "Look into your children's faces. They tell you the truth" (111). Evoking the past, pointing to the loss of a future, and speaking to the present necessity for resistance, Amparo connects the privately lived life with structural and histori-cal oppression. She is the community's mapmaker, charting the deformities, cancers, tumors, miscarriages, and assorted intestinal problems. Amparo, now in her public persona as founder of Mothers for McLaughlin (McFarland), leads the reading of the names of dead children and the protest for reimbursement and relocation to an environmentally safe community (132–133) and, like Dolores Huerta, is severely beaten by the police.

Heroes and Saints climaxes in a definitional ceremony in which Cerezita, draped in the veil of the La Virgen de Guadalupe, embodies her mother's reli-giosity and Amparo's activism as she becomes the welder, sparking, quite liter-ally, the conflagration of the vineyards.[29] Cerezita's action and sacrifice embody Moraga's ethos of democratic visibility and the larger intent of working-class studies: "Nobody's dying should be invisible" (139). Working-class literature is not about a modernist "making it new" or postmodernist "making it indeter-minate," but rather a project of "making it visible." This leads to a much more complex recognition of the shaping force of economic circumstances intertwined with sexuality, race, gender, and place in the formation of culture.

The identities that emerge in the writing of Silko, Viramontes, and Moraga are, in Manuel Castells's term, "resistance identities," voices in opposition to forces of domination and oppression. Working-class studies provides a space where such oppositional identities can be joined to other devalued identities in other locations and cultural contexts to construct what Castells calls "project identities."[30] This is a larger edifice, a collective subjectivity, held together by the mortar of labor. This project has as its common text the inscription of work on the human body. The common struggle is justice. Perhaps working-class studies can be like Estrella's crowbar, a tool to break up the invisibility of the labor pipeline that serves the owning class. It could serve as an arena where bodies inscribed by work can discern each other.

However, such a project must always be dialectically challenged. It is not enough to profess to know an other through a text. Such a transformative project cannot be justly imagined without a recognition of experiential unknowability, especially for the reader whose body is not taxed by labor. Through what I call "respectful not knowing" the assumed "we" is necessarily undermined. Methodologically, the power of institutional language must bow to the materiality of lived conditions and limited choices. John Berger illuminates this crucial distinction:

> To try to understand the experience of another it is necessary to dismantle the world as seen from one's own place within it, and to reassemble it as seen from his. For example, to understand a given choice another makes, one must face in imagination the lack of choices which may confront and deny him. The well-fed are incapable of understanding the choices of the under-fed. The world has to be dismantled and re-assembled in order to be able to grasp, however clumsily, the experience of another. To talk of entering the other's subjectivity is misleading. The subjectivity of another does not simply constitute a different interior attitude to the same exterior facts. The constellation of facts, of which he is the centre, is different.[31]

Working-class studies, as a polyphonic project, has the potential of Moraga's welder, illuminating and fusing multivoiced subjectivity with exterior facts, forging links between stasis and motion, culture and power—but only if it sustains a consciousness of its grounding in human labor.

I may paint flat but I don't think flat.   —*Ralph Fasanella*

Ralph Fasanella

Epic Painter of the Working Class

Self-taught, working-class artist Ralph Fasanella (1914–1997) painted the lives, work, neighborhoods, political struggles, and values of working-class people (mostly New Yorkers) in a broad context of American history and culture for more than fifty years. Fasanella once commented, "My paintings look easy, but they're very complicated. That's why they're so big; that's why people like them."[1] Exuberant, packed, compressed, and haunted by parents' lives, neighborhoods, union struggles, and historical events, Fasanella's paintings challenge canonical categories of art history and raise questions about class and aesthetic judgments.

In the millennial year 2000 the Whitney Museum of American Art presented "The American Century in Art and Culture," staged in two consecutive segments covering 1900 to 1950 and 1950 to 2000, respectively. Somewhat unwieldy, these multifaceted exhibits claimed to present manifestations of American art in their "broader societal contexts," and to offer "examples and analyses of developments in all arts, high and low, visual as well as literary and musical."[2] Whether considered high, low, somewhere in the middle, or, most likely, not considered at all, the paintings of Ralph Fasanella were not included in this celebrated retrospective. While my intent is to center Fasanella's work rather than quarrel with the Whitney, I do question the unacknowledged class biases that exclude working-class cultural and political representation and the absence of a theoretical vocabulary that addresses working-class aesthetics. The Whitney's omission of Fasanella's paintings reflects the elision and neglect of a larger working-class narrative in the cultural legacy of Americans.

Fasanella's capacious visual imagination infuses energy, movement, voice, action, and a kind of grace onto his canvases. But his paintings are not the nostalgic and static scenes of greeting-card folk art. "Fasanella is not an easy artist for some people, not because his work is inaccessible, but because it is too accessible. . . . If, as some people believe, folk art is a distillation of happy memories of a bucolic past, then Fasanella doesn't fit the bill. If folk art is the expression of the most important human passions in a form that transcends the rigid canons of academic art, then Fasanella must stand as one of the most important creative forces of our time," remark art historians Jay Johnson and William C. Ketchum.[3]

Fasanella does fit the bill of an epical painter of working-class life, indeed, in a broader sense, of American history, and very well. He claims a place within any literary study of working-class culture because he is a bard, a great visual storyteller. His paintings invite literary analogies—epic (in a collective sense), bardic (as visual troubadour telling a communal story), and narrative (in a non-linear juxtaposition of the public and private). And what they tell is not a flat tale, nor are Fasanella's paintings solely about individual expression. Bernarda Bryson Shahn's comments on using literary terms to describe Ben Shahn's artistry apply to Fasanella as well: "His [Ben Shahn's] art has, I believe, more than anything else, the character of literature, an entirely visual one. Now epic, now lyric, it is concerned with organization, with form and with style; but it is particularly in the variety of content, its wealth of reference and imagination, and its focus on man that it can justly be called a visual literature."[4]

Fasanella is also an architect, a designer and builder, whose massive canvases resemble (and assemble) the relationship of parts to whole as do great literary epics (and medieval cathedrals or modern skyscrapers?). Reading Fasanella's paintings as narratives expands classical definitions of the heroic and the epical, visually transforming these canonical literary forms into a wider narrative that includes the heroism of survival and struggle. In so doing he affirms the legitimacy of emotional knowledge and an epistemology grounded in workers' lives. He constructs, to draw on Bakhtinian language I have employed before, an architectonics, a set of relationships and tensions between parts and the whole.[5] His paintings are, in a Bakhtinian sense, "aesthetic events" (xxiv), each actively part of a larger vision that conveys the interconnectivity of parts to whole as the painter orchestrates and builds, shouts and wails, this epical story.

Fasanella practices a working-class aesthetic of relationality and solidarity. Whether the scene is a baseball diamond, a family gathered around a kitchen table, a union meeting, a shop floor, a march or demonstration, Fasanella uses the façades that separate and isolate to create an imaginary that while acknowledging oppression, suggests individual and societal possibility and agency. The human figures in his paintings appear diminutive in relation to the powerful structures of work, church, and state that dominate them, but through his painterly body gestures and facial expressions, Fasanella affirms working-class lives as complex and varied, not small. He recognizes individuals, but is not fixated on them. While painting may have been a solitary act (although he seemed capable of painting with a lot of commotion around him), the outcome is communal and grounded in language, history, place, struggle, and joy of life. "Life is together," he once commented. "Fighting together, playing stickball together. People need each other . . . the *charge* of life, the *play* of life, comes with other people, with all its weakness, too."[6] As a political activist and union organizer, he was not naïve about the weaknesses either.

Fasanella paints the story of lived experience through representational gestures—the sway of a man's body, the way a woman puts her hands to her face, the resignation in the shoulders of people at machines, and the claimed relaxation of Sunday afternoon. He accumulates detail, not as so much urban flotsam and jetsam, but as part of the integrated rhythm of daily existence. He offers miniature portraits, not voyeuristic glimpses. His massive paintings are still *and* dynamic; people observe *and* act. Tightly structured and divided, Fasanella's paintings show the connections and relationships of working-class lived experience, both at home and at work. Many groups may claim Fasanella as their own—immigrants (particularly Italians), labor unions, aficionados of city space, especially that of New York City. He belongs to all of them, yet evokes a larger identity of working-class solidarity. His paintings are not just about labor or politics or baseball or the great New York City, but the integration of all these things.

Because he is painting from inside working-class experience, personally and politically, Fasanella achieves a visual vocabulary of representation that reveals without violating, objectifying, or colonizing his subjects. His human figures are frequently presented as attentive *watchers*—of baseball games, parades, labor marches, of their neighborhood kids—as well as involved *listeners*—to political speeches, union reports, and each other. While his subjects emerge out of his own experiences as a worker, union organizer, and political activist, these experiences are often presented within a suggested larger context, an architectonics of relationships and institutional structures. His 1971 painting *Sperry Organizing Committee* pays homage—not to bureaucratic union structure—but to the small storefronts and union halls that are/were the foundation of the industrial union movement. As a field organizer (between 1938 and 1945) for the UE (United Electrical, Radio, and Machine Workers of America), Fasanella helped unionize the Sperry Gyroscope Company in Brooklyn. In *Morey Machine Shop* (1953) he presents the shop floor of a defense industry plant where he washed machine parts during the Korean War and was a UE shop steward.[7]

Fasanella's paintings stand powerfully alone, but viewed as a body of work they narrate episodes or segments in an epical working-class story. In dialogue with the vibrancy of *Sunday Afternoon* (1953), the dark *Wall Street* (1947) appears static. The street is nearly people-less except for the lone cop on the corner. Trinity Church, with its stained-glass windows and tiny graveyard of white crosses, squeezed between the slate, tomblike buildings, is less refuge than reminder of the human costs in the accumulation of great wealth. In contrast, *Sunday Afternoon* exudes activity, centering on Fasanella's favorite street game, stickball. A city neighborhood depicting people smoking, touching, embracing, and acting—a kid climbing onto his father's shoulders, girls jumping rope double dip, buxom madonnas observing the street action, men kibitzing on the corner, a woman pushing a baby stroller, a guy reading the newspaper, kids sitting on a stoop—the painting veritably hums, "Hey, time off! It's Sunday afternoon."

The paintings often evoke music and performance: Italian folk songs in *Festa* and *May Day*, opera in the sweep and passion of his large canvases (such as

Lawrence 1912, "The Bread and Roses Strike"). Texts and voice are integral to Fasanella's visual imagery as well. Fasanella writes back in his paintings through his striking intertextual topography. Texts are integrated into the visual geography through newspaper headlines, banners, slogans, shop signs, advertisements, street signs, mottoes, graffiti, police barricades, union posters, as well as his frequent inclusion of books.[8] Newspaper headlines surround the women garment workers in *Dress Shop* (1970), announcing (nonchronologically) "Nixon Slides In," "RFK Wins California," "King Killed," "Flash President Shot Dallas," reminiscent of the news flashes New Yorkers might see in Times Square. This is a personal, affectionate, perhaps sentimental, painting depicting his mother and sister as seamstresses, but also remembering, in a memorial sign, the fallen Triangle Shirtwaist workers of 1911.

Fasanella often inserts, ironically, consumer messages, slogans, and ads, particularly as they emerged in the postwar 1950s. He appropriates signage, especially the very banality and repetition of ads, for his own political and artistic witnessing. The word *save*, for example, assumes multiple, often ironic, meanings in *McCarthy Press* (1963), which documents through a newspaper pyramid the execution of Ethel and Julius Rosenberg. Embedded in the red sky are advertisements urging consumers to "SAVE," as well as a floating red cross topped with a framed blue religious "SAVE." At the lower left a weeping crowd surrounds a coffin, and a flowered gravesite is arched with "Save the Rosenbergs." The pyramid echoes the pyramidal eye of the great seal on the back of a dollar bill. Eyes of constant surveillance peer out. Fasanella's paintings, depicting the politically oppressive McCarthy period, failed to reach an audience. Or, perhaps better stated, an audience failed to see them. Fasanella believed that critics and galleries ignored him because of the political content of his paintings: "They wouldn't touch them [these paintings] with a ten-foot pole."[9]

Always conscious of praxis, of the relationship of words to actions, the autodidactic Fasanella includes books in his paintings not as static objects, but as the enclosures of powerful, transformative ideas situated in a context of progressive social change. In his unfinished triptych, *Farewell Comrade—The End of the Cold War* (1992–1997), the embalmed body of Lenin rests surrounded by books, his own, *What Is to Be Done?*, as well as those of a hit parade of leftist writers (Arthur Miller, Upton Sinclair, John Reed, Jack London, Bertolt Brecht) and labor and political leaders (Fidel Castro, Mahatma Gandhi, Martin Luther King, Cesar Chavez, Joe Hill, Vito Marcantonio). Fasanella's paintings voice political critique, but refuse postmodern cynicism or posthistorical triumphalism. Never enamoured by institutions, political parties, or union bureaucracies, Fasanella uses signage and textuality to announce the social and material costs of the Cold War mentality: "It Cost U.S.A. 90 Billion $ to *topple* Soviet Union," and "Reagan Triples Deficit with Military." *Farewell Comrade* is as much about the dearth of democratic political leadership nationally and internationally as it is an homage to Lenin. It also echoes a persistent Fasanella concern about the disconnection between the intellectual "movement people" and the working-class masses, as well as the indifference of elite society to the formation of working-class culture.

Grab is a prototypical Fasanella word—an intuitive gesture, a spark, a seizing of meaning through accumulative paint strokes. He's after the process of living—the struggle and pleasure of working out the daily dialectic between individuality and community, freedom and restraint (the street-smart truant and the working stiff), the risks of resistance and the weight of dominant structures, and the search for indigenous heroic models—the radical congressman Vito Marcantonio instead of the phony Horatio Alger.[10] He breaks through elite culture's aesthetic still-life sensibility and unabashedly claims a political vision—a verb, an action, not a doctrine—that acknowledges the possibilities of worker democracy. Ralph Fasanella taught himself how to grab the energy of working-class life, the joy and the grief, to narrate something larger, more public and communal.

In the complex and enormously detailed *Modern Times* (1966) Fasanella portrays class divisions through textured juxtapositions.[11] Carefully groomed ladies lunch inside a corporate museum, while outside, symbolically positioned, a statue of a working stiff literally holds up the world. More sweeping in scope than Charlie Chaplin's 1936 film *Modern Times,* Fasanella's work is less concerned with the Tayloristic measuring of workers' motions and more focused on presenting the technological linkages of modern times. Fasanella disrupts linear time and offers instead an imaginative simultaneity of experiential and historical time, reminiscent of Arthur Miller's technique of constructing a shifting consciousness of internal and external conversations for Willy Loman in *Death of a Salesman.* In Fasanella's vision, historical circumstances take precedence over individual psyches. He presents technological tools as linked to dominant technological systems of war and death—the processing of Vietnam vets, the returning coffins in neat rows, the waiting military planes ready to take on board the next shipment of raw recruits, and the hovering black helicopter in front of a blazing red sky. Below a garish green and black institution of modern art and modern war technology are some Vietnam War protestors burning their draft cards and others being dragged into police vans. People stroll by, barely gazing at the demonstrators. Through his painterly body language Fasanella's diminutive figures convey convenient obtuseness. Instead of mutual and democratic visibility, we have, as the painting demonstrates, technologized blind spots. In contrast, Fasanella sympathetically portrays both the war protestors and the soldiers. The painter's omniscient hand affirms the sacrifice of the vets with the phrase "Welcome Home Boys" and acknowledges the risks of the draft card burners with "Refuse the Draft." After all, these are the little guys. What Fasanella does expose is the permeable line barely separating art and culture (the modern art museum with its gray paintings of war and destruction) from war and destruction (the war industry, i.e., the corporate/government/technical

liaisons producing the knowledge of destruction). And yet, perhaps dialectically, perhaps out of his own quirky humor, Fasanella tells us there's more. A
naval aircraft carrier segues into a baseball stadium. The returning GIs, including a Black soldier with an amputated leg, are surrounded by an ice cream ven-
dor and a guy on what looks like a tractor. A 25-cent rocket amusement ride is
embedded with a baseball catcher positioned below a 7 UP ad, and bursting
from the rocket's cone is a huge, signed baseball surrounded by reverential
flames. Centrally located in the painting are a long shot and close-up of a visiting Pope celebrating mass, surrounded by his religious "fans" as well as attentive outfielders. A Blakean cultural activist, Fasanella dismantles hierarchies as
he visually rebuilds them. The only unoccupied space on this large canvas (104
x 50) is on the top floor of the art museum where unviewed abstract paintings
hang—not Fasanellas.

Some biographical sketches present Fasanella's life in the patronizing tone
used toward the discovered urban exotic.[12] I wonder if this is an unacknowledged strategy on the part of the critic to deflect recognition of how class biases
and perspectives shape aesthetic judgments. Unless presented in the tonalities
of a Hallmark greeting card, or shown in a context of race or ethnic identity, the
diversity of working-class experience rarely has a cultural frame of reference in
the dominant culture. Fasanella's capacious paintings challenge and de-center
elite artistic sensibilities and re-center working-class experience. This is a critical perceptual difference in appreciating his work, which is not to say that
there's a gap between his private life and his work—hardly.

The fourth of six children of Ginevre and Giuseppe Fasanella, Southern Italian immigrants, Ralph embraced the culture and fought the restrictions of
working-class, Southern Italian, New York City neighborhood life. A tough
street kid, baseball fanatic, and frequent truant, Ralph did time at a Catholic
"reform" school, later depicted from memory in *Protectory Games* (1962) and
Lineup at the Protectory (1961). This imposition of rigid order, discipline, and
control resurfaces as a theme of ominous surveillance in many of his paintings,
especially during the McCarthy period.

Joe Fasanella, the iconic crucified iceman in several of his paintings, delivered ice with reluctant help from his son Ralph.[13] In *Iceman Crucified (2)*, the
crucified Joe Fasanella is not Christ incarnate, but Joe/Jesus the proletarian. By
appropriating the crucifixion, Fasanella answers the premodern, Christian narrative of sacrifice, redemption, and otherworldliness with a gritty, modern,
industrial story of immigration, struggle, and for some—defeat.

In his great, open, and expansive painting, *Family Supper* (1972), Fasanella
centers his beloved mother, a skilled buttonhole maker, trade unionist, and
political activist. Ginevre, in dialectical relationship to Joe, is literate, resourceful, skilled, and, ultimately, the family provider. The setting is the kitchen of
their apartment at 173 Sullivan Street. The interior table is set for a continuing
ritual—coffee, pastries, fruit, talk. Seated around the oval table the figures may

seem static, but that would be a false impression. It is the viewer's task to imagine the loud conversations and the friendly family fight to be heard. These are the linguistic rhythms of working-class lives. Telling the family story through the careful placement of artifacts suggests the larger historical narrative. The trundle bed indicates tight sleeping quarters. The immigrant's trunk labeled with the flag of Italy reveals not only Fasanella's parents' arrival, but the emptying-out of Southern Italy between 1880 and 1924. The wine, olive oil, cheese grater, pasta pot, espresso cups, and tomato cans are basics not just

Ralph Fasanella, *Iceman Crucified (2)*. Courtesy of Eva Fasanella.

for physical survival, but for the continuance of culture. The placement of objects—like a Whitmanian catalog—Victrola, trundle sewing machine, framed family photos, school books, vase, comb, brush, and the ubiquitous alarm clock (signifying the omnipresent shadow of work), expands the painting beyond the ethnicity of Italian immigration into a larger narrative of working-class lived experience. Fasanella once remarked, "I never found hopelessness in the working people. Most of the homes were clean and they loved little doodads,

Ralph Fasanella, *Family Supper.* Courtesy of Eva Fasanella.

gadgets. There was always something that would sparkle. In their work these people might be nothing, rejected, empty; the only way they could survive was in their home, having positive colors."[14] Further, *Family Supper* is an homage not just to Ginevre, but to women as sustainers of family and culture, and is suggestive of Ralph's own reliance on his sister Tess and his wife, Eva, so that he could paint. His father's iron ice tongs are transformed into the fluid line of the clothesline.

The setting of *Family Supper* evokes *storia*, public and private, history and narrative. Culture marks every corner. Fasanella enacts his aesthetics of relationality, of human beings connected to each other in time and place. It is *not*, as John Berger avers in his essay, "Fasanella and the City," about the absence of interiority. Berger writes, "The windows *present* the life or lives of their building. They present their interiors in such as way as to show they were never interiors. Nothing has an interior. Everything is exteriority."[15] In this case, John Berger (whose work I admire) gets it wrong. He confuses privacy, an entitlement of economic privilege, with interiority, which is not dependent on physical space. But he is correct that the Fasanella message embedded into the red bricks of the apartment building, "Lest We Forget" is not about nostalgia. It is a reminder that the city and the kitchen table are both deeply historical. Fasanella commented, "In our house, very few little books we had, and our knowledge was at the table."[16]

Quitting institutional school in the eighth grade, Fasanella's education came through the public libraries and his developing epistemology as a union organizer, factory worker, and political activist. In the 1930s he helped his mother publish a small Italian-language antifascist newspaper. In 1937 and 1938 he joined the Abraham Lincoln Brigade to fight fascism in Spain. Fasanella may have been uneasy with middle-class intellectuality, but he was always aware of his own capacious visual imagination. "Now it didn't come from nowhere. It comes from somewhere. I always had images as a kid, you know? Walking around and seeing figures and constant stories all the time. And when I worked in jobs full of monotony I was making ideas in my mind."[17] The public story told by Fasanella, and repeated in articles and books about his life, is that he took up drawing and painting at the suggestion of a friend to relieve what appeared to be arthritis in his hands. A good story, and I have no reason to distrust its credibility, but it raises questions about the conditions and circumstances working-class artists face, a more complicated situation than a chosen bohemian poverty. Artists from the working class do not necessarily have permission from their families and communities—never mind a sense of entitlement or economic independence—to claim for themselves the name "artist." And so, drawing eases the pain in the fingers, yes, so it does.

By the mid-1940s, and with the support of his brothers and his sister Tess, Fasanella structured his days around painting, reading, listening to jazz, and work. In 1950 he married Eva Lazorek, a schoolteacher, and they parented two children. With Eva's steady income, pumping gas at his brothers' filling stations, and occasional factory work where he wasn't blacklisted, Fasanella sustained a routine of painting and working. Postwar McCarthyism and reactionary politics obscured Fasanella not only from artistic fame, but from his working-class audience, but he kept painting. He broke into public awareness in 1972 with Nicholas Pileggi's *New York* magazine cover story, "Portrait of the Artist as a Garage Attendant in the Bronx," followed in 1973 by Patrick Watson's book *Fasanella's City*.[18]

In the mid-1970s, restless with the bucolic surroundings of his new suburban house in Westchester County, Fasanella began thinking about a series of paintings on the history of the working class in America. Inspired in part by William Cahn's book on Lawrence, *Mill Town* (1954), Fasanella found his historic subject in the great Lawrence Bread and Roses textile mill strike of 1912 and its compelling history of interethnic solidarity. In 1975 he temporarily rented a YMCA room in downtown Lawrence and began talking, walking, studying, literally absorbing the history of Lawrence, remarking, "I'm trying to grab this thing [Lawrence] physically and emotionally."[19] Out of that immersion came a series of canvases, initially of the mills and the technology of cloth production (*Mill Workers—Lower Pacific Mill*, 1977, and *Mill Town—Weaving Department*, 1976), culminating in a powerful narrative of historical labor struggle—the working conditions, the dominant, built environment of factories and bridges, the use of police and militia against their own class, the interethnic solidarity of men, women, and children, and the leadership of the IWW (*Lawrence 1912, "The Bread and Roses Strike,"* 1977, and *The Great Strike*, 1978). These paintings restore the event, but also suggest the elision of working-class history, subsequent loss of jobs, and fear of reprisals for union organizing, as well as question the ownership of history. With these paintings Fasanella engages a reciprocal cultural practice: the historic events produce the paintings; the painter witnesses and re-presents history.

All artists face problems of audience, of literally getting the work out to be seen or heard or read. Working-class artists, though, face more complicated problems of access. They have not been schooled in the trade of professional connections; they don't necessarily speak the language of institutions. But they have the power of their work. When, after painting in obscurity for more than two decades, Fasanella's paintings were "discovered" in the *New York* magazine article, he finally had buyers who could offer prices far beyond the yearly wages of Fasanella's working-class subjects. Understandably, after pumping gas in his brothers' filling station for so many years, Fasanella must have welcomed not only the appreciation of his work, but the possibility of some economic freedom. On the other hand, once the paintings are collected and privatized, where is the working-class audience? Are working-class subjects in these paintings then colonized and corralled in the living rooms of the economic elite? Eva and Ralph Fasanella addressed this problem with the help of Ron Carver, a union and community organizer who founded Public Domain to raise money to purchase Fasanellas from private collectors and place them in public spaces. *Family Supper* is now appropriately at the Ellis Island Immigration Museum. *The Great Strike* was purchased by union donations and given to Congress. It hung for years in the hearing room for the House Subcommittee on Labor and Education until it was removed when the Republicans regained the majority (also removing *Labor* from the committee's name). *Subway Riders* (1950) was installed in 1996 under Plexiglas in the subway station at Fifth Avenue and Fifty-third Street. Fasanella posters, note cards, book covers, and Web sites are accessible in part because of the labor politics of the Fasanellas. This is not only about building a Fasanella commercial industry. Rather, it is about recognition of the public purpose of his art, how it rouses consciousness of working-class history and labor struggles. In the photo below Fasanella signs posters to support Yale University clerical workers.[20]

Four years after Fasanella's death in 1997, the New York State Historical Association in Cooperstown, New York, presented a major retrospective of his work curated by Fasanella biographer Paul D'Ambrosio. Given his great love of baseball as represented in many paintings of the game itself whether played in Yankee Stadium or on a neighborhood sandlot, Cooperstown was a natural setting

Margret Hofmeister, *Yale Graduation Rally*, 1996
R. Fasanella sigining posters at "The People's Commencement," Yale University, May 27, 1996. Courtesy of the photographer.

to launch this important exhibit.[21] I would imagine that a goodly number of Fasanella fans traveled to Cooperstown for the chance to see so many of his works in one venue. Others, perhaps visitors to the Baseball Hall of Fame or attendants at Glimmerglass summer opera, may have stumbled on this exhibit as tourists. I overheard one viewer in July of 2001 exclaim, "What a mind this man had!" and another opine, "He was very opinionated, not very tolerant of what he didn't agree with."

Ralph Fasanella was very opinionated, particularly about injustice. His working-class directness, profane idiom, humor, grace, and affection for his subjects can easily distract our attention away from the paintings and onto his biography. What is important is the interrelationship between experience and expression. In many of his paintings, Fasanella includes, perhaps more for himself than his audience, images or composites of family and friends (for example, his mother and sister working in *Dress Shop*) and as a visual signature, images of himself drawing, reading the newspaper, delivering ice and later a refrigerator. These painterly snapshots are part of the Fasanella wit and playfulness ("Ralph loves [his daughter] Gina"), loving filaments of connection, not obsessive self-referential statements.

Fasanella's art narrates working-class lived experience in relation to public history through an aesthetics of relationality and solidarity. Behind the brick walls and curtained windows, Fasanella reveals what Whitman calls "adhesiveness," that is, a "love that fuses, ties and aggregates," a sense of connection—to each other, to jobs, to place, to current events, and to history—that, like it or not, raucous or joyful, comprises working-class lives.[22] It is a cultural expression that recognizes individuals, but is not fixated on, as Whitman writes, "individualism which isolates" (477). Fasanella's paintings are local and historical, lyrical and documentary, and grounded in a sustained belief in the catalytic potential of art. He is a master of visual literature as well as a visual historian, although he never realized his grand plan for a series of paintings documenting labor from colonial times to the present.[23]

Working-class art, if it is recognized at all, is often dismissed by critics as nostalgic and sentimental. Unacknowledged are the critic's own bourgeois sensibilities and assumptions, a discomfort with the untidy, with a spilling over of sentiment. In *The Conspiracy of Good Taste*, Stefan Szczelkun writes forcefully of the oppression of classism on working-class people: "What I learned was the central and murderous denial of our intellectual capacity which is at the heartless core of class oppression" (1).[24] Calling for a "liberatory people-oriented culture" (1), Szczelkun urges working-class people to reconnect "to the hidden working class personal and cultural histories that produced us and find ways to heal ourselves from the terrible legacy of hurt left by class oppression" (4).

Repeatedly in working-class literature characters voice the frustration of their invisibility as human beings to the bosses of the dominant society. It is the job—and I use that word deliberately—as well as the joy and risk of the working-class artist to illuminate working-class epistemology—not as an essentialized single entity but in all its complexity and difference as lived experience. It is risky because the revelation is open to ridicule, to misreadings, and to false bourgeois assumptions. It is also painful because of the necessary reliving of loss, grief, and suffering. The working-class artist/survivor forges cultural expressions that expand loss and grief from the private to the collective and historical.

Fasanella exposes concealed power and testifies to workers' lives. His own life's work constructs a covenant, a testament for the working class. Sometimes playfully, and often didactically, he speaks to the democratic potential of art: rouse consciousness, affirm experience, and become a tool to build a just world. From his Greenwich Village neighborhood to Lenin's tomb, Fasanella's democratic vision never faltered:

> And the point I'm trying to make is, great human leaders have this compassion. . . . But strong guys like Rockefeller and these fucking head men! And a lot of movement people—worried about causes, not worried about people. You've got to have that feeling. It's a kind of artistry."[25]

Fasanella rejected the term "primitive" artist. The term "outsider" art does not apply either, faulty in its assumptions about a center that Fasanella was all too ready to disrupt. Fasanella preferred the simple (but not simplistic) "self-taught." But that too only tells part of the story because, as Fasanella would most likely acknowledge, he taught himself to paint in a technically masterful way, but he relied on his family, friends, block, neighborhood, city, and labor legacy to inspire the work itself, to give expression to his own working-class people. Culture emerges out of reciprocity and imagined and lived solidarity. Perhaps the best way to describe Ralph Fasanella's visual gifts is to say, "communally taught."

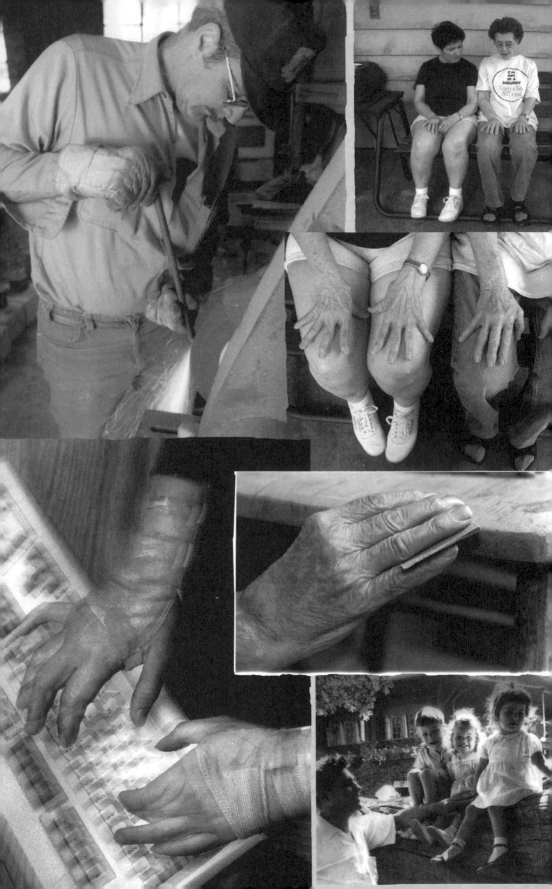

Technologies

On Laboring Bodies

How is the laboring body situated within technological systems of imprisonment, enclosure, exposure, and production? I consider that complicated question by beginning with a tour of a supermax, a maximum security prison. From this brief glimpse into what it means to "do time," I move into various speed zones, short reflections that zigzag from the narratives of "net-slaves" in *Gig* and computer builders in Tracy Kidder's *The Soul of a New Machine,* to time travel in Octavia Butler's *Kindred.* Race and gendered systems of technological production are integral to Butler's depiction of a contemporary Black woman pulled back in time to an antebellum plantation. Tours also take readers into industrial time zones, figuring as narrative strategies to lead bourgeois readers up the dolorous mountain to watch the birthing of paper from bachelors' rags to finished foolscap in Melville's "The Tartarus of Maids," or down into the fog and muck and darkness of Rebecca Harding Davis's *Life in the Iron Mills.* From outsider looking in to insider looking out, the voices from Benita Eisler's *The Lowell Offering* suggest the ambivalence of labor, especially for young women factory operatives. The last speed zone crosses international borders and focuses on the constructive and destructive potential of technology in Christa Wolf's *Accident.* This meditation on the prowess of a surgeon's hands performing delicate brain surgery occurs in the immediate aftermath of the Chernobyl explosion in April 1986 as the fallout drifts over central Europe. Through intricate intertextuality, Wolf opens her text to the reader's own blind spots. But in my reading, the exclusion of the fate of the Chernobyl firemen signifies other class blind spots in the writer's own literary imagination.

Preface: The Prison Tour

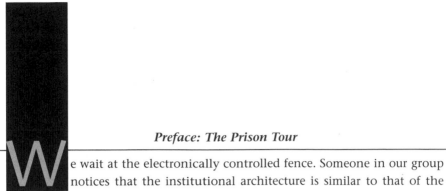

e wait at the electronically controlled fence. Someone in our group notices that the institutional architecture is similar to that of the California campus where he was a student. But this is no college campus. This is a state-of-the-art, $65-million, three-year-old, maximum-security Ohio State penitentiary. A supermax. Inside are incarcerated men, determined by a combination of their own actions and the prison system to be unsafe prisoners. Almost all are Black men. We are a touring group of professors waiting to be admitted. Some of the prisoners can see us from their cells, but we cannot see them. It is a hazy-blue-sky May day in 2001.

Once inside, the deputy warden welcomes us. We listen to his brief lecture; some of us take notes (having learned long ago how to be good students). He is articulate and patient with our questions, acknowledging the lawsuit pending against the prison.[1] Mostly, he describes the penal efficiency of this supermax. He does not let us forget that it houses the most dangerous inmates. We can safely tour it because it is has the best security technology in the world. Cameras are everywhere. We pass through the metal detector after handing over our various cards of identification. We are given visiting tags and march through the first waiting area. One door electronically closes behind us before the next one opens. We are watched constantly. The deputy warden is new to the job. The computer system that recognizes handprints has not yet integrated his hand into the system. He holds up his I.D. card to a smoky glass frame we cannot penetrate.

The halls and walkways are institutional gray with an occasional line of color. The guards we encounter are cheerful, friendly, well groomed. We walk down steps to the receiving area. A clean warehouse. The deputy describes the process of depositing a prisoner and the awesome capacity of the institutional armory (weapons that will never be needed because this is a supermax). We see the waiting cells, the processing arena, the scale (prisoners are weighed at least once a month). Then we proceed toward a vacant pod. The theorists in the crowd mumble, "panopticon." On the way we hear the voices of prisoners— talking to each other, yelling at us, making noises at the professorial tour.

Every man has his own cell in which he exists for twenty-three hours a day. The cells are 7 x 14 feet with built-in compartments for sleeping and minimal living. They are allowed one narcotic, a stripped-down television, in their cells. Fluorescent lights remain on twenty-four hours a day. The deputy warden says they are dimmed at night. He does not say how much. As far as I can tell, the prisoners do not have jobs. For one hour a day, depending on behavior, each prisoner may shower and exercise. All movement is shackled movement. The exercise room is about the size of a cell and is adjacent to the other cells in the pod. A four-inch-wide barred opening constitutes fresh air and outdoor exercise. The deputy warden politely answers my questions about whether the inmates can domesticate their spaces in any way, with their own artwork, perhaps. The answer is no. I ask about visiting hours. He promises to show the space used for visitors, but somehow we don't get to that. No physical contact is allowed. Those prisoners considered most dangerous can visit only with lawyers and clergy. I ask about mental illness as I feel this gray place penetrate my skin. The deputy warden says that inmates receive the best medical care and eat well-prepared food. "If I had to be incarcerated," he concludes, "this is where I'd want to be." No one responds.

The tour ends. We talking professors are subdued. We reclaim our identity cards. We observed "doing time." We are out.

This prison tour—and it is a tour—of the implementation of an imagined space of total confinement resists abstraction. It sits like a massive obstacle challenging my own bookishness. It should resist facile theorizing, on one hand, but also remind us that, as Tom Wicker puts it, "what happens inside the walls inevitably reflects the society outside."[2]

The historic links connecting imprisonment—often as a consequence of race, class, and political oppression—to capitalism are more than barnacles on the bedrock of the United States. Prisons as technological systems developed concomitantly with the Industrial Revolution. As H. Bruce Franklin documents, industrial capitalists of the nineteenth century realized the inherent profitability of cheap prison labor.[3] Franklin also illuminates the racist corners of the Thirteenth Amendment to the Constitution that permitted a rigged criminality to counter the emancipation of slaves: "Neither slavery nor involuntary servitude, *except as a punishment for crime*" [my emphasis] (4). In the Reconstruction South, especially, a crime was defined by a manipulative system of White, owning-class injustice that reaped economic gain from peonage labor. An anonymous "Georgia Negro Peon" narrates the trap of peonage labor in "The New Slavery in the South," a "lifelet" printed in the *Independent* in 1904: "There are hundreds and hundreds of farms all over the state [of Georgia] where negroes, and in some cases poor white folks, are held in bondage on the ground that they are working out debts, or where the contracts which they have made hold them in a kind of perpetual bondage."[4]

Poverty too can be a crime. With characteristic irony, humor, and critique, Jack London described assembly-line injustice after being "pinched" in Niagara

Falls in 1894 for vagrancy and sentenced without lawyer or jury to thirty days in jail.[5] Prison time has also been a mechanism for restricting and silencing political critique. During World War I, Agnes Smedley spent six months in New York's Tombs without trial purportedly for having birth control information in her possession (a federal crime at the time). She and Emma Goldman each wrote powerful accounts of their time served in women's prisons.[6] These brief examples merely point to a long history of how judicial systems can function if you are non-White, poor, and perceived as politically radical.

While I cannot approach what it means to live *inside* a prison wall, I can trace the shadow of that wall on the outside, and how that shadow hides cultural blind spots. The prison tour, like the industrial plant tour, or literary excursions into the pit or mill, permits a controlled glimpse into networks of relationships among capital, technology, work, and imprisonment. This Net is inherently physical, not virtual, yet, ironically, nearly invisible. I tour particular zones of representation between labor technologies that order and control the body and literary formations. I use the word "tour" with all its problematic bourgeois connotations because I wish to acknowledge distance and difference between my analysis and the lived reality of these subjects.

Zone 1: Technological Speed

Prisons in this country are used mainly for those who commit a select group of crimes. . . . Excluded are the criminals of the capitalist class, who cause more of an economic and social loss to the country and the society but who are not often given prison sentences. This means that prisons are institutions of control for the working class, especially the surplus population of the working class.

—Richard Quinney, "The Political Economy of Criminal Justice"

My students wear current technology the way construction workers wear tool belts, the way small-town sheriffs wore their gun holsters. Hooked on instant messaging, tethered to their beepers and cell phones, they barely remember what it is like to be technologically disconnected. They are literally always on call. Technology is attached; humanity is detached. Resistance is futile. The Borg is here. So it goes. Well, not so fast.

In Youngstown, Ohio, the steel mills went down and the prisons (public and private) went up.[7] The Ohio supermax prison could not exist without technological systems and tools. It *is* state of the art, but whose art? My students are designers of cutting-edge computer technology, flexible software programs, fail-safe systems, imaging science, efficient spaces. Who owns their knowledge? How are their technological tools embedded in systems of confinement and liberation? And how have they been taught to ignore these questions?

Each time I teach a course on American literature and technology I begin by asking students to define technology. Invariably, they see it as tool "for making life easier" and inextricably connected to progress, to purposeful forward motion. Some, occasionally the most technologically sophisticated, offer some skepticism. One student noted that "applied science aims to solve problems, but often raises new ones, too." When I ask for a "technological snapshot" of their first encounter with technology as children they frequently describe their first home Mac or early Atari. In a later oral history assignment they link their own memories to those of their parents and grandparents who tell stories about their first television sets, changes in farm equipment, new washing machines, and, more rarely, jobs lost because of technology. My intent is to open a historical lens for students to see beyond the shiny appeal of their current machines and deeper into a continuum of technologies in specific historic circumstances. It is a challenge for them to acknowledge that technology is inseparable from conditions of labor, and, even harder for them to see technology as a system of both production and reduction. To speak of technological systems of slavery, war, or gender control is to evoke polite but blank stares. It is a frame that does not fit into their technological training. But what they do understand, even if they are not quoting Karl Marx or C. Wright Mills, is the difference between alienated labor and satisfying, craft-based work. They hope that their education will lead to a degree of autonomy, control, and satisfaction in the development of a useful finished product. They want to be well paid (why shouldn't they?) and are prepared to shed one job for another in an era of just-in-time production and industrial and technical downsizing. They expect to heed the warnings of their instructors to "retrain," not anticipating how complicated that might get at the age of forty-five or fifty. Before the dot-com bust, some hoped to be "post economic," that is, to make their millions fast, student loans long paid, material desires nearly satisfied, and enter economic bliss by the age of thirty-five. Money made fast and early would free them from grunge work. Someday they might slow down, but now everything has to be faster, faster, because they exist in the technological speed zone.[8]

"Mr. Lessard, in going over your resume, I see that you've had, on the average, one job per year for the past seven years."

"That's correct."

The man let out a tiny, mocking laugh. "Mr. Lessard, if this were California, I'm sure that potential employers would think you're a pretty stable guy. But this is New York. I'm afraid the clients I deal with would think there's really something wrong with you. Is there any reason why you've jumped around so much?"

"You don't understand," I stammered. "I'm in the Internet business. Everything's very unstable. The last place I worked merged and laid everybody off; the place before that went out of business and the place before that . . ."[9]

In *NetSlaves: True Tales of Working the Web*, authors Bill Lessard and Steve Baldwin take up the technological version of the American upward mobility success mythos in their descriptions of "Silicon Schmoes," "real-life Dilberts," or their preferred "Net-Slaves." With fleeting homage to Studs Terkel's *Working*, they explain how, like "two amateur anthropologists," they spent a year interviewing anyone who would talk to them about working in the Net industry.[10] They debunk computer celebrity culture, which assumes that "if you work in the Internet business, you're a 25-year-old with a $30 million initial public offering (IPO). Anything less means that you're an abject loser—after all, how can anyone 'fail' in a business that's grown more explosively and created more wealth than we've seen since the Oklahoma oil boom, if not for some deep personal flaw?" (3). Borrowing the language of blue-collar work and (problematically) the metaphor of slavery, they sketch a system of exploited and insecure labor in which their Dilberts work, for example, as "Garbagemen."[11] Matt, according to the authors, is a typical, sleepless, rumpled, sanitation engineer, on constant call to clean up technological messes. Matt's mind is caught in an ever-lengthening technological speed zone: "Time started to behave in the weirdest way. It stretched and stretched, until Matt's numbed mind could no longer conceive of there being a tomorrow, or a day after that. Time became abstract and unreal—like some cryptic piece of code that might never execute" (22). Machines are anthropomorphized; humans are technologized. But, Matt's critique of technologized capital is limited to e-mail ranting against corporate Darth Vaders and descriptions of giant software companies as something straight out of Fritz Lang's *Metropolis*. Only in this movie, the robotic human laborers might be "perma-temps," temporary technical support with or without IT degrees. These are whiny personal politics; don't look to Matt to start the revolution. What is important, though, is tracing the conditions of labor on the technological continuum.

Like the culture of *NetSlaves*, the world presented in Tracy Kidder's *The Soul of a New Machine* is hierarchical, largely male, socially retarded, and verbally constrained.[12] A technological romance, told as mock-heroic epic, *Soul* is a combination ethnography, materialistic fairy tale, and boy's adventure story with wars, sabotage, feuds, and game playing—all devoid of physical contact. Kidder was hired by boss man/project head Tom West to document the technological and managerial process of building (birthing?) a 32-bit superminicomputer. West applies the mushroom theory of management toward the fresh, young, narrowly focused engineer "racehorses" he hires: "Put 'em in the dark, feed 'em shit, and watch 'em grow" (109). These young software programmers and hardware builders exist in a state of prolonged, sexless, and sleepless adolescence. Their reward is "pinball," successfully completing one project so they catch a chance to play in another one. They do not look up, not even to smell the mushrooms.

What these young engineers and computer technologists possess, part of the allure of the technological speed zone, is a degree of autonomy to pursue their craft, as well as a vested interest in company profits through stock options—a boom in the go-go nineties, a bane in the deflated 2000s. Better paid than the clerks in Wal-Mart's "family" or most free-lance Netslaves, they have what their training has taught them, what Harry Braverman discerned as something more than a commodity exchange, *a share in the surplus*, a managerial stake.[13] They have yet to experience the brunt of engineering de-skilling masked by corporate cheerleading in Kurt Vonnegut's technological dystopia *Player Piano*.[14] Lovers of gadgetry and toys, believers in individual technical prowess, and a depoliticized sense of progress, they are presciently described by John Dos Passos:

> There is a layer: engineers, scientists, independent manual craftsmen, writers, artists, actors, technicians of one sort or another, who insofar as they are good at their jobs are a necessary part of any industrial society. . . . As a writer I belong to that class whether I like it or not, and I think most men who graduate from working with their hands into desks jobs eventually belong to it, no matter what their ideas are. . . . The most important thing you have to buck is the fact that along with the technical education that makes them valuable to the community they have taken in a subconscious political education that makes them servants of the owners. . . . It's the job of people of all the professions in the radical fringe of the middle class to try to influence this middle class, that most of them would rather not belong to, so that at least some of its weight shall be thrown on the side of what I've been calling civilization. It's a tough job, but somebody's got to do it.[15]

Netslaves, computer builders whose souls are given to machines, player pianos without human hands, all are located in worlds where human relationships are at best temporary and at worst ersatz. Indeed, the connective tissue that makes relationships possible, never mind builds community, is frayed or missing. I get blank stares when I ask my students how the new world of so-called "knowledge work" will enable them to care for their elderly parents, balance family and work lives, practice an informed citizenship. No space exists in their careerist curriculum for these questions. Yet they are aware, especially when asked to do generational oral histories, that there is a slippage in what constitutes a career under the pressures of global capital. They intellectualize the distinctions between career—as Richard Sennett explains it as, "a road for carriages, . . . a lifelong channel for one's economic pursuits"—and job, especially the shape-shifting into what resembles older meanings of *job,* "a lump or piece of something which could be carted around."[16] What is more burdensome to intellectualize is how these shifts undermine their own human linkages. Sennett argues that the new world order of flexible capitalism (Matt's world in *NetSlaves)*, has produced a "corrosion of character." Work gigs erode "trust, loyalty, and mutual commitment" (24); "there is history, but no shared narrative of difficulty, and so no shared fate" (147) because "[t]he conditions of time in the new capitalism have created a conflict between character and experience, the experience of disjointed time threatening the ability of people to form their characters into sustained narratives" (31).

Such a sustaining narrative must be more complicated than the post 9/11 embrace of the heroic and the patriotic. It would involve a critique of what constitutes progress and move beyond a mere chronicle of events, beyond Vonnegut's "Forward March," experienced as either fixed bureaucratic systems (the old industrialism) or mobile technologized systems (the new Information Age). To construct that new narrative of self and work and to resist the corrosion of their characters, the children of the technological age need to recover their lost inheritance of labor struggle and disengage themselves from the technology of managerial surveillance. The stakes are high—the sustainability of the earth, a modicum of global economic justice—and individual—their own futures. It is not enough to wring our hands over a loss of purported community. We need to penetrate the problematic of constructed individuality in the technological speed zone. This is not a Luddite-like refusal of technology per se, but a refusal of the technologizing of the self, to move, as Michel Foucault suggests, into "new forms of subjectivity through refusal of this kind of individuality which has been imposed on us for several centuries."[17] Such a resistance subjectivity might be developed through deeper encounters with the physicality of labor.

> I closed my eyes and saw a future of children
> kept in ranks of desks, ranks of identical
> expectations, thousands of pairs of hands
> trained to the keys, and they called it "good."
> I opened my eyes and saw it hadn't happened
> yet. I saw instead the child
> who could still be called a "King" in his way.
>
> This is a chorale, not a solo.
> This is the thunder of our quiet ways, our rowdy Saturdays,
> our clocks wound tight out of duty.
>
> Carolyn Chute[18]

Zone 2: Industrial Tours

> The girls did not so much seem accessory wheels to the general machinery as mere cogs
> to the wheels.   —Herman Melville, "The Tartarus of Maids"

> It is *very* hard indeed and sometimes I think I shall not be able to endure it. I never
> worked so hard in my life but perhaps I shall get used to it.
>
> —Mary S. Paul, letter to her father, 1848, from Lowell

Perhaps it is the memory of the yearly picnic and tour through Trubeck's, my father's chemical plant, in the 1950s, that inspires my interest in literal and literary industrial tours, as sources of nonacademic knowledge and as strategies for writers to bridge imagined and lived worlds. I have traveled into simulated mines in the Black Country of Birmingham, England, and Glace Bay, Nova Scotia, donned earplugs in the restored Boott Cotton Mills Museum in Lowell, and taken Rochester visitors on tours (now discontinued) of the once mighty, always oxymoronic Kodak Park. Perhaps I am an industrial voyeur, a chaser after experience denied to a working-class, college-bound girl. Perhaps I seek to know my parents better through the labor they shielded from me, or perhaps I've recognized what my formal education obscured, the knowledge embedded in the physicality of work.

The plant tour may soon be a vintage of an eroding industrialism, but for some, especially from my generation, it was an epistemic moment. In her memoir, *Packinghouse Daughter*, Cherie Register describes a sixth-grade field trip to Wilson's, the packinghouse where her father worked.[19] As was true with Trubeck's, acrid smells alerted her nose to the plant's presence before her eyes could see it. *Packinghouse* is a euphemism for slaughterhouse, for blood. The tour begins with the literal Judas Goat leading the "mooing and grunting freight" to slaughter (31). The students proceed into the packaging area where women worked, and then they climb up into rooms steamy "from vats of hot water" and others "cold as the inside of a refrigerator, where men hacked at red flesh, ground blades against bone, stripped blue veins still leaking blood, and scraped pale yellow globs of fat from foul-smelling hides" (33). Register defines the tour as horror and warning, a message planted in their sixth-grade heads by their teacher, Miss Kriesel: "*Start planning your escape. Everything you do from now on must help you out of here*" (35).[20]

From a working-class perspective I caution care in interpreting that warning. Escape from dangerous, physical labor is not disdain for the ethos behind the work itself. Register acknowledges her parents' pride of work, and how—denied other choices for themselves—they could simultaneously point their daughter to another world and steadfastly embrace the positive rhythms and fear the imminent dangers of their own.[21]

In the literary analyses that follow, I consider the challenges authors face in representing labor—as place and space, and, more elusively, as complex subjectivity. Who tells the story and to what audience? How does the text bridge differing class-inscribed worlds? The tour becomes a stratagem for illuminating unseen labor production, and, more rarely, for moments of mutuality where workers are not only seen by others, but also see out for themselves. The dynamic of active and passive sight permeates these nineteenth-century writings. But voice is another matter. How reliable are the voices that we hear in the text? And whose voices are heard? Much depends on who is in charge of the tour. And, despite good intentions, can it be anything but a tour—fragmentary, temporal, and, ultimately, unsatisfactory? Perhaps the more penetrating question is how the tour functions as experiential force, how it can turn back on itself, mirror itself, and expose a larger complicity in the oppression of labor.

as I am neither Painter nor Poet I cannot describe them all I can say it was a charming sight we had a faint view of Mount Blanc some of the places we passed they looked very poor many houses were built of stone and clay thatched roofs not any windows sometimes little holes in the side of the house the women were at work as hard as the men their skin was a perfect brown.

—From the 1851 travel diary of domestic servant and nanny
Lorenza Stevens Berbineau, on European tour with the Lowell family

In her 1861 novella, *Life in the Iron Mills,* Rebecca Harding Davis summons the bourgeois reader to "hide your disgust, take no heed to your clean clothes, and come right down with me,—here, into the thickest of the fog and mud and foul effluvia" to see conditions of brutal labor and thwarted humanity.[22] In telling the story of furnace tender, korl carver, and imprisoned suicide Hugh Wolfe, Harding Davis uses the stratagem of a double tour: first, taking the privileged reader into the muck of the story itself, the "incessant labor," and "kennel-like" rooms of the mill hands (15) and, secondly, as plot device, on a tour of the foundry at night taken by a group of male visitors. This sets up the crisis in Wolfe's life involving stolen money, harsh and unjust imprisonment, and existential despair. Read as a novella that illuminates lives hidden and ignored and of genius denied, *Life in the Iron Mills* has become, with Tillie Olsen's biographical interpretation, a classic of working-class literature.

Rebecca Harding Davis employs the synecdochic language of hands to describe the labor and identity of Hugh Wolfe (a "hand") and his cousin Deborah (a textile "picker"). From a mill owner's perspective "these men who do the lowest part of the world's work should be machines,—nothing more,—hands" (34). Truncated hands represent, metonymically, an ignored whole, a lesser human element and species. From a worker's perspective, hands signal class difference, "the contour of the white hand," of a "thorough-bred gentleman" (29). Hands also speak a substitute language for illiterate workers, those denied the cultivation of spoken and written language. Hugh Wolfe observes how his hands narrate his life; how prison would weaken his hands (55). Hugh "thrust[s] his hand out of the [prison] window" in a useless and pathetic attempt at final human connection. Hands that carved korl and tended furnaces become in his prison cell agents of the only liberation he can see, as he takes a "bit of tin" in his hand and "bare[s] his arms" (59). In *Iron Mills* human hands may be extensions of machinery or isolated expressions of compassion and love, but are not linked in solidarity with other workers.

This is a story of the exposure of one class to another, the above- and below-dwellers in the same West Virginia industrial town of Wheeling. Harding Davis is the sympathetic observer of the procession of mill workers, attentive not to the end product of iron ore (unlike the male foundry visitors), but to another technology of labor, "the vast machinery of system by which the bodies of workmen are governed" (19), chained, like prisoners, to their furnaces. Harding Davis challenges her genteel reader to see a sequence of injustices, showing parallels between the procession to the mills and the machinery of the judicial system. Her intent is exposure, to make it "a real thing" (14), to force the dilettante reader to look. But to what ends is that glance? As William Watson critically states, she chooses not to expose a larger labor context of strikes, militancy, labor unrest, and "proletarian self-representation,"[23] labor activism that she no doubt was aware of, particularly the massive New England shoemaker strike of 1860. True, her antebellum story is set thirty years earlier, a stratagem that delimits labor agitation in the present of the story, although there is some worry by the owning class that "these mill-hands are gettin' unbearable" (51). And there is Deb's theft of the dilettante's purse, which becomes the plot device for Hugh's doomed fate, a less radical narrative path than developing the thievery as a break-out act of resistance and transgression initiated by the undervalued Deb. In emphasizing Hugh's unjust fate rather than the emancipation money may permit, Harding Davis both valorizes and victimizes the worker as thwarted great artist. This subtext of thwarted artistic power is crucial to Tillie Olsen's reading of the novella and to any gendered study of the limitations imposed on women writers.[24] What Harding Davis does accomplish, albeit in a patronizing tone, is an exposure of the parallels of institutional confinement between the wage slavery of tending furnaces and the facile criminalization of the worker. Hugh's suicide and Deb's Quaker rescue resolve the author's delineation of class status as a determinant of penalization. The effect is not so much to *represent* the interior lives of workers, but to *present* an unacknowledged labor subjectivity to her audience, her own class. It's a tough job, but as Dos Passos makes clear, somebody's got to do it.

Workers, particularly women, have even less self-representation in Herman Melville's story "The Tartarus of Maids," which is usually paired with "The Paradise of Bachelors." Both stories begin with an "it," a specific place—in one, a paradise of bachelor rooms near the Temple Bar in London, in "Tartarus," a hellish paper processing plant in a Berkshire Mountain hollow.[25] Like Rebecca Harding Davis, Melville invites the outsider into the terrain of the stories, to observe, on one hand, a lavish feast, and, on the other, an efficiently dehumanized production process. Juxtapositions—plenty with penury, warmth with cold, leisure with labor—connect the stories in a commodity chain of cloth. Might the stifling rag room hold "some old shirts gathered from the dormitories of the Paradise of Bachelors" (223)? Melville also uses the trope of the plant tour to take the reader inside the paper mill. The narrator, in the "seedsman's business," looking for cheap paper and a bit of adventure, visits the Devil's Dungeon paper mill. While the atmospheric conditions of Harding Davis's *Iron Mills* are dirty fog, rain, and heat, Melville's are denatured and shrouded icy cold and snow. Conditions and context dominate: the boarding houses of the female operatives are "comfortless"; the factory edifice and the narrator's horse are better protected from the elements than the factory girls with their "thin aprons." In contrast to the spirited Lowell girls, these workers are voiceless, bleached and bloodless, sacrificial maidens to the god of the machine, "mere cogs to the wheels" (221). They become the intended paper pun, "ruled." Melville cast a sympathetic eye on these sexless, blank, thin, and muted factory operatives, but does not open his story to their perspective or voice. One, a former nurse (midwife?), gets fleeting attention as foolscap paper drops into her waiting hands. The narrator does pause to query the factory owner as to why they are "indiscriminately called girls, never women" (228). Why? Because the "off-and-on"-ness of married women would slow down production. Primarily, though, this is a narrative of anxious ideas about the machine in the garden, about commodities, and about the determinism of mechanical production displacing organic reproduction in faster, 9-minute time.[26] The machine, with its "autocratic cunning," "metallic necessity," and "unbudging fatality" (227) trumps all—and offers the seedsman cheaper paper. While Melville demonstrates the nearly complete desexing and technologizing of gender in "The Tartarus of Maids," the female operatives who produced textiles in Lowell have something more to say.

Neither dystopia nor utopia, the boardinghouse textile mills of Lowell offered thousands of Yankee farmer daughters the opportunity to earn hard cash, pursue intellectual interests, and labor for long hours in a mill instead of on a farm. As an example of corporate paternalism, and a vision of how human workers could be inserted into technologically current textile production, the Lowell system is an important model for the study of worker expressivity within corporate controlled space. *The Lowell Offering* is a collection of writings (sketches, stories, poems, letters, reportage) by New England factory women written between 1840 and 1845.[27] *The Lowell Offering* emerged out of Mutual Self-Improvement Clubs, gatherings where mill operatives would read their own literary efforts to each other and even submit the best of their writings to regional annuals, sponsored by local Protestant churches. *The Lowell Offering*, appreciated by an enthusiastic Universalist Church minister, merged with a company-sponsored periodical in 1841, retaining the original name (33–34).

Historian Thomas Dublin cautions a critical reading of the *Offering* as an operatives' literary magazine, finding the mill workers' letters more believable and trustworthy.[28] Some critics outright dismiss it as a company organ. I believe, however, taking into account the context of publication as well as the obscured process of editing and mediation, that the *Offering* is worthy of serious study not only because it is an early example of literary expression by factory women themselves, but because, read carefully (as well as in juxtaposition with the letters the women wrote home), it attests to the subjective ambiguity of the young women, working "half in sunlight—half in shade" (77).

They were young, single, childless, literate, industrious, adventuresome, and accustomed to hard work. At Lowell they had an opportunity to use their modicum of free time to hear lectures, shop, visit, write and read, and take some respite from the incessant factory noise and fast-paced production system. Their wages were less than what the corporate owners would pay men, but they earned cash rather than scrip, and could send money home, save, or spend. The corporate owners convinced Yankee farmers to allow their daughters to leave the farm by sending persuasive agents to rural New England, offering free transportation (which may have been more promise than practice) to mill towns—an early example of interior migrant labor, as Thomas Dublin suggests. Boardinghouses, managed by a combination of house mothers, peer pressure, and stringent rules insured a controlled merger of labor and life.[29]

Frequently described as cheerful rather than contented, many of the Lowell girls saw millwork as temporary, even seasonal, and chose to return to the farm when they had had enough, and, most importantly, when wages were cut. When they did return home, however, they frequently faced the stigma of being a "factory girl," a fact some kept secret so they would be more socially accepted and marriageable.[30] As capital chased cheap labor ("wages were reduced in all the Lowell mills in Nov. 1848"),[31] they left the mills in droves, replaced by newly arrived Irish, Polish, Greek, and French Canadian immigrants who could not return home so easily.

At a time when Emerson was philosophizing about houses as metaphors for the self, some Lowell operatives were composing epistolary tours, taking their readers from the boardinghouse, through the factory gate, and into the rooms of the mills and the integration of the "hands" into a system of textile production: "first, the carding room, where the cotton flies most, and the girls get the dirtiest. . . . Then there is the spinning-room." At this point the perspective shifts from the room itself to a naming of the jobs performed: "In this room are the spinners and the doffers. . . . In some of the factories the spinners do their own doffing." Worker mobility depended on the nature of the specific job. The weavers, especially those in charge of several looms simultaneously, were "the most constantly confined." Further, millwork marked the body physically: "When I went out at night the sound of the mill was in my ears." And, "It makes my feet ache and swell to stand so much. . . . The right hand, which is the one used in stopping and starting the loom, becomes larger than the left; but in other respects the factory is not detrimental to a young girl's appearance."[32] It is important not to read these descriptions as complacency, but rather see them as reflective of the stoic sensibility of these women, who like the Okie poet Wilma Elizabeth McDaniel are simply not whiners. Harriet Farley, one of the *Offering* writers, emphatically insists that the girls (the presumed collective voice was common) were not uncritical and passive about their laboring conditions: "The girls here are not contented; and there is no disadvantage in their situation which they do not perceive as quickly and lament as loudly, as the sternest opponents of the factory system do" (53).

Factory girls "turned out" in 1834 and 1836 when wages were cut and petitioned in 1846 for the ten-hour day. As Josephine L. Baker writing "A Second Peep at Factory Life" in 1845 shows, at least some had a labor consciousness that was collective as well as individualistic, despite the discipline of the factory bell. Baker's rhetorical strategy of inserting an "overheard" conversation into a description of factory life: "'This cutting down wages is not what they cry it up to be. But I wonder how they'd like to work as hard as we do, digging and drudging day after day, from morning till night, and then, every two or three years, have their wages reduced. . . . And besides this, who ever heard of such a thing as their being raised again,' says the first speaker. 'I confess that I never did, so long as I've worked in the mill, and that's been these ten years'" (80).

The Lowell operatives labored at a moment of historical change. Mechanization—a workable power loom—firmly planted the machine in the New England garden; by 1840 there were ten textile corporations and thirty-two mills. While the factory girls were resisting "white slavery" and affirming their right to be considered "ladies," Frederick Douglass was on the abolitionist lecture circuit, having published his first autobiographical narrative in 1845. Lucretia Mott, Elizabeth Cady Stanton, and others presented a Declaration of Sentiments and Resolutions at a women's rights convention in Seneca Falls, New York, in 1848, and, that same year, Karl Marx and Frederick Engels published their *Communist Manifesto*. Out of this zeitgeist, some Lowell operatives imagined alternative labor conditions for women. "Tabitha" (Betsey Chamberlain) describes such a world in "A New Society," holding fathers accountable for the education of their daughters, insisting on an 8-hour work day, fair pay, equal wages between men and women, and the dominance of "industry, virtue and knowledge" over wealth and titles (210).

When working conditions worsened, the Lowell girls exercised an option not readily available to the immigrants who followed them into the mills, nor to Deborah and Hugh Wolfe or Melville's Tartarus maids—they left. Most had homes to return to, but some did not, as noticed by J.L.B. (Josephine L. Baker) in 1845: "For the sake of them, we earnestly hope labor may be reformed; that the miserable, selfish spirit of competition, now in our midst, may be thrust from us and consigned to eternal oblivion" (82). Not revolutionaries and certainly not merely company mouthpieces, the Lowell girls, at least some, held to an ethos of solidarity—"for the sake of them"—one would be hard pressed to find among the Netslaves of today.

Zone 3: The Amputation

No matter how degraded the factory hand, he is not real estate.　　—W.E.B. Du Bois

educated didn't mean smart　　—Octavia Butler, *Kindred*

"I lost an arm on my last trip home. My left arm." So begins Octavia Butler's 1979 novel, *Kindred*.[33] It defies facile genre classification: on one level, a slave narrative, on another, time-travel, speculative fiction, on another, women's interior memoir, on still another, a narrative about work and history. On her twenty-sixth birthday, June 9, 1976, Dana (Edana) Franklin, African American, writer, temp worker, and wife, is unpacking books in the new suburban Los Angeles house she shares with Kevin, her white husband, also a writer. Suddenly she feels dizzy, nauseated, and is pulled back and down into another space, time, and dimension. She finds herself on the ground beneath trees near a river and hears the screams of a drowning child. She rushes into the river, yanks the child to the shore, revives him, and is threatened by someone with a rifle. She has been thrust back into the antebellum South, onto a plantation in the slave state of Maryland. The child is the plantation owner's son, Rufus Weylin. The rifle, threatening her life, propels her forward to the present. She reappears in her living room "wet, muddy, and scared to death" (16). That is the first trip. All together there are five trips. She is called back each time Rufus, as a child and then later as a young man, puts his life in danger. In a move never to be rationally explained, Dana becomes the embodied historical link between her present and her ancestors. The White Rufus is destined to father a child, with the Black Alice, born free. This child, Hagar Weylin, born in 1831, will become Dana's great-great-great-grandmother. Dana's burden is to keep the manipulative and increasingly brutal Rufus alive long enough so that her progenitor can be conceived and born.

Dana is trapped literally and figuratively in a historical moment—with primitive medicine, intensive labor, minimal hygiene and sanitation, and, most immediate and horrific, the brutal fact of slavery. The clarity and accessibility of Octavia Butler's narrative belies its complexity. While it is well documented that slave narratives, as a genre, include descriptions of beatings, escapes, and spirit breaking as integral to their subject's ordeal of slavery, and these description no doubt evoke sympathy and horror, there is still a safety zone and distance for the contemporary reader. That is, the text can be read as artifact. What Butler achieves through the device of time travel and the convincing dilemma of her protagonist is an imagined space where a mind located in the present (1976) must survive and negotiate existence in the antebellum past. Even Kevin, a White, educated man, who is pulled into the past at one point with Dana, suffers psychologically and physically. But it is minimal compared to what Dana faces.

Each time she is forced back because of Rufus's actions, her body endures physical pain, which increases as the episodes lengthen. The first time her shoulders and back ache from a pounding by Rufus's irrational mother. The next time it is 1815 and she is caught, beaten, and almost raped by a white patroller. As her consciousness of the constant unpredictability of life on a plantation increases, Dana is increasingly fearful about her ability to survive there:

> "So the more I think about it, the harder it is for me to believe I could survive even a few more trips to a place like that. There's just too much that could go wrong."

[Kevin:] "Will you stop that! Look, your ancestors survived that era—survived it with fewer advantages than you have. You're no less than they are."

"In a way I am."

"What way?"

"Strength. Endurance. To survive, my ancestors had to put up with more than I ever could. Much more. You know what I mean."

"No, I don't," he said with annoyance. (51)

The third time, 1819, she and Kevin are pulled back together and Dana notices how quickly they slip into the routines of plantation life and how the narrative of the historical past turns on the interpretative position of the present:

"This could be a great time to live in," Kevin said once. "I keep thinking what an experience it would be to stay in it—go West and watch the building of the country, see how much of the Old West mythology is true."

"West," I said bitterly. "That's where they're doing it to the Indians instead of the blacks!"

He looked at me strangely. He had been doing that a lot lately. (97)

Kevin is stranded without Dana for eight days—five years in antebellum time. Separated, Dana endures a beating for running away to find him, described by the elliptical refrain, "He beat me until . . . He beat me until . . . " (176). Finally reunited and threatened with imminent death, Kevin and Dana are propelled back into present time. Butler continually reminds us this is no tour. Even the free, white Kevin returns altered, physically and psychologically, experiencing a dislocation he compares to imprisonment and wonders "how people just out of prison manage to readjust" (197).

With each kidnapping into the past, physical pain increases as the skin of Dana's body absorbs history. Forced into fieldwork, lashed by the current overseer for her slowness, and bossed into a rural speedup, she learns a dimension of labor that leaves her "shaking, humiliated" (212). It is reminiscent of Frederick Douglass's description of fieldwork eroding his "natural elasticity," of being broken and eclipsed by the "dark night of slavery."[34] Dana is saved not only by Rufus's intervention but by the advice of another field hand on the rural production line, "Slow down! Take a lick or two if you have to. You kill yourself today, he'll push you to kill yourself every day" (212).

Dana bears the burden of rescue (as the author finds a narrative form to rescue history for the present). As she is historically compelled to save Rufus's sorry ass, Dana straddles the border between bondage and bonding. She hesitates, but only briefly, before sinking her knife into Rufus as he moves to make her his mistress. Even in death he holds her; her arm, "from the elbow to the ends of the fingers" is caught in the grip of his hand as if it were being "absorbed into something. Something cold and nonliving" (261).[35] At this horrific moment Dana's burden turns to bodily sacrifice, a literal severing of what Douglass called "the bloody arm of slavery" (79). She can no longer see the end of her arm, trapped in the wall of a house and the time zones of history. She pulls, pulls hard, and screams with "an avalanche of pain, red impossible agony!" (261). This final time her body speaks a new tongue of pain.

The amputation of Dana's arm above the elbow is a script of narrative necessity, a body part offered as historical evidence. Like the cuts on the scripted back of Maxine Hong Kingston's warrior woman, Fa Mu Lan, like Sethe's chokecherry-tree scars in *Beloved*, and like the backs of escaped slaves as documented in photographs, these physical scripts challenge textual representation. Dana's scars on her face and back remind us of the difference between texts situated in libraries and classrooms and bodily texts endured historically. In *Kindred*, Butler develops a dialectic between books and body. Dana and Kevin are both writers. As struggling writers they met at a temp agency that regulars called "a slave market" (52).[36] When the first episode occurs, she is unpacking books and putting them in order on shelves. Earlier, Kevin visits a library to research a "certificate of freedom," which they ultimately fail to re-create. They tear a map of Maryland out of their large atlas. Dana reads *Robinson Crusoe, Pilgrim's Progress, Gulliver's Travels*—adventure tales and meditative journeys. Dana is whipped when she is caught reading. She carries a paperback history of slavery with her which Rufus orders her to burn (143).

All these words set against the physical reality of the system of enslavement suggest the limitations of book knowledge. Caught within hours of an attempted escape, stuck in the past but cognizant of the future, Dana says, "Nothing in my education or knowledge of the future has helped me to escape. Yet in a few years an *illiterate* [my emphasis] runaway named Harriet Tubman would make nineteen trips into this country and lead three hundred fugitives to freedom. What had I done wrong?" (177).

Octavia Butler, a prolific and accomplished writer, is, obviously, not antitext; rather, she presses for a deeper query of book-based assumptions. In this dialectic between books and body, she builds a structured epistemology of physicality. Our task as readers and critics is to recognize how knowledge situated outside books and libraries enables an expansion of our intellectuality. But tours are insufficient, as are theories about the body presented in disembodied, abstracted language hermetically sealed for an intellectual elite. The hand/mind dichotomy is defunct; we need a language that will penetrate and present a body consciousness grounded in the physicality of labor, oppression, and struggle. Dana's arm is severed by history; Mrs. C.'s hands are crushed by fact. The linkages between those imagined and lived realities and our educational practices should temper our assumptions about what constitutes knowledge. This is a part of the connective tissue within the larger project of working-class studies.

Zone 4: Blind Spots

I know your hands by heart, brother, can picture them at any time.

—Christa Wolf, *Accident: A Day's News*

In the hospital those last days, if I lifted his hand the bone in his arm would be hanging there; his body had come away from it.

—Ludmilla Ignatenko, speaking about her husband,
a fireman at the Chernobyl nuclear disaster

Where the optic nerve connects to the eye itself there is no light; it is our blind spot. As a metaphor, the blind spot both illuminates and conceals. On one level, it takes us off the hook. Yes, our human bodies have blind spots, just as we do in automobiles, what can we do but acknowledge them and carry on? The blind spot permits a sensibility of the inevitable. Accidents happen, shit happens. More threatening, unacknowledged blind spots enable an arrogance of power wrapped in a cloth of self-interest and private protection. On still another level, probing our myriad blind spots is the catalytic work of writers and artists, and the labor of teaching. Democratic evolution depends on it.

I ask students taking my Literature and Technology course to trace, in a final reflective essay, the blind spots in the texts we've studied and in their own technological education. The textual analysis comes easier than any scrutiny of their significant educational investment. We cover a lot of literary and historical ground in ten weeks, moving from the first generation of factory workers to massive steel production to auto assembly lines, to computer hard- and software construction. I fear this is another castor oil course for students eager to enter what they perceived to be the real world and their own technology-based careers.[37] We conclude with Christa Wolf's short novel *Accident: A Day's News*, a meditative, intertextual tracing of one April day in the life of a woman writer awaiting news of her brother's risky brain surgery as she listens to radio reports of the Chernobyl nuclear accident and the toxic cloud advancing over central Europe.[38]

Images of probing—the delicate membrane of the brain (so close to the optic nerve), the damage of nuclear rods gone amuck in the earth's core, the inevitable and annoying weeds crowding vegetables and flowers, combine rather than dichotomize the organic with the technical, the constructive with the destructive. Wolf brilliantly constructs an archeology of language associations—Grimms' fairy tales, bits of song, news reports, telephone conversations, banal aphorisms, dreams, nursery rhymes, scientific articles, and Joseph Conrad's *Heart of Darkness* to lead the reader into an examination of the core, the DNA, of our collective and individual blind spots:

Now we're getting close, very close, to our blind spot after all. Whether it was actually a requirement of nature, whether there was no other solution to the construction of the human eye than to equip it with a blind spot, that tiny point in the retina where it is joined by the optic nerve, leading to the brain. Speedy consolation. Our other eye is said to compensate for this minimal gap in our perception. But who or what can help us fill that gap in our perception which we inevitably inflict upon ourselves through our special way of holding our own in this world? Where to find consolation for this? (88–89)

Wolf (author and narrator) penetrates the structural flaws of dichotomous thinking. She exposes those blind spots that divide the world into good and evil, or for that matter, technophiles or technophobes, beneficial or harmful science, all forms of antipodal thinking. She casts her net out into a future, seeking, in Konrad Lorenz's words, the "long-sought missing link between animals and the really humane being." She probes the continuum of meanings of pathos from apathy to antipathy to empathy, and worries about technology severing connective tissue, human feelings, in the name of progress. She too slips into too-simple analogies, as when she compares a generation's love for its computers to the shackling of "a slave to his galley" (63). Through her deftly woven free association technique she uncovers the Western humanistic core, the tangled lines of Eros and Thanatos, the forbidden fruit and fall in the garden, Faust's pact with the good old devil, and the Frankensteinian indifference to repercussions and consequences. But it is more complicated than an attack on technology or progress per se; after all, in the simultaneity of the text, it is a surgeon's technical skill that removes the cancer from her brother's brain. In her intertextual mediation on the "roots of our desire for destruction" (81), she turns to a friend's book on the human hand. And the hand leads her to further distinctions, between simian gesture and human language. For her, language and writing are at the core, means and cause, the bull's eye of the blind spot, the "crater in our selves," and "the heart of darkness" (89). In other words, although she recognizes how the stakes ratchet up, how nuclear technology creates new destruction, she does not take herself as a writer off the hook. She comes instead to a recognition of our own "unbearable radioactive feelings"(89), our own blind spot as "an acquired protection against our own insights about ourselves and outside attacks" (93). Ours as individuals and as collective. She ends the single day of the novel with a book, *Heart of Darkness*, and stops her reading with Conrad's image of "six black men, forged together by chains." She recognizes Conrad's capacity to know, or willingness to know, "the meaning of sorrow" (108). She emerges from the travail of the day with a perception of the writer as probing both blind spots and flashes of lightning, situated in a momentary but essential flicker. Her concluding sentence, "How difficult it would be, brother, to take leave of this earth" (109), powerfully and poetically combines the metaphysical and the physical. And that too is the blind spot in the novel.

Despite the narrator's worry over nuclear fallout ruining garden vegetables and tainting water for children's showers, despite Wolf's learned meditation on the complicity of language, the imaginative and empathic world of *Accident: A Day's News* remains middle-class bound. She imagines the surgeon's hand sawing her brother's skull, but not the Chernobyl fireman's hand quelling the fire.[39] The sterile space of the literary text obscures the actual geography of Belarus, at the heart of the radiation fallout, which destroyed 485 villages. "It takes fourteen days for a man to die of radiation sickness" reports the wife of one of the fireman sent without "protective tarpaulin suits, just as they were, in their shirt-sleeves," unwarned, called out to fight "an ordinary fire." Bodies transformed into barely breathing wounds. The subjectivity and physicality of this experience are not beyond the province of the talented Wolf, not imaginatively unreachable. The same technique of intertextuality could include, for example, this account by Ludmilla Ignatenko, a fireman's widow:

> In the hospital those last days, . . . [b]its of his lungs and his liver came out of his mouth. He was choking on his own innards. I would wrap my hand in a bandage and push it into his mouth to fish all that stuff out of him. I can't describe it. It can't be written about. It was all so dear to me; I loved him so much. They just couldn't find any shoes big enough to fit his feet. They laid him in his coffin barefoot. (*Harper's*, 17)

Indeed, "the horror, the horror." I do not wish to single out Christa Wolf for her decision to exclude the physical costs of fighting the Chernobyl fire, the consequences to the surrounding villages and cities, the long-term health effects, not to mention any imagined meditation on the interior lives of the people surrounding Chernobyl. What I wish to suggest is the probability that it was not a decision at all, that for the writer writing about a day in the life of a writer, a day spent in the interior mind of that writer, there is little or no imagined space for experiences outside her own class. It is one example of how great or minor literature, what is read, assigned, included in anthologies, discussed at conferences, reviewed, and critiqued, what is proffered as worthy of study (particularly at the high school level) is and has been thoroughly middle class, sometimes wanting to be upper class, in its perspective. To be sure, it took several generations of brilliant writers of color to dismantle the cultural gates to what the textbooks call the human condition. But we have yet to reveal how class difference shapes that condition, especially for Americans inured to success stories that often belie their own lived experience. We need to probe the class blind spots at the point of connection and cultural production. We need to recognize how the body at work reveals a crucial epistemology. The best writers of working-class experience take us deeper, beyond the tour, into a physicality inseparable from consciousness. The best readers must be ready and willing not to avert their eyes.

Notes

Introduction

1. Jack Salzman, *Years of Protest: A Collection of American Writings of the 1930s* (New York: Pegasus, 1967), 354–355.
2. Agnes Smedley, *Daughter of Earth* (1929; reprint, New York: Feminist Press, 1973), 79.
3. Maxine Hong Kingston, *China Men* (New York: Knopf, 1980), 11.
4. Tillie Olsen, *Yonnondio* (New York: Dell, 1974), 95.
5. Wilma Elizabeth McDaniel, letter to Janet Zandy, June 23, 1997.

How Much Are Two Hands Worth?

The epigraphs in this chapter are from Simon Jennings, general ed., *Ways of Drawing Hands: A Guide to Expanding Your Visual Awareness* (Philadelphia: Running Press, 1994).

1. To protect her privacy, I have not used the real name of Mrs. C.
2. Wayne A. Hall, "Worker Gets $4M for Loss of Arms," *Times Herald Record,* October 31, 1995, 4.
3. Ibid., 4.
4. John Scibelli, "Newburgh Woman's Arms Severed in Factory Accident," *Times Herald Record,* August 4, 1993.
5. Shelly Green, "Doctors Attempt Miracle," *Times Herald Record,* August 5, 1993.
6. Ed Shanahan, "Plastics Firm Fined $5,460 for Hazardous Work Place," *Times Herald Record,* February 3, 1994.
7. New York State AFL-CIO pamphlet, Albany, NY.
8. Hall, "Worker Gets $4M for Loss of Arms," 4.
9. New York State AFL-CIO pamphlet.
10. Letter to attorney Elliot Tetenbaum from Janet Zandy, August 8, 1997.
11. Jennings, *Ways of Drawing Hands.*

Loss: Circumstances and Choices

1. In his essay "A Pedagogy of Respect: Teaching as an Ally of Working-Class College Students," Larry McKenzie dissects the ladder-to-success metaphor and puts the ladder in the context of class circumstances, noting how some folks have not only sturdier ladders, but stairs, even elevators, to the top. In *Coming to Class: Pedagogy and the Social Class of Teachers*, ed. Alan Shepard, John McMillan, and Gary Tate (Portsmouth, NH: Heinemann/Boynton/Cook, 1998), 94–117.

Trubeck Labs

1. In the summer of 2001 I placed an ad in the *Bergen Record* newspaper inquiring whether any former employees of Trubeck Labs, later called UOP Chemical Company, remembered working with my father, Charles Ballotta. I wish to thank Rose and Ralph Limatola for their kind response and Herb Halpern for his telephone conversations and remembrances.
2. This and the next two quotations are from *The Trubeck Laboratories Employees' Handbook* (1946). These well-intentioned rules and guidelines present a commitment to safety that belies the reality of labor performed around dangerous chemicals and toxic lagoons. It is too late for epidemiological studies, but not too late to recognize how millions of workers face hazardous working conditions and long-term occupation-caused diseases. Just as there is a general state of denial about environmental harm, so too there is little public recognition of the hazards of work. See Lawrence White, *Human Debris: The*

Injured Worker in America (New York: Seaview/Putnam, 1983); Rachel Scott, *Muscle and Blood* (New York: Dutton, 1974); Dorothy Nelkin and Michael S. Brown, *Workers at Risk: Voices from the Workplace* (Chicago: University of Chicago Press, 1984).

3. Lizabeth Cohen, in *A Consumer's Republic* (New York: Knopf, 2003), sets the record straight regarding class mobility assumptions and the GI Bill: "But most often, it was the already better educated, middle-class veteran who parlayed GI benefits into a college or graduate degree and a middle-class occupation, while his less educated, lower-class fellow serviceman advanced only within the working class" (157). She cites this comment from an ex-serviceman in one Midwest study, "What good is the GI bill going to do me? No married man could afford it, unless he's got lots of dough" (159). See also Janet Zandy, "Labor Day," in *Calling Home: Working-Class Women's Writings,* ed. Janet Zandy (New Brunswick: Rutgers University Press, 1990), 155–156.

4. See chapter 1 of Nelkin and Brown's *Workers at Risk.* Also, I want to suggest that hazardous working conditions were *worse* prior to the 1970 creation of OSHA, not that OSHA has in any way resolved the continuing problem of occupational safety and health. See Mary Gibson, *Workers' Rights* (Totowa, NJ: Rowman and Allanheld, 1983), on the right-to-know issue: "adequate posting and training in health and safety *versus* blaming the victim and 'safety' competitions on the one hand, and access to, and accuracy of, monitoring data, specifically accident records *versus* recording only lost-time accidents, with emphasis on keeping the numbers as low as possible, on the other" (43). See also Daniel M. Berman, *Death on the Job: Occupational Health and Safety Struggles in the United States* (New York: Monthly Review Press, 1978).

5. *http://www.epa.gov/oerrpage/superfund/sites/rodsites/0200101.htm.* U.S. Environmental Protection Agency Superfund, Record of Decision Abstracts: *Universal Oil Products/Chemical Division.*

6. Editorial, "Pollution Less Secret," *Bergen Record,* April 22, 1990, no p.

7. Donald M. Pitches, letter to the editor, "Cleanup is a step in the right direction," *Bergen Record* May 27, 1990, 8. With appreciation to Reverend Pitches for permission to reprint this letter.

8. Sandra Steingraber, *Living Downstream: An Ecologist Looks at Cancer and the Environment* (Reading, MA.: Perseus, 1997), 235–236. Also, Susanne Antonetta writes, "Being Americans, we don't just dump toxins into our soils but catalogue them, create hierarchies. We have for that the Environmental Protection Agency, which creates lists: lists of sites to watch and investigate, to ignore, to give up on, lists of the worst sites in the United States, the ones that pose an immediate danger" (*Body Toxic: An Environmental Memoir* [Washington, DC: Counterpoint, 2001], 21).

Books of the Dead

1. This essay is based on the research in Claudia Clark, *Radium Girls: Women and Industrial Health Reform, 1910–1935* (Chapel Hill: University of North Carolina Press, 1997).

2. Katherine Schaub, "Radium," *Survey Graphic* 68 (May 1, 1932): 138–141, 156–157. Schaub's complaints about radium poisoning to the New Jersey Health and Labor Departments led to government consideration of dialpainting's dangers (Clark, *Radium Girls,* 17, 211–213).

3. Katherine Schaub as quoted in Clark, *Radium Girls,* 35. Schaub survived until February 1933.

4. Clark, *Radium Girls,* 34–35.

5. For a fuller account see Clark, *Radium Girls,* particularly chapter 3, "Something About That Factory: The Dialpainters and the Consumers League"; for the sustaining importance of the Consumers League see p. 206. See also Alice Hamilton, *Exploring the Dangerous Trades: The Autobiography of Alice Hamilton, M.D.* (1943; reprint, Boston: Northeastern University Press, 1985).

6. See Laura Hapke, *Tales of the Working Girl: Wage-Earning Women in American Literature, 1890–1925* (New York: Twayne, 1992).

7. Clark, *Radium Girls*, 133.
8. Ibid., 135.
9. Adrienne Rich, *The Dream of a Common Language* (New York: Norton, 1978), 3.
10. Janet Zandy, "Dialpainters," *Blue Collar Review* 4, no. 4 (Summer 2001): 20–22.
11. All quotations from Audre Lorde are from her book *Zami: A New Spelling of My Name* (Trumansburg, NY: Crossing Press, 1982).
12. See also "Digger" in Jim Daniels's poetry collection, *Punching Out* (Detroit: Wayne State University Press, 1990). Young Digger, working the line at Ford Motor Company, learns a series of blunt lessons about how to pace his work from other workers: "Look, you got to learn how to survive / around here, kid. If you don't know / how to break your machine / then you shouldn't be runnin' it" (16).
13. See Bill Lessard and Steve Baldwin, *NetSlaves: True Tales of Working the Web* (New York: McGraw-Hill, 2000); and Jill Andresky Fraser, *White-Collar Sweatshop: The Deterioration of Work and Its Reward in Corporate America* (New York: Norton, 2001). On the other hand, Barbara Ehrenreich's *Nickel and Dimed: On (Not) Getting By in America* (New York: Holt, 2001) insists on the distinct physical difference of low-wage work. See "Down and Out in America: Barbara Ehrenreich Talks about Life as a Minimum Wage Employee," *Women's Review of Books* 18, nos. 10–11 (July 2001): 6–7.
14. All quotations are from Muriel Rukeyser, *Out of Silence: Selected Poems*, ed. Kate Daniels (Evanston, Ill.: TriQuarterly, 1992). Rukeyser planned "The Book of the Dead" as part of a "summary poem of the life of the Atlantic coast," *U.S. 1* (New York: Covici and Friede, 1938): "Gauley Bridge is inland, but it was created by theories, systems, and workmen from many coastal sections—factors which are, in the end, not regional or national" (End note, *U.S. 1*). For critical readings of Rukeyser's "The Book of the Dead" see: Louise Kertesz, *The Poetic Vision of Muriel Rukeyser* (Baton Rouge: Louisiana State University Press, 1980), 98–99; Walter Kalaidjian, *American Culture Between the Wars: Revisionary Modernism and Postmodern Critique* (New York: Columbia University Press, 1993), 162–163; David Kadlee, "X-Ray Testimonials in Muriel Rukeyser," *Modernism/Modernity* 5.1 (1998): 23–47; John Lowney, "Truths of Outrage, Truths of Possibility: Muriel Rukeyser's 'The Book of the Dead,'" in *"How Shall We Tell Each Other of the Poet?": The Life and Writing of Muriel Rukeyser*, ed. Anne F. Herzog and Janet E. Kaufman (New York: St. Martin's Press, 1999).
15. The best factual source is Martin Cherniack, *The Hawk's Nest Incident: America's Worst Industrial Disaster* (New Haven: Yale University Press, 1986). He identifies some of the individuals who speak in Muriel Rukeyser's poems, for example, the social worker Philippa Allen who published two articles in the *New Masses* in 1935 under the pen name Bernard Allen. While Cherniack reviews representations of the incident in both the conservative and radical presses, and laments the absence of indigenous songs with the exception of one written in New York by blues musician Josh White as Pinewood Tom, "Silicosis Is Killing Me," he surprisingly fails to recognize Rukeyser's magisterial poem sequence.
16. Cherniack, *The Hawk's Nest Incident*, 89.
17. See similar patterns of intersecting race and class oppressions in Michael Wilson, *Salt of the Earth* (1953; reprint, New York: Feminist Press, 1978).
18. Ashley Lucas and Ariadne Paxton, "About the Hawk's Nest Incident—Background for Muriel Rukeyser's *The Book of the Dead*," *http://www.english.uiuc.edu/maps/poets/m_r/ rukeyser/hawksnest.htm*. For an extended definition see Mary Gibson, *Workers' Rights* (Totowa, NJ: Rowman and Allanheld, 1983): "*Silica dust* causes silicosis, a scarring of the lungs which causes them to become progressively inelastic, making it more and more difficult to breathe, and preventing passage of oxygen to the blood. The scars may join together and form larger scars, which may occupy the entire lung. The process, called progressive massive fibrosis, is often accompanied by increased susceptibility to tuberculosis and other lung infections. The heart, due to the strain of pumping blood through inelastic lungs, becomes enlarged and fails to pump effectively" (59). See also

J. M. Stellman and S. Daum, *Work Is Dangerous to Your Health* (New York: Random House, 1973).

19. Note, similarly, how dialpainter Amelia Maggia's death certificate reflects racist assumptions in Clark, *Radium Girls*.

20. Vito Marcantonio was an American-born Italian protégé of Fiorello La Guardia who headed the American Labor Party. See Ralph Fasanella's paintings "Marcantonio for Mayor" and "Death of a Leader" and my essay on Ralph Fasanella in this collection.

21. Vito Marcantonio, "Dusty Death," *The New Republic*, March 4, 1936: 105–106.

22. Compare Rukeyser's "The Book of the Dead" as imagined geography with William Carlos Williams's *Paterson* (New York: New Directions, 1963), and as documentary with Walker Evans and James Agee, *Let Us Now Praise Famous Men* (1941; reprint Boston: Houghton Mifflin, 1980).

23. See "Workers Memorial Day," in this volume, for the enacted ritual of naming the dead.

24. Quoted in Bernard Allen (pen name of Phillipa Allen), "Two Thousand Dying on a Job: How the Tunnel Workers Lived," *New Masses*, January 22, 1935: 19–21.

God Job

Versions of this essay appear in *Writing Work: Writers on Working-Class Writing*, ed. Larry Smith, David Shevin, and Janet Zandy (Huron, OH: Bottom Dog Press, 1999) and in *Coming to Class: Pedagogy and the Social Class of Teachers*, ed. Alan Shepard, John McMillan, and Gary Tate (Portsmouth, NH: Heinemann/Boynton/Cook, 1998). This essay is dedicated in loving memory to Constance Coiner and her daughter Ana Duarte-Coiner who died in the crash of TWA flight 800 in 1996.

1. Quoted in Walter Rosenblum, foreword to *America and Lewis Hine: Photographs, 1904–1940* (Millerton, NY: Aperture, 1977), 10. The summary of Hine's last years that follows in text is also from Rosenblum (9–15).

2. These images are reminiscent of William Blake's 1789 poem, "The Chimney Sweeper."

3. The comments from *Child Labor Bulletin* (August 1913) and by Hine (from "Baltimore to Biloxi and Back," *The Survey*, May 3, 1913) are quoted in *America and Lewis Hine*, 58. Hine's comments and photographs are reminders that child labor is not an artifact of the past, but still a critical component of migrant farm work and the globalization of labor.

4. *Portraits 9/11/01: The Collected Portraits of Grief from the New York Times*, a hardbound book published in 2002, is a collection of 1,910 portraits of lives abruptly ended on 9/11. Profits from the $30 book will be donated to the *New York Times* 9/11 Neediest Fund, according to a full-page ad in the *Times* (August 26, 2002, B8).

5. Roxanne Rimstead, "What Working-Class Intellectuals Claim to Know," *Race, Gender and Class: Working-Class Intellectual Voices* 4 (1): 119–141, 128. See also Michael Zweig, *The Working Class Majority: America's Best-Kept Secret* (Ithaca, NY: ILR/Cornell University Press, 2000.) Zweig claims that the occupations of one's parents are the single most important predictor of one's class position.

6. Studs Terkel, *Working* (New York: Avon, 1975), xxviii.

7. Mike Wallace, *Mickey Mouse History and Other Essays on American Memory* (Philadelphia: Temple University Press, 1996), x.

8. See also Michael Frisch, "American History and the Structures of Collective Memory," chapter 3 in *A Shared Authority: Essays on the Craft and Meaning of Oral and Public History* (Albany: State University of New York Press, 1990, 29–54).

9. Michael Wilson, *Salt of the Earth* (1953; reprint, New York: Feminist Press, 1978).

10. Thomas Geoghegan offers this summary of Taft-Hartley: Passed into law in 1947 over Harry Truman's veto, it had three effects: "It ended organizing on the grand, 1930s scale. It outlawed mass picketing, secondary strikes of neutral employers, sit downs. . . . Everything we did then is now illegal." Further, it stymied organizing. No longer could workers just sign up (as they do in Canada); now the law requires a much more elaborate process before a union can be recognized. It created union bureaucracies and produced

a new breed of "professional" labor consultants hired by businesses to thwart labor's demands (*Which Side Are You On? Trying to Be for Labor When It's Flat on Its Back* [New York: Plume/Penguin, 1992], 52–53).

11. Muriel Rukeyser, "The Minotaur," reprinted in *Anthology of Modern American Poetry*, ed. Cary Nelson (New York: Oxford University Press, 2000), 688.

12. Carole Anne Taylor, *The Tragedy and Comedy of Resistance: Reading Modernity Through Black Women's Fictions* (Philadelphia: University of Pennsylvania Press, 2000), 8.

13. Thomas Bell, *Out of This Furnace* (1941; reprint, Pittsburgh: University of Pittsburgh Press, 1976); Pietro di Donato, *Christ in Concrete* (1939; reprint, New York: Signet, 1993). Note the influence of *Christ in Concrete* in Ralph Fasanella's *Iceman Crucified* paintings. For a fuller discussion of *Yonnondio* see my essay "In the Skin of a Worker" in this collection.

14. See *Struggles in Steel: The Fight for Equal Opportunity,* produced by Ray Henderson and Tony Buba and distributed by California Newsreel (1996), an important documentary on racial inequality, the steel industry, and the USWA (United Steelworkers of America).

15. A Lewis Hine photograph appears on the cover of the University of Pittsburgh Press reprint edition of Bell, *Out of This Furnace.* See Margaret F. Byington, *Homestead: The Households of a Mill Town* (1910; reprint, Pittsburgh: University of Pittsburgh Press, 1974) for Hine photographs and documentation on the conditions of households and working conditions at the mills. As reported in *Homestead,* insurance was important to workingmen's families because of the rate of industrial accidents. For example, during the months of January, February, and March 1907, sixty-five men in the Homestead area were injured on the job; seven died. Injuries included crushed feet, lacerated hands, sprained ankles, broken limbs, amputated arms, paralysis, and laceration of the eyes, face, and head (92). For a discussion of Hine's role in the Pittsburgh Survey see Alan Trachtenberg's essay "Ever—The Human Document" in *America and Lewis Hine,* 118–131.

16. Terry Eagleton, *The Idea of Culture* (Oxford: Blackwell, 2000), 48.

17. Jimmy Breslin, *The Short Sweet Dream of Eduardo Gutierrez* (New York: Crown, 2002), 191. According to the Bureau of Labor Statistics, on-the-job construction deaths are 20 percent higher for Latinos (who are often unskilled, illegal immigrants with little English) than Whites and Blacks (as reported in the *New York Times,* July 16, 2002). Breslin's important book provides a textured context for the cause of such deaths.

18. Quoted in Daile Kaplan, ed., *Photo Story: Selected Letters and Photographs of Lewis W. Hine* (Washington, DC: Smithsonian Institution Press, 1992), 49–50.

Workers Memorial Day: April 28

1. Year after year, 6,000 is the estimated number of workers killed on the job. The *New York Times* reported 6,210 work-related fatalities in 1995 or five for every 100,000 workers (December 22, 1996, 10). In 1999 there were 6,023 workplace deaths due to traumatic injuries, in 1998 6,055 deaths were reported based on data from the Bureau of Labor Statistics (BLS). These numbers do not include the estimated 50,000 to 60,000 workers who die each year because of occupational diseases according to the annual AFL-CIO report *Death on the Job: The Toll of Neglect,* 10th ed. (April 2001). Also, BLS data covers only private sector workers, is culled from employer reports, and does not recognize workers discouraged from reporting injuries on the job. Labor groups consider the BLS numbers conservative estimates, at best. *America's Forgotten Environment* (1989), a pamphlet published by a coalition of labor, minority, and environmental groups, reports 100,000 worker deaths each year from occupationally caused disease and 10,000 deaths from preventable accidents on the job. The terrorist attacks of 2001 spiked the number of people killed on the job, according to the Labor Department, to 8,786; of those deaths, 2,886 were related to the attacks (The Associated Press, *Democrat and Chronicle,* September 26, 2002, 5A).

2. Daniel Berman claims the actual signing day is December 29, 1970 (*Death on the Job: Occupational Health and Safety Struggles in the United States* [New York: Monthly Review Press, 1978], 33).

3. OSHA is emblematic of a larger struggle, according to Mary Gibson: "The real issue behind that of the right to know (and workplace health and safety generally) is control of the workplace" (*Workers' Rights* [Totowa, NJ: Rowman and Allanheld, 1983], 53). See also Tom Wayman, *Inside Job: Essays on the New Work Writing* (Maderia Park, BC: Harbour, 1983).

4. See Charles Noble, *Liberalism at Work: The Rise and Fall of OSHA* (Philadelphia: Temple University Press, 1986), for a critique of the goals of the act and the manner of implementation. Noble sees a "fundamental disjuncture between the ways in which Americans seek to solve social problems and the ways in which the wider socioeconomic system discourages social change" (14). He offers an alternative approach that shifts policy from standards and penalties to state-enforced rights of workers to plant governance, that is, worker empowerment rather than governmental regulations. Noble uses OSHA to critique the larger failure of liberalism to promote participatory democratic mechanisms rather than bureaucratic, statist reforms (17).

5. See Alice Hamilton, *Exploring the Dangerous Trades: The Autobiography of Alice Hamilton* (1943; reprint, Boston: Northeastern University Press, 1985).

6. Summarized in Kenneth C. Crowe, "Labor's Memorial Day," *Newsday* (April 27, 1989).

7. I describe the yearly rite of Workers Memorial Day in Rochester, NY, in my introduction to *Liberating Memory: Our Work and Our Working-Class Consciousness* (New Brunswick: Rutgers University Press, 1995), 12–13.

8. Barbara Myerhoff, *Number Our Days* (New York: Simon and Schuster, 1978), 32, 185–186. See also Victor W. Turner, *Dramas, Fields, and Metaphors: Symbolic Action in Human Society* (Ithaca, NY: Cornell University Press, 1974).

9. E. P. Thompson, *The Making of the English Working Class* (New York: Vintage, 1966), 9.

10. Excerpts from testimony reprinted in Joyce L. Kornbluh, ed., *Rebel Voices: An I.W.W. Anthology* (Ann Arbor: University of Michigan Press, 1968, 1972), 181. Mrs. William Howard Taft (wife of the president) happened to be present at the hearings; her shocked response helped trigger national attention to the plight of the workers and the cause of the strike.

11. My father also was persuaded by his family to use the birth certificate of a deceased elder brother so he could go to work to support the family. See my "Labor Day," in *Calling Home: Working-Class Women's Writings*, ed. Janet Zandy (New Brunswick: Rutgers University Press, 1990), 155–156.

12. Paul Cowan, introduction to William Cahn, *Lawrence 1912: The Bread and Roses Strike* (1954; revised, New York: Pilgrim Press, 1980), no p.; a revision of the work published in 1954 under the title *Mill Town*. The cover illustration is one of Ralph Fasanella's Lawrence 1912 paintings. Fasanella lived for a time in Lawrence while he was researching his series of paintings of the famous strike. See my essay on Fasanella in this collection.

13. Dee Garrison, ed., *Rebel Pen: The Writings of Mary Heaton Vorse* (New York: Monthly Review Press, 1985), 32.

14. Raymond Williams, *Marxism and Literature* (New York: Oxford University Press, 1977), 128–135.

15. Pamela Fox, *Class Fictions: Shame and Resistance in the British Working-Class Novel, 1890–1945* (Durham, NC: Duke University Press, 1994).

16. What if April 28, Workers Memorial Day, became a day when every teacher and every school child learned a small piece of labor history from a worker's perspective?

17. See Jacqueline Jones, op-ed, "Solidarity Helps Ensure Security," *New York Times,* August 2, 2002. For an analysis of working conditions in this nonunion mine, see Charles McCollester, "Less Than Miraculous," *The Nation,* March 17, 2003, 21–23.

18. Ellen Smith, "Eroding Federal Support, Funding Threaten the Safety of Coal Mining," [Rochester] *Democrat and Chronicle,* August 1, 2002.

19. Aram Roston, "Fire in the Hole," *Mother Jones* (September/October 2002).
20. Raymond Williams, *Politics and Letters: Interviews with New Left Review* (London: New Left, 1979), 252.
21. See Jim Hightower, "Tony Mazzocchi, 'Labor Guy,'" *The Nation,* October 28, 2002, 9.

Articulations

1. Quoted in Philip S. Foner, *Helen Keller: Her Socialist Years* (New York: International, 1967), 38.
2. See H. Bruce Franklin, *Prison Literature in America,* especially "The First Literary Genre of the United States: The Slave Narrative" (Westport, CT: Lawrence Hill, 1978).

Worker Writers: Where Do You Keep Your Writing?

1. Tillie Olsen, in conversation with Janet Zandy.
2. Tillie Olsen, *Silences* (New York: Dell, 1978).
3. Janet Zandy, ed., *Calling Home: Working-Class Women's Writings* (New Brunswick: Rutgers University Press, 1990).
4. Marge Piercy, "Out of the rubbish, " in *My Mother's Body* (New York: Knopf, 1985), 11–13. Reprinted in Zandy, *Calling Home,* 122–124.
5. Tillie Olsen, *Yonnondio,* 1974 (New York: Delta, 1989), 6. See also the poignant and angry passage where Olsen addresses the bourgeois reader after a mine blowup: "And could you not make a cameo of this and pin it onto your aesthetic hearts?" (20).
6. "The Kizaemon Tea-bowl" from *The Unknown Craftsman* by Soetsu Yanagi, adapted by Bernard Leach, in World Crafts Council, *In Praise of Hands: Contemporary Crafts of the World* (Greenwich, CT: New York Graphic Society 1974), 7.
7. Alice Walker's often anthologized story "Everyday Use" (in *In Love and Trouble: Stories of Black Women* [New York: Harcourt Brace Jovanovich, 1973], 47–59) and B. Traven's "Assembly Line" (in *The Night Visitor and Other Stories* [Chicago: Elephant Paperback/Ivan R. Dee, 1993], 73–88) offer fictional representations of the linkages between use and aesthetic values.
8. Octavio Paz, "Use and Contemplation," trans. Helen R. Lane, in World Crafts Council, *In Praise of Hands,* 17–24.
9. See the important work of Michael Denning, *The Cultural Front* (New York: Verso, 1996); Barbara Foley, *Radical Representations: Politics and Form in U.S. Proletarian Fiction, 1929–1941* (Durham, NC: Duke University Press, 1993); and Laura Hapke's comprehensive *Labor's Texts: The Worker in American Fiction* (New Brunswick: Rutgers University Press, 2001).
10. Antonio Gramsci, *Selections from Cultural Writings,* ed. David Forgacs and Geoffrey Nowell-Smith, trans. William Boelhower (Cambridge, MA: Harvard University Press, 1991), 38.
11. "Feds Under the Bed" was originally devised by Fed member Roger Drury for the twenty-first anniversary of the FWWCP. It was performed to an appreciative audience at the 1999 Working-Class Studies conference in Youngstown, Ohio. See http://www.the-fwwcp.org.uk.
12. Dave Morley and Ken Worpole, eds., *The Republic of Letters: Working Class Writing and Local Publishing* (London: Comedia, 1982), 18.
13. Gramsci's distinctions between traditional and organic intellectuals are relevant here, particularly for noting the formation of the social conditions that enable the development of human intellectuality. Gramsci writes, "The most widespread error of method seems to me that of having looked for this criterion of distinction in the intrinsic nature of intellectual activities, rather than in the ensemble of the system of relations in which these activities (and therefore the intellectual groups who personify them) have their place within the general complex of social relations" (304). See "Intellectuals and Education" in *An Antonio Gramsci Reader,* ed. David Forgacs (New York: Schocken, 1988), 300–311.

14. Nicholas Coles, "Joe Shakespeare: The Contemporary British Worker-Writer Movement," in *Popular Literacy: Studies in Cultural Practices and Poetics*, ed. John Trimbur (Pittsburgh: University of Pittsburgh Press, 2001), 189–208.

15. Ken Warpole, afterword to *Writin: Worker Writers and Community Publishers* (London: Federation of Worker Writers and Community Publishers, 1978), 244–245.

16. The archival work of annotating these numerous publications is in process. For reviews of publications see *Federation Magazine* and for further contact information write to Tim Diggles at the Feds' e-mail address, *thefwwcp@tiscali.co.uk*.

17. Warpole, afterword to *Writin*, 244.

18. Notes from the Editor, *West End Press: Twenty-five Years of Outstanding Multicultural Literature*, catalog (Albuquerque, 2001).

19. See Constance Coiner, *Better Red: The Writing and Resistance of Tillie Olsen and Meridel Le Sueur* (New York: Oxford University Press, 1995).

20. See Florence Howe's account of Tillie Olsen giving "her tattered copy of *Life in the Iron Mills*" (9) to the fledgling press in "Learning from Teaching" in *The Politics of Women's Studies: Testimony from 30 Founding Mothers*, ed. Florence Howe (New York: Feminist Press, 2000), 3–15.

21. Fred Whitehead, "The Sage of Moberly," *People's Culture* 24/25 (November 1994–February 1995): no p.

22. Douglas Wixson, *Worker-Writer in America: Jack Conroy and the Tradition of Midwestern Literary Radicalism, 1898–1990* (Urbana: University of Illinois Press, 1994).

23. I call this trajectory—of moving with consciousness of working-class solidarity into the larger world—working-class *bildung*. It is distinct from the Horatio Alger model of "making it," and refutes the societal message to forget working-class roots. See my *Liberating Memory: Our Work and Our Working-Class Consciousness* (New Brunswick: Rutgers University Press, 1995) and my essay "Traveling Working Class" in *What We Hold in Common: An Introduction to Working-Class Studies* (New York: Feminist Press, 2001).

24. See Thomas Bell's novel of Slovakian steelworkers, pejoratively called "Hunkies," *Out of This Furnace* (1941; reprint, Pittsburgh: University of Pittsburgh Press, 1976).

25. Larry Evans, "The Mill Hunk Anthology: An Organizer's Odyssey," in *Overtime: Punchin' Out with the* Mill Hunk Herald *Magazine, 1979–1989*, ed. Larry Evans (Pittsburgh: Piece of the Hunk Publishers and Albuquerque: West End Press, 1990).

26. Mihal Pecio, "Our Hunk Heritage," *Mill Hunk Herald* 5 (Spring 1980), reprinted in Evans, *Overtime*, 119.

27. *Mill Hunk Herald* 4 (Winter 1979–1980), reprinted in Evans, *Overtime*, 171.

28. See David Joseph's moving account of his struggle to find a public voice in "Breaking Through the Sounds of Silence," in Zandy, *Liberating Memory*. Joseph's *Working Classics* is not to be confused with *Working Classics: Poems on Industrial Life*, ed. Peter Oresick and Nicholas Coles (Urbana: University of Illinois Press, 1990). See also the now-defunct, Maryland-based *Talkin' Union*, produced by Saul Schniderman, an AFSCME member working in the Library of Congress. See also the graphically hip *Processed World* out of San Francisco.

29. Meridel Le Sueur, "On the Continuity of Peoples Culture" (presented at The Midwest Conference on Alternative Journalism and Popular Culture, 1978), *Midwest Alliance* 1, no. 1: 3–4 (Wichita, KS: Midwest Alliance, 1979?). This journal was a continuation of the short-lived *Midwest—A Review*, edited by Meridel Le Sueur and Dale Kramer for three issues in 1936 and 1937.

30. See Paul Buhle, ed., *Labor's Joke Book* (St. Louis: WD Press, 1985).

31. See Walter Benjamin, "The Storyteller," in *Illuminations*, ed. Hannah Arendt, trans. Harry Zohn (New York: Schocken, 1969), 83–109.

32. John Crawford, personal correspondence with Janet Zandy, May 15, 2002.

33. Emmanuel Cooper, *People's Art: Working-Class Art from 1750 to the Present Day* (Edinburgh: Mainstream, 1994), 10.

34. See Wixson's comments about the worker writer's dual consciousness in Joseph Kalar's poem about the proletarian night in *Worker Writer in America,* 212.
35. Tim Diggles, correspondence with Janet Zandy, May 16, 2002.
36. Sue Doro, *Blue Collar Goodbyes* (Watsonville, CA: Papier-Mache Press, 1992), 6. See also "Worker Ghosts" in this volume.
37. Quoted in *Midwest Alliance: A Continuation of Midwest: A Review* 1, no. 1: 15 (Wichita, KS, 1979?); see note 32.
38. Wilma Elizabeth McDaniel, "Moving Away"(unpublished ms.), 36.
39. Wilma Elizabeth McDaniel, correspondence with Janet Zandy, December 8, 1999.
40. Quoted in Lillian Vallee, "Tulare Poet Gives Valley Residents a Voice," *Connections* (May 1995): 9.
41. Wilma Elizabeth McDaniel, correspondence with Janet Zandy, July 17, 1993.
42. *Down an Old Road: The Poetic Life of Wilma Elizabeth McDaniel,* produced and directed by Christine Simon (Film Arts Foundation), 34 min.
43. Quoted in Roxanne Dunbar-Ortiz, *Red Dirt: Growing Up Okie* (London: Verso, 1997), 222.
44. Wilma Elizabeth McDaniel, "The Journey," in *The Ketchup Bottle* (St. John, KS: Chiron Review Press, 1996), 24.
45. Joan Jobe Smith, "The Almost-Interview of Wilma E. McDaniel," *Chiron Review* (Autumn 1999).
46. Wilma Elizabeth McDaniel, "The Summons," *Broomstick* (May–July 1985): 13.
47. Quoted in Peter H. King, "On California," *Los Angeles Times,* August 11, 1996, 1, A17.
48. Wilma Elizabeth McDaniel, correspondence with Janet Zandy, July 4, 2002.
49. Benjamin, "The Storyteller," 83.
50. On the unreliability and complexity of experience see Joan W. Scott, "Experience," in *Feminists Theorize the Political,* ed. Judith Butler and Joan W. Scott (New York: Routledge, 1992). See also Alessandro Portelli, *The Death of Luigi Trastulli and Other Stories: Form and Meaning in Oral History* (Albany, NY: State University of New York Press, 1991).
51. See Leslie Marmon Silko, *Storyteller* (New York: Seaver, 1981), for making and remaking the world through story. Silko's dedication: "This book is dedicated to the storytellers as far back as memory goes and to the telling which continues and through which they all live and we with them."
52. Wilma Elizabeth McDaniel, *A Primer for Buford* (New York: Hanging Loose Press, 1990), 70.
53. Ibid., 77.
54. Wilma Elizabeth McDaniel, correspondence with Janet Zandy, July 4, 2002.

In the Skin of a Worker; or,
What Makes a Text Working Class?

1. See Richard O. Boyer and Herbert M. Morais, *Labor's Untold Story: The Adventure Story of the Battles, Betrayals, and Victories of American Working Men and Women* (Pittsburgh: United Electrical, Radio and Machine Workers Union, 1997).
2. See Sharon O'Dair, *Class, Critics, and Shakespeare: Bottom Lines on the Culture Wars* (Ann Arbor: University of Michigan Press, 2000), 8–9.
3. See Michael Denning, *The Cultural Front: The Laboring of American Culture in the Twentieth Century* (New York: Verso, 1996); and Laura Hapke, *Labor's Text: The Worker in American Fiction* (New Brunswick: Rutgers University Press, 2001).
4. Alexander Saxton, *The Great Midland* (1948; reprint, Urbana: University of Illinois Press, 1997); Harriette Arnow, *The Dollmaker* (1954; reprint, New York: Avon, 1972).
5. I am currently co-editing with Nicholas Coles the anthology *Working-Class Literature in the United States* (New York: Oxford University Press, forthcoming).
6. Raymond Williams, "The Writer: Commitment and Alignment 1980," in *Resources of Hope,* ed. Robin Gable (London: Verso, 1989), 77–87.
7. Williams, "Culture Is Ordinary," in Gable, *Resources of Hope,* 15.

8. Peter Hitchcock, "They Must Be Represented? Problems in Theories of Working-Class Representation," *PMLA* 115 (January 2000): 20–32. See other references to answerability in this collection, particularly "Worker Ghosts."

9. To contextualize Thompson's comments further: "There is today an ever-present temptation to suppose that class is a thing. . . . That was not Marx's meaning." Class is "a social and cultural formation, arising from processes which can only be studied as they work themselves out over a considerable historical period" (*The Making of the English Working Class* [New York: Vintage, 1966], 10–11).

10. All quotations from Michael Ondaatje are from his *In the Skin of a Lion* (New York: Penguin, 1988).

11. All quotations from Tillie Olsen are from her *Yonnondio: From the Thirties* (New York: Dell, 1975). For an extensive analysis of Tillie Olsen's writing see Constance Coiner, *Better Red: The Writing and Resistance of Tillie Olsen and Meridel Le Sueur* (New York: Oxford University Press, 1995).

12. Raymond Williams, *Marxism and Literature* (New York: Oxford University Press, 1977), 132.

13. See "Worker Writers" in this collection.

14. See poetry on the Triangle fire in "Recoveries" in this collection. Olsen's poem is reprinted in *Calling Home: Working-Class Women's Writings*, ed. Janet Zandy (New Brunswick: Rutgers University Press, 1990), 91–94.

15. Agnes Smedley, *Daughter of Earth* (1929; reprint, New York: Feminist Press, 1973).

16. Denise Giardina, *Storming Heaven* (New York: Ivy, 1987).

17. Florence Reece, "Which Side Are You On?" in *Hillbilly Women*, ed. Kathy Kahn (New York: Avon, 1974), 9–11.

18. Mary Casey, "The Class Game," in *Once I Was a Washing Machine: The Working-Class Experience in Poetry and Prose*, ed. Ian Bild et al. (Brighton: The Federation of Worker Writers and Community Publishers, 1989), 2.

19. Mike Gold, "Go Left, Young Writers!" Editorial, *New Masses* (January 1929).

20. A version of this essay appeared in *The Heartlands Today*, vol. 11, ed. Larry Smith (Huron, OH: Firelands Writing Center, 2001).

Worker Ghosts

1. Thomas Hardy, *Jude the Obscure* (1896; reprint, New York: Penguin, 1985).

2. Bill Hutchinson, *Daily News*, July 1, 1998, 3. The *New York Times* reported the story, titled "Turbulent Labor Rally Snarls Midtown Manhattan" (July 1, 1998, A21), less enthusiastically than the working-class *Daily News*.

3. A pre-Teutonic etymology (*The Compact Edition of the Oxford English Dictionary* [New York: Oxford University Press, 1971], 1138).

4. "We are talking about characteristic elements of impulse, restraint, and tone; specifically affective elements of consciousness and relationships; not feeling against thought, but thought as felt and feeling as thought; practical consciousness of a present kind, in a living and interrelated continuity. We are then defining these elements as a 'structure': as a set, with specific internal relations, at once interlocking and in tension" (Raymond Williams, *Marxism and Literature* [New York: Oxford University Press, 1977], 132; cf. Bakhtin's architectonics).

5. Bill Bamberger and Cathy N. Davidson, *Closing: The Life and Death of an American Factory* (New York: Norton, 1998), 138.

6. Kurt Vonnegut, *Player Piano* (1952; reprint, New York: Dell, 1980). Hereafter cited in text.

7. "Eased into governance by years and years of conservative ideology, the corporations of America today effectively oversee the Congress, the regulatory agencies and indeed the presidency itself. There is no Article in the Constitution that recognizes the supracitizenship of conglomerates; nothing is written that grants enlarged and pre-emptive voting rights to business organizations and their trade groups" (E. L. Doctorow, "In the Eighth Circle of Thieves," *The Nation*, August 7–14, 2000, 13–18).

8. See also "Ghost Dance Songs," in *The Heath Anthology of American Literature,* vol. 2, ed. Paul Lauter (Lexington, MA: Heath, 1990), 742–745.

9. See Daniel Grossman, "Neo-Luddites: Don't Just Say Yes to Technology," *Utne Reader,* March/April 1990, 44–53, and Kirpatrick Sale, *Rebels Against the Future: The Luddites and Their War on the Industrial Revolution: Lessons for a Computer Age* (Reading, MA: Addison-Wesley, 1995).

10. See Janet Zandy, "Traveling Working Class," *Women's Studies Quarterly* (Spring/Summer 1998): 228–242.

11. This booklet includes the caveat "not intended as a substitute for your company's policies or professional health care" ("Coping with CHANGE: How to Manage the Stress of Change" [San Bruno, CA: Krames Communications, 1987]).

12. See Daniel Singer, *Whose Millennium? Theirs or Ours?* (New York: Monthly Review Press, 1999).

13. See *Corporate Power and the American Dream* (New York: Labor Institute and Public Health Institute, 1996). For an analysis of the eroding American middle-class see Paul Krugman, "For Richer: How the Permissive Capitalism of the Boom Destroyed American Equality," *New York Times Magazine,* October 20, 2002, 62–67, 76–77, 141–142. See also Joel Blau, *Illusions of Prosperity: America's Working Families in an Age of Economic Insecurity* (New York: Oxford University Press, 1999).

14. Manning Marable, *How Capitalism Underdeveloped Black America* (Boston: South End Press, 1983); William Julius Wilson, *When Work Disappears: The World of the New Urban Poor* (New York: Vintage, 1997).

15. Thomas Geoghegan, *Which Side Are You On?: Trying to Be for Labor When It's Flat On Its Back* (New York: Plume/Penguin, 1992), 84–85.

16. See Barry Bluestone and Bennett Harrison, *The Deindustrialization of America: Plant Closings, Community Abandonment, and the Dismantling of Basic Industry* (New York: Basic, 1982); Donald L. Barlett and James B. Steele, *America: What Went Wrong?* (Kansas City: Andrews and McMeel, 1992) and *America: Who Stole the Dream?* (Kansas City: Andrews and McMeel, 1996); *New York Times, The Downsizing of America* (New York: Crown, 1996); Jeremy Rifkin, *The End of Work: The Decline of the Global Labor Force and the Dawn of the Post-Market Era* (New York: Putnam, 1996); Stanley Aronowitz and William DiFazio, *The Jobless Future* (Minneapolis: University of Minnesota Press, 1994); and Michael Moore, *Downsize This!* (New York: Random House, 1996). Also, for an important analysis of the "mismeasure" of the gross domestic product (GDP) see Clifford Cobb, Ted Halstead, and Jonathan Rowe, "If the Economy Is Up, Why Is America Down?" *Atlantic Monthly,* October 1995, 1–15.

17. In her documentary film *Stranger with a Camera,* Elizabeth Barret examines the literal risks of representation in her story of a Canadian filmmaker, Hugh O'Connor, who was shot and killed by Kentucky landowner Hobart Ison for filming without his permission one of the renters on his property in 1967. The renter, a poor miner, gave O'Connor permission to film. (*Stranger with a Camera,* produced and directed by Elizabeth Barret [2000; American Documentary, *POV*]) See also Julie Salamon, "He Turned His Camera on Appalachia, and One Man Wouldn't Stand For It," *New York Times,* July 11, 2000, B1.

18. James Agee and Walker Evans, *Let Us Now Praise Famous Men* (1941; reprint, Boston: Houghton Mifflin, 1980). Hereafter cited in text.

19. *Blue Collar Goodbyes,* by Sue Doro, was self-published in 1991 in a print run of 500 copies which, according to the author, are "all out 'there' somewhere, many in factories, labor union halls, and adult literacy classes." The second edition, with snapshots of co-workers by Doro and a foreword by Tom Wayman, was published by Papier-Mache Press in 1992 (73 pages). This edition includes the section "Plant Closure/Layoff/Stress Information" that lists resources such as the Plant Closures Project in Oakland, California, and a bibliography of worker writer books and other publications. Unfortunately, Doro experienced another kind of closing when Papier-Mache press was sold and she had to

buy back her books to prevent their destruction, but she soon found another distributor in Bottom Dog Press.

20. *Portraits in Steel,* with photographs by Milton Rogovin and interviews by Michael Frisch, was published by Cornell University Press in 1993. It includes a foreword by Robert Doherty and a lengthy introduction by urban historian Frisch describing Buffalo's industrial history as well as the authors' approach to gathering the material and shaping the final book (318 pages).

21. *Closing: The Life and Death of an American Factory,* by Bill Bamberger and Cathy N. Davidson, is a DoubleTake Book published in 1998 by the Center for Documentary Studies in association with W.W. Norton. It includes a preface, seven chapters, and an epilogue all written by Davidson and many black-and-white and color photographs by Bill Bamberger (223 pages).

22. *"I Was Content and Not Content": The Story of Linda Lord and the Closing of Penobscot Poultry* was published by Southern Illinois University Press in 2000 and includes a foreword by Michael Frisch, interviews by Alicia J. Rouverol and Stephen A. Cole, an essay, "Faces in the Hands," by Carolyn Chute, and black-and-white photographs by Cedric N. Chatterley (134 pages).

23. Peter Hitchcock, *Dialogics of the Oppressed* (Minneapolis: University of Minnesota Press, 1993), 24. In his interpretation of Bakhtin in "Problems in Theories of Working-Class Representation" (*PMLA* 115 [January 2000]: 20–32), Hitchcock describes answerability as "a form of social responsibility that allows workers to 'speak' to one another across a range of discourses . . . of memory, of experience, of alienation, of solidarity" (28). See also Jeffrey T. Nealon's distinction between Bakhtinian answerability and Levinasian responsibility in "The Ethics of Dialogue: Bakhtin and Levinas," *College English* 59 (1997): 129–148.

24. See my commentary on Sue Doro in "Worker Writers" in this volume. For further analysis on the concept of community see Raymond Williams, "The Importance of Community," in *Resources of Hope,* ed. Robin Gable (London: Verso, 1989), 111–119.

25. See Douglas Wixson, *Worker Writer in America: Jack Conroy and the Tradition of Midwestern Literary Realism (1898–1990)* (Urbana: University of Illinois Press, 1994), 214.

26. Raymond Williams recognizes such neighborly behaviors as "certain kinds of mutual responsibility" (Gable, *Resources of Hope,* 114).

27. Michael Frisch, *A Shared Authority: Essays on the Craft and Meaning of Oral and Public History* (Albany: State University of New York Press, 1990).

28. See Williams, "The Importance of Community" in Gable, *Resources of Hope,* 111–119.

29. Cathy Davidson writes, "It was not furniture for the masses. A dining room set, in 1993, sold for between fifteen and twenty thousand dollars, more than some White workers earned in a year" (Bamberger and Davidson, *Closing,* 21).

30. For literary representation of meat processing see Tillie Olsen, *Yonnondio* (New York: Dell, 1975) and Upton Sinclair, *The Jungle* (1906; reprint, New York: Signet, 1980); for oral histories see "Voices from the Yards" in *Calling Home: Working-Class Women's Writings,* ed. Janet Zandy (New Brunswick: Rutgers University Press, 1990).

31. Raymond Williams, *Marxism and Literature* (New York: Oxford University Press, 1977), 207.

32. Remarks made in a keynote address at Youngstown State University, June 1999, as quoted in Jeff Sharlet, "Seeking Solidarity in the Culture of the Working Class," *The Chronicle of Higher Education* (July 23, 1999): 1, 19–20.

33. See, for example, Dale Maharidge and Michael Williamson, *Journey to Nowhere: The Saga of the New Underclass* (New York: Dial, 1985), and the more recent Thomas Dublin and George Harvan, *When the Mines Closed: Stories of Struggles in Hard Times* (Ithaca, NY: Cornell University Press, 1998); Margaret K. Nelson and Joan Smith, *Working Hard and Making Do: Surviving in Small Town America* (Berkeley: University of California Press, 1999); and Sherry Lee Linkon and John Russo, *Steeltown U.S.A.: Work and Memory in Youngstown* (Lawrence: University Press of Kansas, 2002).

34. Michael Holquist and Vadim Liapunov, eds., *Art and Answerability: Early Philosophical Essays by M. M. Bakhtin*, trans. Vadim Liapunov and Kenneth Brostrom (Austin: University of Texas Press, 1990), x. Hereafter cited in text.

35. Frisch, *A Shared Authority*, xxi.

36. With appreciation to Florence Howe, John Crawford, Carole Anne Taylor, and Laura Hapke for reading drafts of this essay and offering critical observations.

Recoveries

1. "What It Is I Think I'm Doing Anyhow" in *The Writer on Her Work,* ed. Janet Sternberg (New York: Norton, 1980), 153–168.

Fire Poetry on the Triangle
Shirtwaist Company Fire of March 25, 1911

1. A recurring phrase in newspaper accounts of the fire, "bale of dark dress goods" is from Leon Stein's *The Triangle Fire,* the definitive account of the fire (New York: Carroll and Graf, 1962), 14, reprinted with an introduction by William Greider (Ithaca, NY: Cornell University Press, 2001). I begin, like Stein, with the mood of early spring and the end of the work day.

   For assistance in researching documents, poetry, and images for this essay I wish to thank the staff of the Tamiment Institute Library/Robert F. Wagner Labor Archives at New York University. I also appreciate the support of a Faculty Research Grant from Rochester Institute of Technology. A version of this essay originally appeared in *College Literature* 24.3 (1997): 33–54. See also David Von Drehle, *Triangle Fire: The Fire That Changed America* (New York: Atlantic Monthly Press, 2003), which was published after the completion of this essay.

2. E. D. Hirsch, Jr., *Cultural Literacy: What Every American Needs to Know* (Boston: Houghton Mifflin, 1987); Rich Simonson and Scott Walker, eds. *The Graywolf Annual Five: Multi-Cultural Literacy* (Saint Paul: Graywolf, 1988). For analysis of the concept "useable past" see Casey Nelson Blake, *Beloved Community: The Cultural Criticism of Randolph Bourne, Van Wyck Brooks, Waldo Frank, and Lewis Mumford* (Chapel Hill: University of North Carolina Press, 1990). Blake asserts that for these intellectuals the past was "indispensable" to an understanding of American culture and to "full citizenship" in a democratic community (296). I want to suggest that knowledge about the Triangle fire is crucial to a full citizenship in a democratic state and in an intellectual community unbiased by class differences. For an analysis that couples gender and a useable past see Ava Baron, ed., *Work Engendered* (Ithaca, NY: Cornell University Press, 1991).

3. David Melman, phone conversation with Janet Zandy, February 1991. Founded in 1900, the ILGWU merged in 1995 with Amalgamated Clothing and Textile Workers' Union to form a new organization called UNITE, Union of Needletrades, Industrial, and Textile Employees.

4. See Evan Watkins's "use of Gramsci" in *WorkTime: English Departments and the Circulation of Cultural Value* (Stanford: Stanford University Press, 1989), 68, and David Forgacs, ed., *An Antonio Gramsci Reader* (New York: Schocken, 1989).

5. See Benita Eisler, ed., *The Lowell Offering: Writings by New England Mill Women 1840–1845* (New York: Harper and Row, 1977); Dan Tannacito, "Poetry of the Colorado Miners 1903–1906," *Radical Teacher* 15 (December 1979), and Jim Daniels, *On the Line* (Bellingham, WA: Signpost Press, 1981).

6. Janet Zandy, ed. *Calling Home: Working-Class Women's Writings* (New Brunswick: Rutgers University Press, 1990).

7. Evan Watkins's critical approach was particularly useful in conversing with this poetry. See *The Critical Act: Criticism and Community* (New Haven: Yale University Press, 1978). I wish to make a case for a working-class epistemology, a way of knowing and viewing the world that comes out of direct experiences with the physicality of labor.

8. *New York Call,* March 28, 1911.

9. "Budgets of the Triangle Fire Victims," *Life and Labor* (September 1912): 265–269. The women shirtwaist workers did not fit the socially constructed Victorian definition of womanhood. By the very nature of their labor, they were not "ladies," nor were they "angels in the house." They were frequently viewed by bourgeois society as morally deficient because they labored, and often cross-class concerns were expressed in moralistic terms rather than those of economics and justice. See Laura Hapke's *Tales of the Working Girl: Wage-Earning Women in American Literature, 1890–1925* (New York: Twayne, 1992). Hapke claims that "widespread condemnation of the single woman as worker, and the corollary tendency to blame the sweatshop victim for her plight, had certainly abated by the mid-1920s" (14). See also Anita Levy, *Other Women: The Writing of Class, Race, and Gender, 1832–1898* (Princeton: Princeton University Press, 1991).

10. Bertha Rembaugh, "The Triangle Fire: The Court's Decision," *Life and Labor* (April 1912): 117–119.

11. Quoted in Martha Bensley Bruere, "The Triangle Fire," *Life and Labor* (May 1911): 137–138.

12. Emma Goldman, "Observations and Comments," *Mother Earth* 6, no. 11: 325.

13. Louis Duchez, "The Murder of the Shirt Waist Makers in New York," *International Socialist Review* 2: 666–673.

14. Carrie W. Allen, "Triangle Shop Like Other Hell Holes," *New York Call* (March 28, 1911).

15. Alice Henry, "The Way Out," *Life and Labor* (April 1912): 120–121.

16. Violet Pike, "New World Lessons for Old World Peoples," ibid.: 115.

17. Constance Lounsberry, "The Future," *Life and Labor* (May 1911): 142.

18. I have limited my study of contemporary poets to those whose work is in print and with whom I have had some conversation and correspondence. All the quotations are from private letters from the individual poets to Janet Zandy.

19. Safiya Henderson-Holmes, "rituals of spring," in *Madness and a Bit of Hope* (New York: Harlem River Press, 1990); Julia Stein, "Downtown Women," in Zandy, *Calling Home*; Carol Tarlen, "Sisters in the Flames," *Women's Studies Quarterly*, ed. Janet Zandy (Spring/Summer 1995): 171–172; Mary Fell, "The Triangle Fire," in *The Persistence of Memory* (New York: Random House, 1984); Chris Llewellyn, *Fragments from the Fire: The Triangle Shirtwaist Company Fire of March 25, 1911* (New York: Penguin, 1987), reprinted as *Steam Dummy and Fragments from the Fire* (Huron, OH: Bottom Dog Press, 1993).

20. The process of cultural production as evidenced in this poetry suggests ways in which readings of working-class poetry can open and democratize/secularize critical practices. Particularly useful are Edward Said's insights about the social and political transformative possibilities of moving from a genealogy of "filiation" based on ties of kinship, ethnicity, race, or religion to an "affiliative" social habitat aspiring toward economic justice. See Edward Said, *The World, the Text, and the Critic* (Cambridge: Harvard University Press, 1983). Also, we need to expand the affiliation of worker/poets transnationally and explore, for example, how these fire poems relate to the migration of textile work onto the global assembly line and how resistance literature is generated out of the material existence of those who have been denied access to their own (labor and political) histories. See Barbara Harlow, *Resistance Literature* (New York: Methuen, 1987).

21. James Scully, *Line Break: Poetry as Social Practice* (Seattle: Bay Press, 1988), 5.

22. Alicia Ostriker, *Stealing the Language* (Boston: Beacon, 1986), 10.

23. Remarks made by Rose Schneiderman at the memorial service held at the Metropolitan Opera House on April 2, 1911. Rabbi Wise's comments (epigraph to this chapter) were also made at that memorial service. Quoted in Leon Stein, *Out of the Sweatshop* (New York: Quadrangle/*New York Times* Book Co., 1977).

24. Stein continues, "Its [the sweatshop's] work day is of no fixed length; it links pace of work to endurance. It demeans the spirit by denying to workers any part in determining the conditions of or pay for their work" (Leon Stein, ed., *Out of the Sweatshop*, xv) .

25. Elaine Hedges, "The Needle or the Pen: The Literary Rediscovery of Women's Textile

Work," in *Tradition and the Talents of Women*, ed. Florence Howe (Urbana: University of Illinois Press, 1991), 338–364.

26. See Barbara Myerhoff's use of "definitional ceremonies" in *Number Our Days* (New York: Simon and Schuster, 1980).

27. The Triangle fire was not the first nor the last industrial fire. On March 19, 1958, five city blocks away from the site of the Triangle fire, another textile factory fire occurred. The building had one worthless fire escape, no sprinklers, and the workers had no fire drills. Twenty-four died that day. On September 3, 1991, at the Imperial Food Products chicken processing plant in Hamlet, NC, twenty-five workers, mostly African American women, perished under conditions similar to those at Triangle. In that fire there was no sprinkler system, there were no fire drills, and there was no inspection for eleven years. As at Triangle, the doors were locked to prevent theft—in this case, the stealing of a few chicken parts instead of fabric. In Bangkok, Thailand, in May 1993, an estimated 240 workers died in a doll factory fire. The workers were locked in to control theft and had only one exit on each floor when the fire started. Workers were forced to jump from windows when they couldn't open the locked exits. In November 1993, eighty-one Chinese workers, mostly women who were making Christmas toys for Western markets, died in a Hong Kong–owned factory. In all of these incidents, the cause of death was not an unforeseen natural catastrophe, but rather unsafe working conditions where profits took precedence over human lives.

Stillness, Motion, Bodies, and Possibilities for Working-Class Studies

1. *Bread and Roses*, directed by Ken Loach (2001; Parallax). For a viscerally compelling representation of a literal pipeline, see *El Norte*, directed by Gregory Nava (1983). See also the photographs of Ken Light in *To the Promised Land*, introduction by Richard Rodriguez (New York: Aperture/ California Historical Society, 1988).

2. *Salt of the Earth,* Director: Herbert Biberman, Independent Productions Corp. (1954).

3. Michael Wilson, *Salt of the Earth* (screenplay) (New York: Feminist Press, 1978), 82.

4. See Etienne Balibar, "From Class Struggle to Classless Struggle?" (trans. by Chris Turner): "Less than ever are citizens in modern society equal in respect of the arduous nature of their everyday lives, their own autonomy or dependence, the security they enjoy in their lifetime or the dignity they have in death, or the consumption and education, or information, to which they have access. And more than ever these different 'social' dimensions of citizenship are coupled with collective inequality with regard to political power and decision-making, whether in the areas of administration, the economic system, international relations or peace and war" (*Race, Nation, Class: Ambiguous Identities*, ed. Etienne Balibar and Immanuel Wallerstein [New York: Verso, 1991], 179–180).

5. David Joseph, "Breaking Through the Sounds of Silence," in *Liberating Memory: Our Work and Our Working-Class Consciousness*, ed. Janet Zandy (New Brunswick: Rutgers University Press, 1995), 136.

6. Marla Brettschneider, *Democratic Theorizing from the Margins* (Philadelphia: Temple University Press, 2002).

7. See John Berger and Jean Mohr, *A Seventh Man: The Story of a Migrant Worker in Europe* (Harmondsworth, England: Penguin, 1975) for the correlation between prison time and labor time. See also Jimmy Breslin's journalistic treatment of waiting for work in *The Short Sweet Dream of Eduardo Gutierrez* (New York: Crown, 2002). For an analysis of time-space compression see Doreen Massey, "A Global Sense of Place," in *Space, Place, and Gender* (Minneapolis.: University of Minnesota Press, 1994), 146–156, especially her commentary on different modes of mobility along an economic continuum, what she calls the "power geometry of it all," and "differentiated mobility: some people are more in charge of it than others; some initiate flows and movement, others don't; some are more on the receiving end of it than others; some are effectively imprisoned by it" (149).

8. Roxanne Rimstead, *Remnants of Nation: On Poverty Narratives by Women* (Toronto: University of Toronto Press, 2001), 4–5. Hereafter cited in text.

9. Berger, *A Seventh Man*, 141.

10. James Baldwin, "Stranger in the Village," in *Notes of a Native Son* (1955; reprint, Boston: Beacon, 1983), 166.

11. It should be noted, although it is beyond the purview of this book to discuss, that *literacy* is a word that evokes both ambivalent and negative response among some contemporary Indians. See Paula Gunn Allen's comments about literacy in her introduction to *Spider Woman's Granddaughters* (New York: Ballantine, 1989), 18.

12. All citations from "Lullaby" are from Leslie Marmon Silko's *Storyteller* (New York: Seaver, 1981).

13. Leslie Marmon Silko, *Ceremony* (New York: Signet, 1978). Hereafter cited in the text. Economic sustainability is only one aspect of this extraordinarily deep and complex novel. My comments are not intended as a full discussion of the novel.

14. Paula Gunn Allen, introduction to *Spider Woman's Granddaughters* (New York: Ballantine, 1989), 10.

15. Raymond Williams, "The Writer: Commitment and Alignment," in *Resources of Hope*, ed. Robin Gable (London: Verso, 1989), 87. Note also Bakhtin's commentary about classical autobiography: "To be exterior meant to be for others, for the collective, for one's own people" (M. M. Bakhtin, *The Dialogic Imagination*, trans. Carl Emerson, ed. Michael Holquist [Austin: University of Texas Press, 1981], 135, as cited in Ramon Saldivar, *Chicano Narrative* [Madison: University of Wisconsin Press, 1990], 169).

16. All citations to "The Cariboo Café" are from Helena María Viramontes, *The Moths and Other Stories* (Houston: Arte Publico Press, 1995). If I *had* to choose one story for its pedagogical power with students, it would be "The Cariboo Café." The structure of the story becomes a kind of awakening as students construct narrative and ideological meaning and reflect on what it means to be lost.

17. See Elaine Scarry, *The Body in Pain: The Making and Unmaking of the World* (New York: Oxford University Press, 1985), and *Resisting Representation* (New York: Oxford University Press, 1994). Scarry notes "our habit of inattention to work is the natural counterpart to our intense . . . preoccupation with courtship and desire" (61). See also Bruce Robbins, *The Servant's Hand: English Fiction from Below* (Durham, NC: Duke University Press, 1993); Mark Seltzer, *Bodies and Machines* (New York: Routledge, 1992); Dennis Patrick Slattery, *The Wounded Body: Remembering the Markings of Flesh* (Albany: State University of New York Press, 2000); Nicholas K. Bromell, *By the Sweat of the Brow: Literature and Labor in Antebellum America* (Chicago: University of Chicago Press, 1993).

18. Helena María Viramontes, *Under the Feet of Jesus* (New York: Dutton, 1995). Hereafter cited in text.

19. Drawing on the work of Victor Turner, *Dramas, Fields and Metaphors* (Ithaca, NY: Cornell University Press, 1974), Barbara Myerhoff in *Number Our Days* (New York: Simon and Schuster, 1980) describes *communitas* as "intense camaraderie" evoking both physicality and spirituality.

20. Bertolt Brecht, "The World's One Hope," in *Against Forgetting*, ed. Carolyn Forché (New York: Norton, 1993), 219.

21. For the significance of these precious papers from a global perspective see Alistair Davidson and Stephen Castles, *Citizenship and Migration: Globalization and the Politics of Belonging* (New York: Macmillan, 2000), and especially Davidson's "Fractured Identities: Citizenship in a Global World" and the account of the *sans papiers* in France.

22. Cherríe Moraga, "The Welder," in *This Bridge Called My Back: Writings by Radical Women of Color,* ed. Cherríe Moraga and Gloria Anzaldúa (1981; reprint, Latham, NY: Kitchen Table/Women of Color Press, 1983), 219–220.

23. Cherríe Moraga, *Heroes and Saints and Other Plays* (Albuquerque: West End Press, 1994). Hereafter cited in text.

24. Don Mitchell, *The Lie of the Land: Migrant Workers and the California Landscape* (Minneapolis: University of Minnesota Press, 1996).
25. See Lois Gibbs, *Love Canal: My Story*, as told to Murray Levine (Albany: State University of New York Press, 1982). Gibbs recalls, "The small children suffered the most. They did not understand *chemicals, dioxin,* or exactly how they might be harmed. . . . Many had nightmares imagining what 'chemicals' looked like and then having an imaginary 'thing' attack them" (172). The story of an environmental poison is a continuous narrative. See also Susanne Antonetta's more recent *Body Toxic: An Environmental Memoir* (Washington, DC: Counterpoint, 2001), and her chapter on "Radium Girls."
26. Mitchell makes this important distinction: "Baudrillard's emphasis on hypermobility ignores the rather different mobility of the army of California migratory farmworkers whose lives are grounded not in an empty immense space, but in a ruthless, severe landscape that Baudrillard is incapable of understanding" (22).
27. For a recent incorporation of the canary-in-the-mine image see Lani Guinier and Gerald Torres, *The Miner's Canary: Enlisting Race, Resisting Power, and Transforming Democracy* (Cambridge: Harvard University Press, 2002).
28. See Berger, *A Seventh Man,* for the psychic parallels between migratory labor and imprisonment.
29. Anthropologist Myerhoff describes "definitional ceremonies" as dramas "contrived to allow people to reiterate their collective and personal identities, to arouse great emotion and energy which [is] . . . then redirected toward some commonalities, some deep symbols, and stable shared norms," in *Number Our Days,* 185–186.
30. Manuel Castells, *The Power of Identity* (Malden, MA: Blackwell, 1997), 8.
31. Berger, *A Seventh Man,* 93–94.

Ralph Fasanella

1. Quoted in Peter Carroll, "Ralph Fasanella Limns the Story of the Workingman," *Smithsonian* 24, no. 5 (August 1993): 58–69, 64.
2. Maxwell L. Anderson, "Foreword," in Barbara Haskell, *The American Century: Art and Culture, 1900–1950* (New York: Whitney Museum of American Art and Norton, 1999), 9.
3. Jay Johnson and William C. Ketchum, Jr., *American Folk Art of the Twentieth Century* (New York: Rizzoli International Publications, 1983), 94.
4. Bernarda Bryson Shahn, *Ben Shahn* (New York: Abrams, 1972), 18.
5. Michael Holquist and Vadim Liapunov, "The Architectonics of Answerability," introduction to their *Art and Answerability: Early Philosophical Essays by M. M. Bakhtin,* trans. Vadim Liapunov and Kenneth Brostrom (Austin: University of Texas Press, 1990).
6. Quoted in Patrick Watson, *Fasanella's City* (New York: Ballantine, 1974), 44.
7. See Paul D'Ambrosio, *Ralph Fasanella's America* (Cooperstown, NY: New York State Historical Association, 2001), 68, 141.
8. For the intertextuality of public topography—signs, advertisements, slogans, posters, warnings, etc., see James Thrall Soby, *Ben Shahn* (London: Penguin, 1947) and *Walker Evans at Work* (New York: Harper and Row, 1982).
9. Quoted in D'Ambrosio, *Ralph Fasanella's America,* 92.
10. For a portrait of New York Congressman Vito Marcantonio see Gerald Meyer in *The American Radical,* ed. Mari Jo Buhle, Paul Buhle, and Harvey J. Kaye (New York: Routledge, 1994), 269–277. For New York's working-class history see Joshua B. Freeman, *Working-Class New York: Life and Labor Since World War II* (New York: New Press, 2000).
11. It is regrettable that it was not possible to reproduce the large canvases, given the scale and black-and-white limitations of this book. See the color reproductions in Watson's *Fasanella's City* and D'Ambrosio's *Ralph Fasanella's America.* My appreciation to Eva Fasanella for permission to include two smaller canvases.
12. See, for example, Roberta Smith, "Ralph Fasanella, 83, Primitive Painter, Dies," *New York Times,* December 18, 1997.

13. Fasanella acknowledged the influence of Pietro di Donato's novel *Christ in Concrete* (1939; reprint, New York: Signet, 1993) in presenting his father as the crucified average Joe. See "God Job" this volume. Joe Fasanella is also reminiscent of Agnes Smedley's (Marie's) father in *Daughter of Earth*, and the butcher, Kracha, in *Out of This Furnace*, failed small businessmen and low-end entrepreneurs.

14. Quoted in Watson, *Fasanella's City*, 99.

15. John Berger, "Ralph Fasanella and the Experience of the City," in *About Looking* (New York: Pantheon, 1980), 98–99.

16. Quoted in Watson, *Fasanella's City*, 147. See also Jerre Mangione and Ben Morreale, *La Storia* (New York: HarperPerennial, 1992); Dorothy Bryant *Miss Giardino*, 1978, reprinted with an afterword by Janet Zandy (New York: Feminist Press, 1997); and Fred Gardaphe, *Italian Signs, American Streets: The Evolution of Italian American Narrative* (Durham, NC: Duke University Press, 1996).

17. Quoted in Watson, *Fasanella's City*, 10.

18. Nicholas Pileggi, "Portrait of the Artist as a Garage Attendant in the Bronx," *New York* 5, October 30, 1972, 37–45.

19. Quoted in D'Ambrosio, *Ralph Fasanella's America*, 121. See Paul Cowan, introduction to William Cahn, *Lawrence 1912: The Bread and Roses Strike* (1954; reprint, New York: Pilgrim Press, 1980). Fasanella pays homage to Cahn, who died before he could complete the revision of his book, by placing a memorial plaque on the contemporary bridge in *Mill Town—Weaving Department*. A Fasanella Lawrence painting is the cover art for the new edition. Using labor history as a catalyst and cultural antecedent is an element in the formation of working-class culture. See "Fire Poetry" on the 1911 Triangle Shirtwaist fire in this book. See also Jeanne Schinto, "The Guy in the Street," *DoubleTake* (Winter 2000): 114–120.

20. Summary of Public Domain information from D'Ambrosio, *Ralph Fasanella's America*. Photo courtesy of Margret Hofmeister, who provides this context for the photo: "The photo was taken on Memorial Day—May 27, 1996. Because it was the same day that Yale held their commencement ceremonies, the event was called The People's Commencement. Union members from all over the East Coast participated—clerical and technical workers from Harvard to coal miners of West Virginia. Earlier that year, Fasanella donated signed prints to the Yale unions to be sold for fundraising. Naturally, he was invited to participate in this event" (correspondence with Janet Zandy, April 28, 2003).

21. When I learned that there were open venues for the traveling "Ralph Fasanella's America" exhibit I approached Rochester's Memorial Art Gallery and asked if they would consider showing the forty paintings in either 2002 or 2003. I explained that the collection would generate an understanding of American labor history, and would likely bring people to the museum who may not ordinarily come. The cost, around $25,000, was rather modest; clearly, that was not the issue. I received a polite but firm "no."

22. Walt Whitman, "Democratic Vistas," in *Leaves of Grass and Selected Prose*, ed. John Kouwenhoven (New York: Random House/Modern Library, 1950), 477.

23. See D'Ambrosio, *Ralph Fasanella's America*, 117.

24. Stefan Szczelkun, *The Conspiracy of Good Taste* (London: Working Press, 1993). Szczelkun also writes: "Even when the Enlightenment philosophical tradition did produce its inevitable negation and Marx looked at the origins of what is consumed, and the financial basis of middle class power was clearly described, we end up with something which is still from the mind cage of one class—which is expressed predominantly in the cultural codes of that class . . . money and book knowledge. It does not relate to the daily cultural experience of those who would be liberated. It does not empower the lives and struggles of the oppressed. Marx produced a grand narrative which explained economic exploitation but did not find the heart of working class liberation" (102). See also the remarks of former steelworker Doris McKinney ("They know nothing about you, nothing whatsoever") in Milton Rogovin and Michael Frisch, *Portraits in Steel* (Ithaca, NY: Cornell University Press, 1993), 185, and the essay "Worker Ghosts" this volume.

25. Quoted in Watson, *Fasanella's City*, 103.

Technologies: On Laboring Bodies

My uncle died quite unexpectedly while serving time in a Pennsylvania prison. This essay is dedicated to his memory.

1. American Civil Liberties Union, "ACLU Class Action Lawsuit Targets Brutal Conditions at Ohio's 'Supermax' Prison," January 9, 2001, *http://www.aclu.org/news/2001/n010901b.html*.

2. Quoted from the Foreword to *Prison Writing in Twentieth-Century America*, ed. H. Bruce Franklin (New York: Penguin, 1998), xii.

3. Franklin, *Prison Writing*, 3. The literature on prisons and prison studies is voluminous, and is not the subject of this essay. Rather, I wish to suggest the critical importance of recognizing continuums of labor and imprisonment in relation to technology as tool and system. For further study see H. Bruce Franklin, *Prison Literature in America* (1978; reprint, Westport, CT: Lawrence Hill, 1982); Mary Helen Washington, "Prison Studies as Part of American Studies," *American Studies Newsletter* (March 1999): 1, 3. See the response to the 1998 conference "Critical Resistance: Beyond the Prison Industrial Complex" organized by Angela Davis and Ruth Gilmore and the work of Ellen Barry, founder of Legal Services for Prisoners with Children (LSPC). Belle Gale Chevigny, ed. *Doing Time: 25 Years of Prison Writing* (New York: Arcade, 1999) and "Prison Activists Come of Age," *The Nation*, July 24–31, 27–30. For international perspectives see Judith A. Scheffler, ed., *Wall Tappings: An International Anthology of Women's Prison Writings 200 to the Present* (New York: Feminist Press, 2002). For insights on the relationship between doing time and migrant labor see John Berger and Jean Mohr, *A Seventh Man: The Story of a Migrant Worker in Europe* (Harmondsworth, England: Penguin, 1975) and Jimmy Breslin, *The Short Sweet Dream of Eduardo Gutierrez* (New York: Crown, 2002), previously cited. For historical theory see Michel Foucault, *Discipline and Punish: The Birth of the Prison*, trans. Alan Sheridan (New York: Random House, 1977), and Colin Gordon, ed., *Power/Knowledge: Selected Interviews and Other Writings, 1972–1977* (New York: Random House, 1977). For photographic parallels see Michael Jacobson-Hardy, *Factories Schools Prisons*, catalog (Worcester, MA: Iris and B. Gerald Cantor Art Gallery, College of the Holy Cross, 1996).

4. Anonymous, "The New Slavery in the South" (1904) reprinted in *Plain Folk: The Life Stories of Undistinguished Americans*, ed. David M. Katzman and William M. Tuttle (Urbana: University of Illinois Press, 1982), 154–163. The *Independent* editors (between 1902 and 1906) were determined to tell "representative" rather than extraordinary stories of workers' lives, either through the narrator's own written text or through interviews that were read and approved by the person telling the story (xi).

5. Jack London, "Pinched: A Prison Experience," in Franklin, *Prison Writing in Twentieh-Century America*, 38–49.

6. Agnes Smedley, *Daughter of Earth* (1929; reprint, New York: Feminist Press, 1973). Emma Goldman, *Living My Life*, 2 vols. (1931; reprint, New York: Dover, 1970).

7. See Sherry Lee Linkon and John Russo, "From 'Steel Town' to a 'Nice Place to Do Time'," chapter 4 in *Steel-Town U.S.A.: Work and Memory in Youngstown* (Lawrence: University of Kansas Press, 2002).

8. See James Gleick, *Faster: The Acceleration of Just About Everything* (New York: Pantheon, 1999) and *What Just Happened: A Chronicle from the Information Frontier* (New York: Pantheon, 2002).

9. From the introduction to Bill Lessard and Steve Baldwin, *NetSlaves: True Tales of Working the Web* (New York: McGraw-Hill, 2000), 3. Hereafter cited in text. See also their Web site: *www.netslaves.com*.

10. *Working* (New York: Avon, 1974) is a model for any oral history approach to the study of work, and though Lessard and Baldwin pay homage, they give it and Studs Terkel short shrift. Their intent is more immediate and narrow. See also John Bowe, Marisa Bowe, and Sabin Streeter, eds., *Gig: Americans Talk about Their Jobs at the Turn of the Millennium* (New York: Crown, 2000). My thanks to Todd Vogel for introducing me to

NetSlaves and *Gig*. See his excellent syllabus "Working, Buying, and Becoming: Race, Labor, and the High Life, from the Plantation to the Internet" in *What We Hold in Common: An Introduction to Working-Class Studies*, ed. Janet Zandy (New York: Feminist Press, 2001), 275–282.

11. Other writers have used blue-collar language to describe and compare contemporary white-collar working conditions. While useful in illustrating a labor/technology continuum, they slight the significant physical differences and occupational hazards of industrial jobs. See Jill Andresky Fraser, *White Collar Sweatshop: The Deterioration of Work and Its Reward in Corporate America* (New York: Norton, 2001) and Barbara Garson, *The Electronic Sweatshop: How Computers Are Transforming the Office of the Future into the Factory of the Past* (New York: Simon and Schuster, 1988).

12. Tracy Kidder, *The Soul of a New Machine* (New York: Avon, 1982).

13. Harry Braverman, *Labor and Monopoly Capital: The Degradation of Work in the Twentieth Century* (New York: Monthly Review Press, 1974), 405–406. See also Michael Zweig, *The Working Class Majority: America's Best Kept Secret* (Ithaca, NY: Cornell University Press, 2000). The incorporation of the working class into the managerial stake game accelerated with the replacement of the old-fashioned monthly pensions with mobile 401(k)s. See William Wolman and Anne Colamosca, *The Great 401(k) Hoax: Why Your Family's Financial Security Is at Risk, and What You Can Do about It* (New York: Perseus, 2002).

14. See "Worker Ghosts" in this collection for a fuller discussion of *Player Piano*.

15. John Dos Passos, *The New Masses* (1930), quoted in Michael Denning, *The Cultural Front: The Laboring of American Culture in the Twentieth Century* (New York: Verso, 1996), 179.

16. Richard Sennett, *The Corrosion of Character: The Personal Consequences of Work in the New Capitalism* (New York: Norton, 1996), 9. Hereafter cited in text.

17. Quoted in Paul Rabinow, ed., *The Foucault Reader* (New York: Pantheon, 1984), 22.

18. Carolyn Chute, "Word Pictures" in Olive Pierce, *Up River: The Story of a Maine Fishing Community* (Hanover, NH: University Press of New England, 1996), 65, 88. My appreciation to Carole Anne Taylor from Bates College for the gift of this book.

19. Cheri Register, *Packinghouse Daughter: A Memoir* (St. Paul: Minnesota Historical Society, 2000). Hereafter cited in text.

20. The best known exposé of the meat industry is, of course, Upton Sinclair's *The Jungle* (1906; reprint, New York: Signet, 1980); see also the parallel scenes of slaughterhouse and domestic labor in Tillie Olsen's *Yonnondio* (New York: Laurel Edition/Dell, 1974). For oral histories of women workers in the meat-packing industry see "Voices from the Yards," recorded in the 1930s and reprinted in *First Person America*, ed. Ann Banks (New York: Random House, 1980), 54–62. See also Rick Halpern and Roger Horowitz, *Meatpackers: An Oral History of Black Packinghouse Workers and Their Struggle for Racial and Economic Equality* (New York: Monthly Review Press, 1999).

21. This is an underrecognized complexity that refutes generalized sociological assumptions about workers' efforts to cheat the clock. See my "Labor Day" in *Calling Home*, 155–156, and analysis of labor inheritance in the introduction to *Liberating Memory*, 1–15.

22. Rebecca Harding Davis, *Life in the Iron Mills or The Korl Woman*, with a biographical interpretation by Tillie Olsen (New York: Feminist Press, 1972), 13. Hereafter cited in text.

23. William L. Watson, "'These mill-hands are gettin' onbearable': The Logic of Class Formation in *Life in the Iron Mills* by Rebecca Harding Davis," in *Women's Studies Quarterly: Working-Class Lives and Cultures* (Spring/Summer 1998): 116–136, 131.

24. See Laura Hapke's important analysis in *Labor's Text: The Worker in American Fiction* (New Brunswick: Rutgers University Press, 2001), 76–79.

25. Herman Melville, "The Paradise of Bachelors" and "The Tartarus of Maids," *Selected Tales and Poems by Herman Melville*, ed. Richard Chase (New York: Holt, Rinehart and Winston, 1968), 206–229.

26. For an dystopic contemporary reading that parallels "Tartarus" and *The Lowell Offering* as well as illuminates the technology of gender see Margaret Atwood, *The Handmaid's Tale* (New York: Ballantine, 1985).

27. Benita Eisler, ed., *The Lowell Offering: Writings by New England Mill Women (1840–1845)* (New York: Norton, 1998). See also Thomas Dublin, *Women at Work: The Transformation of Work and Community in Lowell, Massachusetts, 1826–1860* (New York: Columbia University Press, 1979) and *Lowell: The Story of an Industrial City* (Washington, DC: Division of Publications, National Park Service, 1992). For a painter's imagined portrayal of textile production see Ralph Fasanella, especially the Lawrence paintings. On memory, history, and culture see William Cahn, *Lawrence 1912: The Bread and Roses Strike* (New York: Pilgrim Press, 1977).

28. Thomas Dublin, ed., *Farm to Factory: Women's Letters, 1830–1860,* 2nd ed. (New York: Columbia University Press, 1993), 23.

29. Note the similarity of the Lowell widow-housekeepers to the "aunts" in Atwood's *The Handmaid's Tale.*

30. See Laura Hapke, *Tales of the Working Girl: Wage-Earning Women in American Literature, 1890–1925* (New York: Twayne, 1992).

31. Dublin, *Farm to Factory*, note, 129.

32. Harriet Farley, "Letters from Susan," in Eisler, *Offering*, 51, 52.

33. Octavia Butler, *Kindred* (Boston: Beacon, 1979, 1988). See also Phyllis Alesia Perry, *Stigmata* (New York: Hyperion, 1998) and Lisa A. Long's "A Relative Pain: The Rape of History in Octavia Butler's *Kindred* and Phyllis Alesia Perry's *Stigmata*," *College English* 64, no. 4 (March 2002): 459–483, for the authors' treatment of the physical markings of historical forces.

34. Frederick Douglass, *Narrative of the Life of Frederick Douglass*, ed. David W. Blight (Boston: Bedford), 74. Octavia Butler commented on the "scars of history"—physical and psychological—at a lecture in March 2003 in Rochester, NY, where *Kindred* was widely read as the community book. She described *Kindred* as a "grim fantasy" and the plot of the book as an attempt "to make history something people felt."

35. For a literary analysis of the disembodied hand see Katherine Rowe, *Dead Hands: Fictions of Agency, Renaissance to Modern* (Stanford: Stanford University Press, 1999).

36. Butler resists casual contemporary references to slavery: Dana was working out of a "casual labor agency—we regulars called it a slave market. Actually, it was just the opposite of slavery. The people who ran it couldn't have cared less whether or not you showed up to do the work they offered" (52).

37. For a fuller description of this course see my essay "Human Labor and Literature: A Pedagogy from a Working-Class Perspective," in *Changing Classroom Practices: Resources for Literary and Cultural Studies*, ed. David Downing (NCTE, 1994).

38. Christa Wolf, *Accident: A Day's News*, trans. Heike Schwarzbauer and Rick Takvorian, (New York: Noonday Press/Farrar, Straus and Giroux, 1991). On April 26, 1986, during a test of emergency systems, reactor number four at the Chernobyl nuclear plant overheated, causing a steam explosion, fire, and partial meltdown of the reactor core while shooting reactor fuel into the atmosphere, contaminating some ten thousand square miles reaching as far as western Europe. Technical information as well as the medical consequences of the explosion are widely available. See Jay M. Gould, "Chernobyl—The Hidden Tragedy," *The Nation*, March 15, 1993, 331–334, and his review of a firsthand account by Vladimir Chernousenko, *Chernobyl: Insight From the Inside* (Berlin/New York: Springer-Verlag, 1992).

39. Svetlana Alexiyevich, "Half-Lives: Chernobyl Revisited," *Harper's*, May 1998, 17–18; reprinted from accounts collected by Alexiyevich, *A Prayer for Chernobyl* (Moscow: Ostojie, n.d.).

Index

Index

Index

Index

About the Author

JANET ZANDY is Professor of Language and Literature at Rochester Institute of Technology. Her books include *Calling Home: Working-Class Women's Writings, Liberating Memory: Our Work and Our Working-Class Consciousness,* and *What We Hold in Common: An Introduction to Working-Class Studies.* She is currently co-editing an anthology of working-class literature in the United States. She has written and spoken widely on working-class studies.